The College Student's Research Companion FIFTH EDITION

Finding, Evaluating, and Citing the Resources You Need to Succeed

ARLENE R. QUARATIELLO WITH JANE DEVINE

Neal-Schuman Publishers, Inc.

New York   London

Published by Neal-Schuman Publishers, Inc.
100 William St., Suite 2004
New York, NY 10038

Printed and bound in the United States of America.

The paper used in this publication meets the minimum requirements of American National Standard for Information Sciences—Permanence of Paper for Printed Library Materials, ANSI Z39.48-1992.

Library of Congress Cataloging-in-Publication Data

Quaratiello, Arlene Rodda, 1966-
    The college student's research companion : finding, evaluating, and citing the resources you need to succeed / Arlene R. Quaratiello with Jane Devine. — 5th ed.
        p. cm.
    Includes bibliographical references and index.
    ISBN 978-1-55570-729-3 (alk. paper)
    1. Library research—United States. 2. Internet research. 3. Electronic information resources. 4. Report writing. I. Devine, Jane, 1947- II. Title.

Z710.Q37 2011
025.5'24—dc22

                                                          2010041999

Contents

List of Figures and Tables

FIGURES

TABLES

Preface

Before writing your first college research paper, you should have mastered the fundamentals of using twenty-first-century information resources. After reading this book, you'll not only know how to find the best information on your topic using all kinds of sources, but you'll also have learned how to evaluate and use the information you find.

The College Student's Research Companion: Finding, Evaluating, and Citing the Resources You Need to Succeed, Fifth Edition, upholds the philosophy that information should be judged for what it conveys, not how it is conveyed—in other words, for its content rather than its format. You may think that Google is great and Wikipedia is wonderful, and that they are so much easier to use than other harder-to-access sources like books and journals. Although these websites are useful for some purposes, as this book will explain, if you think adequate research consists only of using web sources that are freely accessible to anyone, you will not write very good college research papers . . . and you won't get very good grades, either.

To be information literate and succeed not only in college but also in life, you certainly need to be able to find information, but being able to judge it, utilize it, and integrate it is also essential.

The chapters that follow explain the research process step-by-step.

- Chapter 1, "Library Logistics: Devising a Research Plan," discusses topic selection and provides an overview of research.
- Chapter 2, "Reliable Resources: Evaluating Information," appearing as a separate chapter for the first time in this edition, offers a process for choosing the best sources for your research. With the ever-increasing amount of junk that is out there on the web these days, evaluation has become an essential component of information literacy.

- Chapter 3, "The Wayward Web: Finding Good Sites," describes what can be found on the free web and explains how to find good information using web search engines.
- Chapter 4, "Database Directions: Honing Your Search," explains what a database is and how to search it. Use the skills learned in this chapter to effectively search the library catalog, periodical databases, online reference sources, and the web.
- Chapter 5, "Book Bonanza: Using the Library Catalog," discusses the specifics of how to search the online catalog to find records for books and other library material and then explains how to actually get the items you need.
- Chapter 6, "Pertinent Periodicals: Searching for Articles," like the previous chapter, explains how to search databases, this time to locate records for articles in journals, magazines, and newspapers and then how to obtain these articles.
- Chapter 7, "Ready Reference: Getting Answers," provides an overview of how reference sources can help improve your research papers.
- Chapter 8, "Integrated Information: Using Sources," explains how to take good notes, cite your sources correctly, and avoid plagiarism.

The world of information changes rapidly. Fifteen years ago when I was writing the first edition of *The College Student's Research Companion*, Pluto was still considered the ninth planet and road maps were used instead of GPS devices. Although "google" was an obscure term that had something to do with the English sport of cricket, many people were familiar with the math term "googol" (pronounced like "google") to denote a number 1 followed by a hundred zeros.

As times have changed, so has this book. The fifth edition that you are now reading has been completely revised, updated, reorganized, and enhanced so it can be an integral text in any required first-year composition or information literacy course.

Since the last edition of *The College Student's Research Companion* was published, I have been helping students as an English instructor rather than as a librarian. The previous editions of *The College Student's Research Companion* were written solo, but since I now work with students in the classroom rather than in the library, academic librarian Jane Devine, co-author of *Going Beyond Google: The Invisible Web in Learning and Teaching*, has collaborated with me to ensure that this book gives you the most up-to-date and accurate guidance about research today.

Acknowledgments

CHAPTER 1

Library Logistics: Devising a Research Plan

Why are you reading this book? Your answer may likely be "Because I have to." Perhaps you are in a required information literacy course, or you are taking a freshman composition class that includes a research assignment. You may be wondering why you can't just google your topic and be done with your research. Is the library even necessary anymore? Why should you read this book when Google, among other web resources, seems like a great "research companion" for a college student such as yourself?

Why are you in college? Answering this broader question might help you understand better why learning how to use the library and its resources is so essential. Are you studying for a potentially lucrative career? Or have you not decided what you want to be "when you grow up," but you know that a college education is mandatory in today's competitive job market? Maybe you just enjoy learning and want to expand your knowledge. In any case, information is the foundation of education and, ultimately, knowledge. But how do you obtain the information you need? That's what this book is all about.

The reality is that the research techniques that served you in high school will not be sufficient for college-level research. Using Google and other web search engines reveals only the tip of the information iceberg. As you progress in your studies and focus on a major, you will need to become familiar with more specialized research tools—and because informational resources are always changing, you can never stop learning about them.

To help you understand more clearly why the research skills discussed in this book are essential for every college student to possess, consider the following analogy. Route 66, the first highway constructed between Chicago and Los Angeles in the 1920s, wasn't like the interstate highways on which we travel today. Automobiles had only recently come into widespread use, and it took a long time, compared to today, to get to your destination along what was commonly referred to as the Mother Road. Although you couldn't cruise along at 65 miles per hour, Route 66 remained the major east-west route until the superhighway Interstate 40 was built parallel to it in the 1970s. Since then, Route 66 has become a scenic byway that is traveled by tourists who have come from all over the world to "get [their] kicks on Route 66." Although some sections have been marked with "Historic Route 66" signs, it is sometimes difficult following this road. Parts of Route 66 have even started to disintegrate but other parts are thriving with roadside pit stops, hamburger joints, neon signs, teepees, ghost towns, and other quirky attractions that reflect the highway's heydey. Route 66 is a fascinating road into the past where you can easily spend a lot of time and perhaps get lost if you haven't planned your trip well, but on the way you'll learn a lot about American culture. But if you're in a hurry to get somewhere, don't take Route 66. Drive along Interstate 40 instead. There's not as much to see along the way, but you can drive at speeds unheard of in the heyday of Route 66.

You're probably wondering what Route 66 has to do with research. Think of the World Wide Web as an interstate highway like I-40. During the 1990s, the term *information superhighway* was actually used to describe the emerging phenomenon of the Internet, but you don't often hear that phrase in 2010. Although the World Wide Web has revolutionized the way we do research, many students have come to rely on it exclusively, avoiding sources like traditional books and print sources, or limiting themselves to Google searches rather than delving into the variety of more useful sources that are buried a bit more deeply online. What seems like the fastest way is not necessarily the best way, and the resources that may prove most valuable to your research might not be the easiest to access. In your rush to get your research paper done, taking an exit off the "highway" to get to some informational byways is often a good choice, and this book explains how to do this.

While *The College Student's Research Companion*, Fifth Edition, certainly explains how to use Google and similar resources more effectively to find information on the Internet, it also prepares you to go beyond the sources you have come to rely on, to find the most useful information both online and offline. There's no need to simply make do with search results that aren't quite what you need just because there isn't enough time to find something better. This book shows you how to use your time wisely, do research effectively, and ultimately get better grades.

Although you may not use exactly the same resources in your library that are described in this book, the examples given demonstrate fundamental principles to help you best use the particular resources available. Unavoidably, the sources discussed in this book will undergo modifications in the ever-changing world of information technology. Because much of this change will certainly prove to be superficial, understanding the basic theories of doing research is what matters rather than getting bogged down in details. The examples in this book demonstrate the fundamentals that endure rather than dictate specific instructions that might become obsolete even before this book is published. With knowledge of the underlying theories, you will be able to find your way through unfamiliar territory.

CHOOSING YOUR RESEARCH TOPIC

If you feel confused and overwhelmed after your professor assigns a research paper, it's likely because you don't yet have a clear idea of what information you need. A crucial step in the research process is defining what your topic requires. What ultimately is your informational need? Answering this question will give you a firm foundation upon which to proceed.

To avoid frustration in doing research, first clarify with your professor anything you don't understand about the assignment. Whether the whole assignment or just one area of the project is difficult to interpret, it's important to understand the full scope of the effort that lies ahead, so ask before you begin. If you are unable to paraphrase the assignment in your own words and pick out the important concepts in it, make sure you talk to your instructor.

Once you understand the assignment, you are ready to select a topic. Common sense will tell you that you can't begin your research until you choose a topic because you won't know what information you need. How can you find something if you don't know what you're looking for? You won't find what you need by browsing through the library or the web, especially if you have waited until the night before the paper is due—a practice that is highly discouraged in this book.

Choose a topic you can be enthusiastic about. You need to be interested—even fascinated—by it so you don't become bored with researching it. When selecting a topic, it's always wise to choose something that will engage your curiosity—something that will motivate you when the going gets rough. Think about the discussions in your English class that roused you from an impending nap or something you saw on YouTube that left you thinking long after you finished watching it. Brainstorm by writing a list of possible topics.

Even if you're not given a great deal of latitude in choosing a topic for a particular class assignment, you can come up with a twist that will make researching the assigned topic interesting. Relate it to something that does interest you. For instance, if you are really interested in computers but are taking a freshman composition class because it's required, relate the given assignment to computers—perhaps to the use of the web or, in particular, social networking sites like Facebook. Maybe you're taking a required world civilization course and the assignment concerns some aspect of ancient Greek civilization. Unless you're a history or classics major, this assignment probably doesn't sound too thrilling. But perhaps you are interested in sports. You could study the ancient Olympic Games and the role that athletics played in Greek society.

Narrowing Your Topic

Let's suppose your assignment is one that's common in many freshman composition courses: a research paper on a current controversial issue. You have to choose a side, present the pros and cons, and ultimately persuade your reader to agree with your opinion. For this type of paper, it is especially important to choose a topic that interests you because it is much easier to argue a position about which you feel strongly.

You may have a few ideas right away. Consider these broad subjects, and then try to think of some narrower relevant topics. Suppose you are interested in animal rights but also find the issue of prayer in public schools intriguing. These subjects are too large to address in an average freshman research paper, which is generally fewer than ten pages in length. Make a list of more specific subtopics. See Table 1.1 for some suggestions.

Ultimately, for an assignment such as this, you need to choose a side and write a concise statement in the beginning of your paper that summarizes your argument and purpose in writing the paper. This statement, called a thesis, generally develops out of your research and is not necessary when starting out. A thesis is basically a further narrowing of your already narrowed topic. For example, if your paper concerns the abuse of circus animals, a possible thesis is, "Animals that perform in circuses are routinely abused by their trainers and should be treated more humanely." But initially for re-

Table 1.1. Narrowing Down Research Topics	
Broad Subject	**Narrower Topics**
Animal rights	Treatment of circus animals
	Use of animals in cosmetic testing
	The ethics of wearing leather clothing
Prayer in public schools	Singing Christmas songs at holiday concerts
	Saying "under God" in the Pledge of Allegiance

search purposes, just narrowing down your broad subject to a particular topic is enough. You may need to do some preliminary research in order to decide which side you are on. Or you may already be a firm supporter of one side; if this is your situation, finding some information on the subject will help you to home in on a thesis.

If you are stuck, a variety of websites can help you think strategically about topic selection. A particularly useful resource, not only for topic selection but also for every step of the research and writing process, is Purdue University's Purdue Online Writing Lab, also known as OWL (http://owl .english.purdue.edu). The homepage of this site is displayed in Figure 1.1. This web resource includes such helpful pages as:

- "Choosing a Topic" (http://owl.english.purdue.edu/owl/resource/ 658/03)
- "Introduction to Prewriting (Invention)" (http://owl.english.purdue .edu/owl/resource/673/01)
- "Tips and Examples for Writing Thesis Statements" (http://owl.eng-lish.purdue.edu/owl/resource/545/01)

Keep in mind that while you may need a topic to get your research started, the topic may transform as you move ahead with the project. Things that you learn along the way may alter your expectations and interests. As you proceed with your research, your opinions may change. This evolution is also why you should not set your thesis in stone right away. Give yourself some wiggle room to explore your topic.

You may find that you can focus your topic in a number of ways. For example, if you are writing about illegal immigration, you could limit this topic geographically and focus on a particular state like Arizona or a country

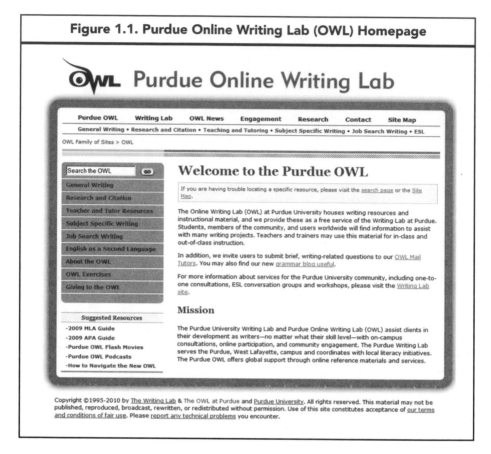

Figure 1.1. Purdue Online Writing Lab (OWL) Homepage

other than the United States. You can also limit a topic by focusing on a particular time period or group of people. If you are writing about the politics of space exploration, you could focus on the Apollo moon landings of the 1970s or the space shuttle flights of the 1980s. A topic such as bullying could focus on elementary school students, middle school students, or high school students. You may find other similar ways to focus your research.

Once you feel that you have zoomed in on an interesting subject, write down a topic phrase that includes important terms defining your topic. These phrases may sound a bit like research paper titles, but your paper will likely have a different title. Underline or circle the keywords, and brainstorm any other synonymous words. Maintain a list and add to it as you think of related terms. These keywords will be very important when it comes time to search online resources. For example:

significance of Olympics in Greek society
- **significance**: importance; influence
- **Olympics**: sports, athletics, Olympic games, Olympiad, marathon
- **Greek**: Hellenistic, Grecian, classical, ancient world
- **society**: culture, civilization

abuse of animals in circuses
- **abuse**: maltreatment, harm
- **animals**: elephants, lions, tigers, horses
- **circuses**: "Greatest Show on Earth," Ringling Bros. and Barnum & Bailey Circus

You may also find it helpful to write down the major research questions that you'll want to answer. Like a journalist would, ask yourself, "Who, what, why, where, when, and how?" To return to the sample topic of social networking websites, here are just a few questions you would need to address:

- Who uses Facebook and other social networking sites?
- Why do people use these sites?
- What are the pros and cons of using these sites?
- How do these sites work?
- How else do young adults use the web as a social network?

If you can write such a list of questions, you'll have a clearer understanding of your needs. The process of writing them down also makes your topic more concrete.

You don't have to pinpoint your topic in great detail. In fact, if you're too narrow in your selection, you will limit yourself. Finding a balance between too broad and too narrow is an art often mastered through trial and error. You may find that once you start your research, your original topic will evolve into something different from what you had imagined. Something you come across in your reading may take you down another road. But such detours don't have to take you out of your way—in fact, they often take you on a shortcut to your ultimate goal.

PLANNING YOUR RESEARCH

Without a research plan, you'll probably end up wasting precious time wandering through the library or browsing online. So after you've determined your topic, you should make a plan by:

- identifying the types of sources that will provide you with the information you need,
- determining where and how you will find these sources, and
- estimating how much time you will need to do your research.

Although browsing can be effective in the preliminary phase of research by helping you select a topic and perhaps find some general information, it's not a very good method once you've chosen a topic—especially if your topic is very narrow. So think of browsing as a joyride: you have no particular destination, but you may see some interesting things along the way. There's nothing wrong with browsing. It's actually a great way to learn. But some students go to the library the day before a paper is due and try to get information by surfing the web, flipping through issues of magazines, or wandering through a section of the library that seems to have books relating to their subjects. These students are not only at risk for anxiety attacks, they will probably not do very well on their papers.

Types of Sources

Informational Formats

Although we may think of information as being textual, information may come in many formats. For example, if you browse the Library of Congress American Memory website (http://memory.loc.gov/ammem/index.html), you will find many traditional printed resources, such as the text of the Declaration of Independence and the official papers of various presidents, as well as fascinating multimedia sources, such as the famous Coca-Cola television commercial from 1971 in which young peaceniks converge on a hilltop singing, "I'd like to buy the world a Coke." Within a few clicks, you can listen to interviews with former slaves recorded in the 1930s (see Figure 1.2) or view the heart-wrenching artworks created by schoolchildren to commemorate the attacks of September 11, 2001. As the Internet has made evi-

Figure 1.2. "Voices from the Days of Slavery," from the Library of Congress American Memory Website

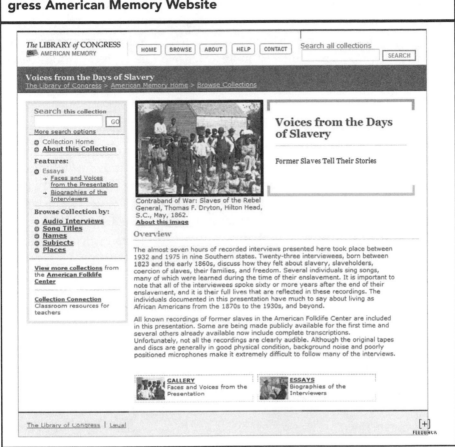

dent, information can come in various media aside from traditional print resources: video, audio, photographs, maps, etc.

The Information Cycle

In addition to being categorized by format, informational resources can also be distinguished by the length of time that passes before they become available. For example, news stories are reported immediately online as well as through television and radio broadcasts. When Sarah Palin was chosen as U.S. Senator John McCain's running mate for the 2008 presidential election, for example, the country was quickly introduced to this relatively unknown governor from Alaska when TV shows were interrupted for "breaking news" announcements. The next day, newspapers carried stories about this event and editorials that commented on McCain's surprising choice. Magazine articles appearing a week or a month later, such as *Newsweek*'s cover story "McCain's Mrs. Right," offered more extensive biographical information and a broader perspective, since journalists had had some time to reflect on the situation.

Academic journal articles that appeared after the campaign ended explored the ramifications of Palin's candidacy; for example, "The Contemporary Effects of Vice-Presidential Nominees: Sarah Palin and the 2008 Presidential Campaign" appeared in *The Journal of Political Marketing* in 2009. Books are usually the final informational resource to emerge on a particular subject. More than a year after losing the election, for instance, Palin's memoir, *Going Rogue*, was published. The immediacy with which a type of resource becomes available needs to be considered when evaluating the information it contains, which will be discussed at length in Chapter 2.

Web-Based Resources

In the past fifteen years, the web has transformed the informational landscape. Because it does have the advantage of allowing the immediate distribution of information, it has become the preferred mode of doing research in our fast-paced society. The web, however, includes two types of information: sources that were originally published in print and sources that are found only on the web. Magazine articles that you can obtain through web-based periodical databases or electronic books available from such subscription services as NetLibrary or ebrary should not be confused with websites that have no print equivalent. Also, searching the resources provided on your college library's website is not the same as searching the web. Googling your topic can often be like rummaging through free stuff left at the side of the road after a garage sale, while using library resources is more like a shopping trip to the mall.

While evaluating the information you find in book and periodical sources remains important, evaluating web-based material is even more crucial. Anyone can put anything on the web, and sites often lack depth, authority, and accuracy. Although there is a great deal of interesting material available on the web and it can be a good source of quick information, proceed with caution.

Books

We can no longer think of a book only as a bunch of pages bound together between two covers. Despite the emergence of electronic books, however, books in their traditional format are probably what first come to mind when you think of a physical library, and books do make up the bulk of most library collections. Two main types of books are housed in libraries: circulating books (those you can check out) and reference books (those you must use within the library). These distinct collections are generally kept in two separate areas of the building and are arranged by Library of Congress or Dewey Decimal Classification call numbers.

Although a growing number of students seem to have developed an aversion to books and prefer to rely on the World Wide Web, books provide a depth of coverage that is hard to beat. Although, technically, anyone can become an author by paying a vanity press to publish a book, most books printed by reputable publishers are written by authors with some expertise and must go through a rigorous editorial process before being published. Facts must be checked and sources of information confirmed. This level of editorial control is lacking on the web, where anyone can post information. To gain a thorough knowledge of your topic, you must search for relevant books.

If you're still uncomfortable about the prospect of using books in your research, remember that you don't have to read these books cover to cover. Maybe there's just one pertinent chapter. Review the table of contents and index to determine which parts of a book to focus on. Your goal should be to find the best information for your project, and books are often the best way to go about getting that information.

Traditional ideas about what constitutes a book are certainly changing, as a growing number of books in print are also published in electronic format. Reference sources such as encyclopedias, dictionaries, and handbooks, which are useful for obtaining quick and concise factual information on a broad range of topics, are increasingly available electronically. A website called Credo Reference (http://corp.credoreference.com), for example, provides online versions of hundreds of reference sources. Classic works that are no longer restricted by copyright and so are considered to be in the public domain (such as the Bible or Herman Melville's *Moby-Dick*) have been available via Project Gutenberg (http://www.gutenberg.org) since the early days of the Internet. Another commercial site, eBooks (http://www.ebooks .com), contains more than 100,000 titles. Many colleges subscribe to a web-based resource called NetLibrary (http://netlibrary.com), which provides full texts of more than 200,000 books, still merely a sampling of the books that have been published. On Amazon.com (http://www.amazon .com) you can now search inside many books; this feature can help you determine whether particular books will be useful. You can also download more than 630,000 e-books to the popular Kindle Wireless Reading Device.

According to the Library of Congress website (http://www.loc.gov/about), there are 32 million books contained in the collections of this massive national library. In contrast, only a fraction of those sources originally published in book form are currently available via the web. Therefore, you should not rely solely on electronic books, since printed books still make up the vast majority of a library's collection. It's also important to evaluate the contents of each book and not just choose one because it is available as an e-book.

Periodical Articles

Finding articles in periodicals is another essential component of doing research. Periodicals include all publications that come out on an ongoing basis, including magazines and journals. As with books, a standardized editorial process is usually employed, which gives the material added validity. As any writer will tell you, it's easy to have an article rejected from a periodical, and it often takes a good deal of persistence to get published.

Types of periodicals include:

- newspapers,
- popular magazines, and
- scholarly journals.

The difference between popular magazines and scholarly journals will be discussed at greater length in Chapter 6. Students sometimes confuse the two terms and tend to use them interchangeably. The main difference between the two types of publications is that when your professors require you to use journal articles rather than those in magazines, they mean you should use resources of a more scholarly nature. The word *magazine* usually indicates a publication of nontechnical articles aimed at a wider, more generalized audience; the word *journal* is more often used when referring to an academic source, but the distinction can be blurry. Sometimes periodicals are the best sources for information on very narrow or very current topics.

Other Resources

Of course, a library provides more than just books, periodicals, and web access. As mentioned earlier, there are many other types of informational resources, such as videotapes and DVDs, government documents, conference papers, dissertations, maps, and photos. Many libraries also have special collections that may relate in some way to the college curriculum or local history. These resources often don't neatly fit into the broad categories just mentioned. Sometimes there is overlap, and you will find references to these kinds of items while searching for books, periodicals, and websites. For example, some libraries include nonbook material in their online catalogs, while government documents are covered in various other databases.

How and Where to Find Sources

To do effective research, you have to know how to use the traditional library as well as the virtual one. In addition to knowing the basics of how libraries are organized, you will need to learn how to use web search engines to find websites, periodical databases to find articles, and online catalogs to find books. All of these resources can be defined as databases, and Chapter 4 will explain how to search a database to find the information needed.

To find websites, you must know how web search engines work. Surfing the web, like browsing in the library, can be very ineffective. Just as online catalogs enable you to find books, and periodical databases help you find articles, search engines locate websites. Google is currently the most popular web search engine, so much so that *google* has emerged in everyday conversation as a verb to denote looking for information by using Google. But numerous other sites also enable you to find websites. When you use these tools, which are far from perfect, you often find a lot of irrelevant material. This problem is due partly to the amount of junk that is on the web, partly to ineffective use of the search engines, and partly to the design of the tools themselves. You can never be quite sure what you're going to find. Although you can't control the content of the web or the way search engines work, you can learn to use them as effectively as possible.

Chapter 5 will explain how to use an online catalog most efficiently to find books and other library material on your topic. From the catalog, you obtain titles and library call numbers. This information is essential for obtaining the items described in the catalog, as is an understanding of the organizational system (either Dewey Decimal or the Library of Congress classification) at your library.

To find articles in periodicals, it's inefficient to browse through issues of magazines or journals or surf the web, hoping to find the complete text of an article on your topic. Instead, you should select the appropriate periodical databases available online through your library's website. Each one of these databases covers a different set of periodicals. Some databases cover broad ranges of subjects, and others focus on more narrow disciplines. Often there is a lot of overlap, and many periodical databases are available.

Using Other Libraries

Planning your research also involves such decisions as whether to use the resources of another library. Not every library can buy every book or provide access to every periodical source, so you may have to go elsewhere for the material you need, particularly if another college library has a special collection that relates to your subject. Many smaller academic libraries have very limited budgets and select books based on the specific academic programs of the school. A college that specializes in technology will likely choose a great number of science books for its library, but it may not contain a great collection in literature and the fine arts. Your library, however, might be a member of a consortium, which is a group of libraries in the same area that shares resources.

You can also get materials through interlibrary loan (ILL), a service that locates a hard-to-find book or article elsewhere in the country and delivers it to your library. This helpful system is available at most libraries, but plan on allowing at least a week or two for the material to arrive. In some cases it can take much less time—especially if what you need is an article that can be photocopied and faxed or e-mailed—but don't depend on ILL at the last minute.

Planning Your Time

Although waiting until the last minute is a common practice among busy college students, you should expect to be particularly stressed if you do this. The research process is time-consuming, no matter how many time-saving hints you learn. Another important aspect of the planning stage is determining how long you will need to do your research and complete your paper.

There are two phases to completing a research paper: doing the research and writing the paper. These processes, each of which takes about an equal amount of time, often overlap. However, many students consider the research process a painful task to endure and get out of the way quickly. Doing research, however, should be a rewarding and even enjoyable process, especially considering how much time you will devote to it. Research is a major component of a research paper; that's why it's called a *research* paper. Without good information, you have nothing to write about. Effective research is the first step in writing papers that will get high marks from your professors.

The required length of the paper as well as your own research experience will, of course, determine when you should start your research. The University of Minnesota Libraries' website has an "Assignment Calculator" tool (http://www.lib.umn.edu/help/calculator) that helps break down the process of writing a research paper into manageable steps. As displayed in Figure 1.3, there are boxes in which to enter the date you plan to start your research and the date the paper is due. The calculator will respond to your input with a personalized day-by-day guide to the steps you should be taking, including

Figure 1.3. The University of Minnesota Libraries' "Assignment Calculator"

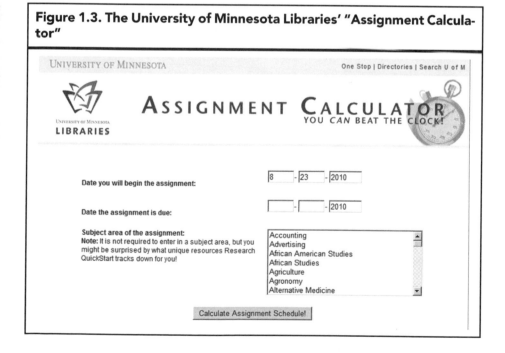

selecting a topic; finding and evaluating books, articles, and websites; and writing a first draft.

Allow yourself time for problems along the way—for example, the results from your Google search all seem to be ads in disguise, a book you need at the library has been checked out, you realize that you'll have to go to another library or get a book through interlibrary loan, the computer system has crashed; any number of scenarios can occur. Then again, sometimes your gut instinct tells you when it's time to start the research process, as a mild anxiety comes over you.

Since the cure for worry is action, just getting started will make you feel better. Set aside a short time for an initial visit to the library well in advance of your paper's due date or spend some time exploring the library's online resources. Spend an hour each day on your research, but don't put any pressure on yourself. You don't even have to be successful in finding anything. Just spend that hour each day on research. Chances are, the time you spend will have positive results. Then try again the next day. Take small steps, and you'll see that everything will slowly come together.

EXERCISES

Using your particular assignment, answer the following questions to help you choose a topic and formulate a research plan.

1. In your own words, what is your research assignment?

   _____

   _____

   _____

2. No matter how bizarre they may seem, what are the first three ideas that come to mind when thinking about this assignment?

   _____

   _____

   _____

3. What is your major or favorite subject area?
   How can you relate your assignment to this interest?

   _____

_____

_____

4. After homing in on a topic, write a phrase describing it:

    _____

    _____

    _____

5. What do you consider to be the most important keywords in the phrase
    you wrote in question 4? Think of at least one synonym for each term.

    _____: _____

    _____: _____

    _____: _____

6. Can you limit your topic in any of the following ways to narrow it down
    further?

    Chronologically: _____
    Geographically: _____
    Culturally: _____
    Other: _____

7. What are five major research questions that you will need to answer?

    (1) _____
    (2) _____
    (3) _____
    (4) _____
    (5) _____

8. How would you rank the following types of informational sources ac-
    cording to how useful you think that type of resource will be for finding
    information on your topic (1 being the most useful)?

    _____ newspaper articles
    _____ books
    _____ scholarly journal articles
    _____ websites
    _____ reference sources

_____ magazine articles
_____ interviews
_____ other material (maps, DVDs, and so on); specify:

9. What other libraries are located in your area? Do any of these libraries have resources that your library does not have which might help you with your research?

_____

_____

_____

Chapter 2

Reliable Resources: Evaluating Information

Imagine going to the mall to buy some clothes. Walking into the first clothing store you see, you start pulling items from the racks without regard to their size, color, or style. You purchase these items without trying them on. This would be absurd and a waste of money. When you go to any store, you evaluate items before buying them. Similarly, you shouldn't just google your topic or search your library's online catalog or periodical databases and use the first few sources you find, regardless of their content.

Doing research is not about finding any kind of information on your topic; it's about finding good, credible, and relevant information. An important research skill, therefore, is the ability to evaluate any type of informational source to determine whether it satisfies your needs and will be appropriate for your particular research assignment. After developing this skill, you will be able to answer the following questions:

- After an initial web search of your topic, how do you decide which particular links to click in the long list of choices that appears?
- When you search the online catalog for books, how do you pick which books you will actually pull from the shelves?
- When you retrieve numerous articles about your topic through a periodical database, how do you know which ones are worth printing?

With the constantly increasing amount of information available out there and the powerful electronic tools we now have for accessing it all, you may actually discover, to your surprise and dismay, that you're overwhelmed with too many resources. Don't select a source simply for the sake of adding one more item to your bibliography. The quality of your information is more important than the quantity. The search strategies explained in this book certainly enable you to find resources related to your topic, but evaluation better enables you to further narrow your search and select the most relevant items from the many that you find. Although assignments vary and more will be expected of you as you advance in college, you may only need a dozen—or maybe even fewer—sources for your first research papers. How do you find the best sources?

While evaluating the information you find in books and periodicals is important, evaluating web-based material is absolutely crucial. Because anyone can publish to the web, many sites that appear legitimate lack depth, authority, and accuracy. Although a great deal of interesting material is available on the web, and it can be a good source of quick information, be skeptical.

Librarians certainly evaluate material—both web-based and in print—before purchasing anything for their libraries. They want to be sure that their choices are reliable and credible and have been edited by reputable publishers. But they evaluate these materials with a broad audience in mind, not for your specific research topic. Even though library sources don't require the scrutiny that free websites do, you still need to apply the principles of evaluation that are discussed in this chapter to all information.

THE PACAC METHOD

The evaluation method discussed in this chapter is referred to throughout this book by its acronym, PACAC. Focusing on the five following characteristics is important for websites, articles, books, and any other type of information.

- Purpose—the reason or reasons the item was written
- Authority—the qualifications of the writer
- Currency—the time when the item was written
- Accuracy—the absence of errors and use of reliable information
- Content—the information provided by the item

When evaluating sources, one thing you should not consider is whether they are available on the web, in a magazine or journal, or in book form. Although the format shouldn't matter, many students still consider format the most important criterion for selecting sources. They prefer websites they can access from their dorm rooms to books that require a trip to the library. They choose only the articles that are available through the web and ignore any article that is available only in hard copy. A source should be judged for what it contains, not for how it is stored or produced. The most useful sources for your research may not be the material that is easiest to obtain. At the same time, don't rely exclusively on written material. Visual material in the form of photographs and DVDs and audio material such as recorded interviews can provide a wealth of pertinent information.

Purpose

The first step in evaluating an informational resource is determining why the source was written. (In this chapter, the words *written*, *writer*, and *writing* will refer to any source of information, regardless of format, whether it is a written text, a videotape, a photograph, an audio recording, etc.). Determining a writer's intent is important when evaluating your sources, especially for websites but also for any other informational resource. Some of the primary purposes of writing are to inform, instruct, or educate the reader. But writers might also want to entertain or inspire their audience. They might seek to promote a cause or product or to persuade their readers to agree with them on a particular issue.

Ask yourself if a particular resource is intended to promote a product, cause, or organization or if its only purpose is to provide information. An encyclopedia article, for example, is written primarily to convey factual information. Although an online version of an encyclopedia may display advertising on the webpage, the content of the articles is generally unbiased. Other resources may serve ulterior purposes. Perhaps a magazine article is written to promote a particular cause. The author of a book can also promote a certain viewpoint. Reference sources, either in print or online, tend to be the most unbiased resources, while free websites must be evaluated for purpose with the most scrutiny.

Although the purpose of a free web source may not be to make money directly from the user, many sites, including Google, derive their profit from advertising revenue. If commercial use does not seem to be the purpose of the site, there must be another reason for its existence. Although this reason could be the desire of the writer to share information freely, more likely it is not so magnanimous. This is why it is best to consult web resources that your library subscribes to before searching the rest of the web.

Persuasion and the Use of Appeals

A major purpose of writing is persuasion—to convince the reader of a particular point of view or the superiority of a certain thing. If this appears to be the purpose of a source, it's important to understand the ways in which writers try to persuade readers. There are three main ways to persuade someone—ways that have been recognized since the ancient Greeks referred to them as *pathos*, *ethos*, and *logos*:

- Emotional appeals (*pathos*) take advantage of the power of human emotions (the Greek term *pathos* is the root of the words *pathetic*, *sympathetic*, and *empathetic*).
- Ethical appeals (*ethos*) utilize experts and other figures that the reader respects to add credibility to a cause (because the word *ethical* can be confusing, as it can evoke unrelated ideas about morality, this type of appeal is also called a *credibility appeal*).
- Logical appeals (*logos*) present the facts and let them speak for themselves.

Unless you have been successfully shielded from the web, television, magazines, and newspapers, you are already familiar with these three classical appeals even if you weren't aware of them. Advertisers have always taken advantage of these techniques to sell their products. Consider vintage Coca-Cola ads. (Although permission to reprint some of these ads was not received before the publication of this book, a variety of them can easily be viewed on the web by searching Google for "**coca-cola ads**." This book's companion website also provides links to a number of these images.)

- **Emotional appeal (*pathos*):** One thing that is immediately apparent when looking at old Coke ads is that everyone looks very happy. One famous image shows two people who appear to be a father and son sharing a special moment at the local soda fountain, which is where people used to go for refreshment. The man waiting on them is also smiling; so is the woman pictured at the bottom of the page. Why are they all so happy? Because they are drinking (or serving) Coke, of course. Happiness is a powerful emotion. Advertisers often take advantage of this emotion to sell their products. Consumers want to buy what makes them and those they care about happy. Another powerful emotion that is often harnessed when trying to persuade is fear. For example, if you don't do something, like buy a particular item or vote for a certain candidate, bad things could happen.

- **Credibility appeal (*ethos*):** In a number of old Coke ads, some of the happy people depicted are nurses working in hospitals. The locations depicted as well as the nurses dressed in traditional white uniforms exude an atmosphere of authority and harken back to the early days of Coca-Cola when it was marketed as a medicinal beverage. The ad implies: If medical personnel drink Coke, it must be good for you. This is the essence of the ethical appeal—people are more likely to agree with you if authority figures that they respect agree with you.

- **Logical appeal (*logos*):** In the very early days of Coca-Cola, print ads often contained text only with no happy faces and not even a picture of the product. One such ad states the fact that Coca-Cola "contains the valuable tonic and nerve stimulant properties of the Coca plant and Cola nuts" which makes it not only a refreshing "temperance drink" but "a valuable Brain Tonic, and a cure for all nervous affections." The primary appeal of this ad is logical: Drink Coke because it will make you healthy.

Although analyzing ads can help you understand the three classical appeals, you should realize that the way these appeals are utilized by some writers would not be appropriate in legitimate sources for your research paper. What is acceptable in advertising may be unacceptable in other sources. The best sources for your research are those which rely on the presentation of logical information. In such sources, the facts speak for themselves. A source that uses some specific anecdotes may rouse your sympathy to generate interest, but if a writer seems to be taking advantage of your emotions this source may not be the best choice. Citing experts is also fine and quite appropriate, especially in scholarly sources, but if a source seems to be appealing to your admiration for famous figures or extolling celebrities as authorities, be wary of the source's content.

What Web Addresses Reveal about Purpose

You can tell a lot about the purpose of a website simply by analyzing its address. As will be explained in Chapter 3, sites with domain names ending in

.com are commercial sites. Such sites are usually trying to sell something; they are often just advertising in disguise. As with all advertising, these sites often make emotional appeals. Keep this fact in mind when evaluating the informational content of the site. If the domain name ends in *.org*, the site is put up by a nonprofit organization. Therefore, it is likely that the purpose of the site is to promote the cause of the organization. This bias will add a certain slant to the information. Sites affiliated with educational institutions have domain names ending in *.edu*. Although you might think that the information included in such sites would be free of propaganda, this is not a valid assumption. Also watch for students' personal pages. The problem with using such pages as reference material is that there is absolutely no editorial control. They may contain bad poetry, family photos, or a student's research paper. As previously mentioned, even government websites (those ending in *.gov*) can take a biased perspective and must be evaluated critically.

Audience

In determining the purpose of a resource, it is helpful to identify the audience for that particular source of information. Whom is the writer addressing? Answering this question is also important in evaluating a source and its usefulness to you. If you're writing a paper about the reasons many people do not want to get the H1N1 vaccine despite the 2009–2010 global pandemic, for example, you will probably not want to use a highly technical medical journal article that is written for medical professionals because you won't be able to fully understand it. Consider your own level of knowledge when selecting sources. If you try to use something that is beyond your comprehension, you will be frustrated. Conversely, if you use resources that are obviously written for a juvenile or high school audience, your paper will not reflect the depth of research expected of a college student.

Authority

Who wrote the source you are evaluating? An author with credentials or extensive experience adds reliability to a source. While you can't always find out much about an author, books often contain brief biographies. You can also google an author or use such reference sources as *Marquis Who's Who Biographies* or *Contemporary Authors* highlighted in Chapter 7 to answer such questions as the following:

- Does the author have an academic affiliation?
- What academic degrees has the author earned?
- What other books has the author written?
- Does this author's work appear in many scholarly journals or other periodical sources?
- What life experiences has the author had which would make him an expert in his field?
- What other credentials does the author have?

Authority is easier to establish for authors of journal articles than for magazine articles because most articles in scholarly periodicals are written by experts in the journal's specialty field. Journal contributors have often been selected by the their peers as having written articles that are important, help advance the study of the field, and are worthy of publication. This process is called *peer review*, and it greatly enhances the authority of an information source.

When evaluating the authority of websites, remember that anybody can publish one. Many sites have no editorial control. It is important to know who is behind the information that you see on a webpage, whether it is an individual or an organization. This can sometimes be more difficult than with print resources, since the author is not always identified on a website. The webmaster, or the person who designs or maintains the site, may be named or credited at the bottom of the webpage, but this person is not necessarily the author. If you are having difficulty finding out who is responsible for a website, look for an About link on the homepage.

You should always be a little suspicious of websites and be prepared to do a bit of detective work. A site with the address http://martinlutherking.org, for example, appears to be a legitimate research source. If you click on the link at the bottom of the page, Hosted by Stormfront, however, you will discover that Stormfront is, surprisingly, a white supremacist organization. Many sites do not provide links to the sponsoring organization. To determine who is responsible for such sites, you can go to Whois? (http://www.whois.com) and use their Lookup tool, which will reveal the identity of the party, complete with mailing address, that originally registered the website.

Primary versus Secondary Sources

When evaluating for authority, you also need to determine whether your source is primary or secondary. Let's say you are writing that previously mentioned paper about the abuse of circus animals. You learn that the circus is coming to town, and you decide to get tickets and actually see those animals you are reading about in books, journals, magazines, and websites. You take notes at the show and even talk to one of the trainers afterward. Eventually, you incorporate this information into your paper. What you have done, through your observations and interview, is called primary research.

Getting back to the other sources you have located, ask yourself if the authors obtained their information through actual experience by conducting interviews; observing people, things, and events; or even conducting experiments. If they have, the source can be classified as a primary source. Any book, magazine, or journal article that contains the actual observations or experiences of the author is primary. These sources also include interviews, diaries, letters, and autobiographies, as well as any original work of literature, like a novel or a poem. The source doesn't have to be a printed text. Photographs and recordings of television shows, radio programs, or speeches are also very useful primary sources. The web provides access to a multitude of primary source material. Visit the American Memory site sponsored by the Library of Congress, mentioned in the previous chapter, to examine photos, recorded interviews, diaries, and numerous other primary historical documents.

Secondary sources are those in which the authors, who are more removed from what they are writing about, use and interpret primary sources. Authors who do not write about their own firsthand experiences or observations provide secondary sources of information. Articles or books that comment on events that were not observed by their authors are secondary. An article about circus animal abuse, for example, written by an animal rights advocate who has not actually observed a circus or interviewed a trainer is a secondary source. This type of source is fine to use as long as the information is accurate and based on other legitimate sources.

A third type of source is referred to as tertiary. These sources include such reference material as almanacs, encyclopedias, and bibliographies, all of which are described in detail in Chapter 7. Tertiary sources distill the information contained in many other primary and secondary sources and are useful for learning basic background information on your topic.

Currency

If you're researching the World War II Japanese attack on Pearl Harbor, an eyewitness account might be very useful. Therefore, you could search for newspaper articles written shortly after December 7, 1941. Certainly many authors have written and will continue to write about this day, but a source written around the time of the attack will have a unique perspective. Conversely, if you were writing about how social networking sites are changing society, you would probably want the most up-to-date information about this topic.

Sometimes it's important to have the most recent information available, especially for scientific and business-related topics. At other times, particularly with historical topics or those related to the humanities or literature, you may prefer older sources in order to obtain primary information. In either case, as you search for material on your subject, you should determine the date that each item was written in order to evaluate the item thoroughly.

It's easy enough to determine the date that a book was written because the copyright date will be shown on one of the first few left-hand pages; it will also be listed in the online catalog record. The dates for articles are included in the citations you find through periodical databases. Many subscription databases allow results to be displayed in chronological order, either from newest to oldest or oldest to newest. Finding out how old a webpage is can be problematic (like so many things about the web) because websites are constantly updated. If the webmaster has followed the rules of good design and maintenance, the date when the site was last updated should appear prominently on the homepage and on each page that has been revised within the site. Even if a date does appear on a webpage, however, you often have no way of knowing if it is the date of initial creation or the date of most recent revision. Search engines such as Google and Yahoo! offer an advanced search option to limit results to webpages updated within certain time frames: the past 24 hours, the past week, the past month, etc.

The cycle of information, as explained in the previous chapter, should also be considered in evaluating an item. Websites can be updated instantly, while television and radio broadcasts can report about events in real time. Most daily print newspapers report news the following day, while magazines appear later, followed by journals, and finally books. The perspective of each of these resources is different due to the amount of time that has passed between the event and its analysis. Most students prefer more recent information because it is usually easier to obtain. Many older articles are still available only on microfilm, and to find citations for this material you may have to use a print index rather than a periodical database. While full-text electronic sources are definitely convenient, don't rely exclusively on the sources available online because this format favors current rather than retrospective information. An exception to this generalization, however, is that the most recent issues of some periodicals are not available online because the publishers want to encourage sales of the print version.

Accuracy

The basic question when evaluating a source for accuracy is whether the information provided by the source is correct. Accuracy is related to content and is most applicable to evaluating websites. A book or article should have gone through an editorial process that included fact-checking. On the other hand, most websites are often unedited and, as a result, they can contain erroneous information. After reading a number of articles and books on your topic and gaining a working knowledge of it, you may have learned enough to notice inaccuracies in some of your other sources. If a website about the Civil War gives the wrong date for the Battle of Gettysburg, for example, it would be difficult to trust the accuracy of the statistics it provides on the number of casualties. When you detect inaccuracies in a source, you should simply pass it by and use something more reliable.

You should be cautious even if you notice minor errors like misspellings, because they reflect poorly on the source as a whole. Here's an example that points out the weakness of googling your topic and finding sources that have not been edited by reputable publishers: Let's say you always thought that gardeners were more likely to get warts because you had heard about "planters warts." Maybe that's why you never strived to have a green thumb. But gardening does not cause this condition—the correct spelling is *plantar*. *Plantar* refers to the sole of the foot and has nothing to do with plants.

If you googled the inaccurate term **planters warts** you would find nearly as many sites under this misspelling as under the correct search term **plantar warts**. Google searches also turn up mostly *.com* sites, which promote products for treating warts. If you are looking for an authoritative source, such as the Mayo Clinic, you may have to scroll through a few screens. Contrast this with a search of MEDLINE, a periodical database that covers medical journals. Not a single record misspells the term "plantar warts." Databases like MEDLINE also help guarantee that search results will be informative rather than merely commercial. For instance, MEDLINE lists the Mayo Clinic, as well as several other reputable consumer health sites, in the first few hits.

If you use a secondary source, the information upon which it is based should be clearly identified or documented. Even the often-maligned *Wikipedia* appreciates the value of good documentation. Before some articles, the following message appears: "This article does not cite any references or sources. Please help improve this article by adding citations to reliable sources. Unsourced material may be challenged and removed." For books and journal articles to be considered reliable, notes and a bibliography should be included. Otherwise, there's no way to tell whether the author fabricated the information. With clear documentation, a reader can hypothetically check the accuracy of a given source.

Content

Perhaps the most fundamental question to ask when evaluating a source is whether it adequately provides the information you need. You must determine if a resource addresses your topic enough. Does it answer the main questions that you have? The records you find using online catalogs and periodical databases and the results you get from search engines do not always have enough information to evaluate the material described. Even when you are given an abstract in an article citation or a table of contents in an online book record, you may not get a clear idea of what the source will really provide.

An effective way to thoroughly evaluate content is to skim through the actual book, article, or website to see how extensively your topic is addressed. For a book, also look up your topic in the book's index to get a sense of how many pages are devoted to it. Even though the source may have seemed ideal initially, you may realize that it won't really help you. Although you may decide not to use a source and it may feel like you have wasted your time, this is certainly not the case because you increase your knowledge through the evaluation process.

Evaluating content on the web is facilitated by the ability to search a particular page for keywords using the Find feature. Using Internet Explorer, for example, you can click "Find on this page" under Edit in the menu toolbar. Some webpages can be very long. Search for a particular term to see how many times your topic is actually addressed. Although the site may have been located by Google, if your keywords are mentioned only in a parenthetical note, the source will probably not be that useful. Some websites have site indexes that work in much the same way as book indexes, so you can click on a link in this index and go directly to the page within the site that addresses your topic.

The time and effort you spend evaluating resources is well worth it. Think of how much time you spend picking out a new cell phone. If you bought the first one you saw on display, you might be very sorry later on when you realize that this particular phone doesn't really serve your needs. Just like picking the right cell phone, choosing your informational sources requires some critical evaluation. Using the PACAC method to help you choose the most relevant resources for your topic will result in a well-researched paper!

EXERCISES

See Appendix A for answers.

1. For each of the following examples, indicate what type of argumentative appeal is being utilized. (E = emotional/pathos; C = credibility/ethos; L = logical/logos)

    a. A newspaper editorial on lowering the drinking age cites statistics from government reports indicating that automobile accidents did not increase when some states lowered the drinking age in the 1970s. _____

    b. A page on the People for the Ethical Treatment of Animals (PETA) website states, "From hosting *G4s Attack of the Show!* to appearing in summer blockbusters *Date Night* and *Iron Man 2*, Olivia Munn is entertaining audiences all over the globe. Olivia also has a soft spot for animals and was shocked to learn that elephants used in circuses are torn from their mothers at birth." _____

    c. A newspaper article shows one candidate shaking hands with a popular politician, while the same article shows the opposing candidate standing with an unpopular former politician. _____

    d. A writer claims that an environmental disaster will occur in this country if people don't stop driving their cars. _____

    e. A journal article analyzes data from a scientific experiment suggesting that an asteroid will likely collide with the earth in the next century eradicating human beings just as a previous asteroid collision killed off the dinosaurs. _____

    f.   A writer argues that school vouchers do not violate the First Amendment of the U.S. Constitution, which advocates separation of church and state, because the U.S. Supreme Court has decided in a number of cases that school vouchers are indeed constitutional. _____

    g.   A book about the organization Mothers Against Drunk Driving (MADD) begins with the true story of the founder's child being killed by a drunk driver. _____

2. Briefly evaluate the authority of a hypothetical source written by each of the following hypothetical authors. Which would probably be the best source? The worst?

    a.   The owner of a Fortune 500 company who received an honorary degree from a prestigious university

_____

    b.   A former U.S. governor who ran for president

_____

    c.   A college professor who has written numerous journal articles and three previous books

_____

    d.   The founder of an organization that promotes legalization of marijuana

_____

    e.   An award-winning journalist whose articles helped expose a corrupt politician

_____

3. Identify each of the sources below as either primary (P) or secondary (S):

    a.   _____ A book about diaries kept by Civil War soldiers
    b.   _____ A discussion with a member of the Tea Party movement
    c.   _____ A journal article about the author's scientific study of whales
    d.   _____ A magazine article about motion pictures featuring whales
    e.   _____ The diary of a former slave
    f.   _____ A book chapter about the Boston Tea Party written by a twentieth-century historian

Chapter 3

The Wayward Web: Finding Good Sites

The time has come to begin your research. Where do you begin? If you're like most students today, you turn to the World Wide Web, and, like most users of the web, you go to Google, the most popular search engine. But do you know what you're actually doing when you use Google or another search engine such as Yahoo! or Bing? Do you believe you are searching the sum total of human knowledge? Do you consider the web to be one-stop shopping for all your research needs? You expect a list of sites, perhaps containing millions of links, to appear once you click the search button, but the relevance of these sites for your research needs will depend, to a large extent, on the words you choose to enter in the search box. Since you should know what you're actually searching through, you should be aware of a few myths many people have regarding the web.

Myth #1: Everything is on the web.
Reality: Not yet—and maybe not ever.

Myth #2: Any information can be found on the web for free.
Reality: There are many things on the web that you have to pay for.

Myth #3: Google searches the entire web.
Reality: Google, like all the other search engines, covers only part of the web. Microsoft (http://www.pcworld.com/article/111789/microsoft_takes_sides_on_search.html) estimates that 30 to 40 percent of the web is indexed and searchable. The web can be compared to an iceberg: The visible tip of an iceberg constitutes only a fraction of the entire ice-

berg, while the hidden portion underwater is the largest part. In the same way, what you can find using Google is only a fraction of what is out there. All the rest of the web, including important research materials, is found in the part known as the "invisible web," the "deep web," or the "hidden web."

Myth #4: Every search engine returns the same results.
Reality: According to a recent study by Dogpile.com (http://dogpile .com/dogpile/ws/about/_iceUrlFlag=11?_IceUrl=true), there is little overlap, less than 12 percent. This low overlap rate means that it is always a good idea to use more than one search engine or other kinds of search tools when doing serious research.

The web has evolved tremendously since its early days when it was all text, had no graphics or videos, and offered much less interactivity. It has emerged as another essential home and mobile appliance and a tool we use on a daily basis. How could we live without it? What began as a resource mostly used in government and academia has emerged as a predominantly commercial medium. Most businesses rely on it to conduct their daily affairs. Buying things and paying bills online used to be novelties; now they are, for some people, the preferred way of doing business.

An unfortunate side effect of these developments for research purposes is that the web has become overrun by advertising—and sometimes by advertising in disguise. For example, you enter your search words in Google and a results list appears. Most of the sites listed on the first screen of results are probably commercial sites. On the right-hand side of the screen are sponsored links, which are results that appear because companies have paid for them to be included. If you choose a .com site from the sponsored links section, you will likely be directed to a site advertising a product rather than providing information on your topic.

Using the web requires you to vigilantly evaluate sites if you are looking for objective and trustworthy sources of information. As explained in Chapter 2, you must question the purpose of a site. Is it there to sell something or make money? Is its purpose to promote a certain cause or persuade the reader on some issue? You should identify who produced the site or contributed to it in order to determine the authority of the information provided. You should try to determine when the site's information was last updated; many websites are neglected and outdated.

You also must go beyond the first page of sites listed. Don't just rely on the top ten results. Your search may have yielded thousands or even millions of sites. If you don't find anything relevant in the first few screens, narrow down your search to retrieve fewer items. This chapter gives some tips on improving your web search results.

THE CONTENT OF THE WEB

The web is a lot like television. It doesn't cost anything to watch TV—as long as you are content to watch the small number of major network or local stations that are available for free. But if you want to see the big game on ESPN, find out what a life-size statue of Michael Jackson is worth on the History Channel's *Pawn Stars*, or watch that big family on TLC with enough kids to form not one but two baseball teams, you have to pay a monthly fee to a cable company or satellite service. The situation is similar on the web. You can view lots of sites for free. These free sites are the focus of this chapter. As with just about anything that appears to be free, however, there are often hidden costs in the form of advertising and propaganda. What can you find on the web for free? Because of the sheer bulk of information available, only some broad generalizations can be offered here based on the categories of information providers.

Companies

Companies provide information about their products and services on the web. Most of this information is advertising, but sometimes such information can be helpful. If you're writing a paper about lawsuits against a particular cigarette company, you will certainly want to take a look at its website. Many commercial sites are not only sources of information but interactive sites where customers can purchase products and perform transactions.

Nonprofit Organizations

Nonprofit organizations also have a strong presence on the web. These organizations are formed to promote causes, so their sites are designed to help in their missions. No matter how altruistic this mission is, it's important to beware of propaganda and bias when viewing these sites. They're certainly not out to make a profit the way the commercial sites are, but they often have an agenda, including fundraising for their cause.

Government

Departments and agencies of the U.S. government have always had a strong presence on the web, since the basis of the Internet originated in the late 1960s as a project of the Department of Defense. Government websites can be very useful objective sources of information, including statistics, reports, and so on; however, it's important to remember to think critically about any information you find on them.

Schools

Every college and university has a website. Most secondary and elementary schools have their own sites as well. In addition to lots of information about events, student services, courses, and individual departments, colleges often let students and faculty post their own personal pages. While these webpages can be excellent sources for research, be sure to evaluate the material using the PACAC method. You might have at your disposal the wisdom of a world-renowned expert in Shakespearean studies who has made his research available with no thought of financial gain. Or you might be able to view a fraternity site that explains how to brew your own beer.

Individuals

Anyone can create a website. Even a child can easily construct one with no help from an adult. With the current ease of creating websites, information is present and accessible on the web at a level that is unprecedented in human history, and the availability of these primary sources is a significant development. Much of this information is personal and useless to most viewers. Information on a research topic that's found on a personal website might be incorrect. Be critical when using personal sites, and make sure that the original source of any secondary information is clearly cited.

One popular category of personal website is the blog, which has evolved from the original term *web log*. Blogs are online diaries or journals in which bloggers can post anything they want: personal opinions, daily activities, poems, pictures, etc. As with any source of information, determining the identity of the author is important. If the author of a blog is a known expert in your subject, this site may prove to be a valuable primary source. Otherwise, a blog will likely be as useless to you as someone else's junk mail.

While blogs can be considered current primary sources, the web is also rich in historical primary documents. For example, the diary of a nineteenth-century American slave named Adam Plummer (http://anacostia.si .edu/Plummer/Plummer_Diary.htm) would be an excellent primary source if you were doing a research paper about the history of slavery in the United States. This rare document provides a primary account of history from a unique perspective because very few slaves could read or write. The Plummer diary, which in pre-Internet days might have been stored in the bowels of a college library archive where only historians might read it, is now accessible to any student who googles the phrase **slave diary**. The Plummer diary website not only provides links to a transcription of the diary but also photographs of its actual pages. The web abounds in such valuable resources.

Social Networking

Social networking sites have emerged in recent years as one of the predominant uses of the web. Facebook (http://www.facebook.com), the most popular of these sites, is also the most visited site on the entire web, having surpassed Google according to a 2010 Compete.com study. If your research involves particular people who have Facebook pages, this could be a useful resource for primary research. An increasing number of libraries also use Facebook sites as platforms to help guide students to the services they offer.

Twitter (http://twitter.com) is another popular social networking site that allows users to communicate by posting brief 140-character statements. Plurk (http://www.plurk.com) is a similar site that is gaining in popularity. Are these sites, which provide such small pieces of information, of any real use? If your research topic concerns a current issue, take a look and see what comes up. You may find a link to a great website on your topic, an answer to a particular question you have about it, or an announcement about a relevant event happening in your area.

Some social networking sites have emerged to provide users with a means of sharing their bookmarks, or links, to their favorite websites. These bookmarking sites, like Digg (http://digg.com) and Delicious (http://www .delicious.com), can be searched, and the results provide a wide variety of recommendations from around the world. All of these social networking sites provide a mixed bag for your research; they're definitely an interesting gateway to primary sources, but be cautious in evaluating the information provided.

Another mixed bag for research purposes is YouTube (http://www .youtube.com), a website that provides access to videos posted by users. Both trash and treasure can be found on YouTube, just as on the web in general. You can find videos of everything from an elementary school field trip to a butterfly museum to a lecture given by a highly respected astronomer on the origins of the universe. You can also use the general search engines like Google to search for videos. Visual information can be very valuable for your research.

Wikis

Another interesting development on the web has been the emergence of the wiki—a site that can be altered by anyone who can access it. The most popular wiki is *Wikipedia* (http://www.wikipedia.org), an online encyclopedia containing articles on a staggering range of topics. This site can be edited by anyone, expert or not, who wants to add to, delete from, or revise something in an article. Jimmy Wales, the creator of *Wikipedia*, has said that the site shouldn't be used as a scholarly source. While it has mechanisms in place to police controversial topics, incorrect information can still sneak into even the best articles. *Wikipedia* has cleaned up its act recently and is much better about handling bad information and hackers. Some professors recommend *Wikipedia* as a good starting point to their students, demonstrating it in class and referring students to the bibliographies and links that it provides. Other professors tell their students not to use it or at least not to cite it as a resource for their research. Make sure you know what your professor's opinion is about using *Wikipedia*.

THE STRUCTURE OF THE WEB

The web is appropriately named because it certainly is as intricate as a spider's web and very easy to get caught in. The web is composed of millions and millions of websites. These sites include one or more pages. Think of each site as a street; using this image, picture each page as a house on that street. Some streets only have one house; others have many. Every house on the same street will have a similar address except for the unique house number. In the same way, all the pages in a site have the same basic web address but also a unique component. Of course, all the streets are interconnected, just as sites on the web are intricately joined.

Addresses, also called URLs (which stands for uniform resource locators), are entered in the location box of a browser like Internet Explorer in order to access a particular webpage. These addresses used to always start with *www.*, but that is no longer the case. Web addresses may also begin with *http://*, but you can omit this when entering the URL. The domain name, the first part of the address that takes you to a homepage, ends with one of the following codes (called top-level domains) that give an indication of the source of the information:

- *.com*—commercial sites; two other commercial top-level domains are *.pro*, which is specifically for doctors, lawyers, and accountants; and *.biz*.
- *.org*—nonprofit organizations; the specific top-level domain *.museum* is reserved for—you guessed it—museums.
- *.edu*—educational institutions.
- *.gov*—government agencies; the related top-level domain *.mil* specifies a military site.
- *.net*—Internet service providers, which are companies that provide access to the web; personal websites often have this top-level domain.
- *.name*—a top-level domain for personal websites.
- *.info*—a general top-level domain for individual sites, businesses, or organizations.
- Each country has a top-level domain; for example, *.it* for Italy and *.kw* for Kuwait.

Specific addresses for pages in a website beyond the homepage are lengthier and often more complicated, with backslashes to separate each portion of the URL. The term *webpage* is a misleading term because the web does not confine the designer of a website to a certain amount of space. Pages can be of all different lengths. A page on the web is defined as the space that you can scroll through at a particular URL. In addition to providing information, most webpages also contain links to other webpages. You can access other pages by clicking on these hypertext links. Links can be either highlighted text or a graphic or icon.

Your school's homepage probably allows you to connect to all of the different departmental pages, as well as pages about events, services, and the library. The library homepage will likely enable you to connect to its various online resources. There may even be a list of webpages that connects you to different sites throughout the web pertaining to particular topics. Each one of these connections is called a link. When following links, it is easy to lose track of your online location. You may think you are still on your school or library's site when, in fact, you have ventured away from it. Although sites are constantly being added to the web, many are also removed. If you click on a link to a removed site or one that has a new URL, you will be directed to an error page that states the sought-after site cannot be found.

As an example of following links within a site to find specific information within that site, let's suppose you never watched the hit TV show *Lost* and, now that the series has ended and you have time to begin watching it over winter break, you're wondering what all the fuss was about. Midway through your viewing of the second season of *Lost* on DVD, you're a bit confused by the plot of the twelfth episode. You go to the official *Lost* website and get more information about that episode to understand what's going on. While the address for the ABC network homepage is http://abc.go.com and you can actually just enter abc.com to reach the same location, the specific address for the page providing information on the second season's twelfth episode is http://abc.go.com/shows/lost/episode-guide/fire-water/40668, probably not an address you would know off the top of your head unless you are really obsessed with *Lost* trivia. You are more likely to get to this page by clicking on links within the ABC site.

To get to the *Lost* episode page just mentioned:

- Click on the link Shows, which brings up a list of programs.
- From this list select *Lost*, which brings up a page dedicated to the show.
- Click on Episode Guide, which brings up a pull-down menu from which you can select a season and then a particular episode.
- After choosing Season 2 and Episode 12, you will see a summary of this episode as well as a link to view the episode itself.

Clicking through four links is all it took to get from the homepage to the specific page you wanted.

You are not restricted, however, to browsing within one website. As its name has always suggested, the web is a collection of interconnected sites. For example, Bill Arnett, a software engineer interested in astronomy who lives in Arizona, maintains an award-winning website called The Nine Planets (http://nineplanets.org). Arnett has crossed out the "nine" on the homepage, however, and replaced it with the digit "8" to acknowledge Pluto's demotion to dwarf planet status. But if you enter the URL eightplanets.org, you are redirected to nineplanets.org. Let's say your topic for a persuasive essay is to argue that Pluto should still be considered a planet, as Arnett seems to suggest by not simply changing the title and URL of his site to reflect the eight-planet model of the solar system. You've googled **Pluto** and among the results is the page displayed in Figure 3.1 from Arnett's site, referred to hereafter simply as The Nine Planets (http://nineplanets.org/pluto .html).

Among the facts that Arnett cites regarding Pluto is that the planet is named after the Roman god of the underworld; in Greek mythology, this god is referred to as Hades. The name Hades is highlighted because it is a link. Click on this link and you will be taken to an entirely different website, *Encyclopedia Mythica*, not just another page in Arnett's site. This website (http://pantheon.org) provides information on mythology, including a detailed description of the Greek god Hades. Returning to The Nine Planets page about Pluto in Figure 3.1, you will also see a link to the "new definition of 'planet'" if you scroll down the page a bit. Clicking on this link will take you to the website of the International Astronomical Union (http://iau.org), the organization that sets the criteria for determining which objects in the solar system are planets.

Figure 3.1. The Pluto Page from The Nine Planets: A Multimedia Tour of the Solar System

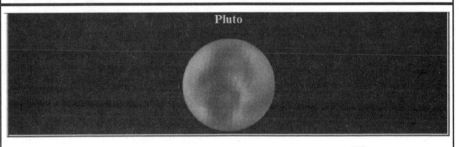

Pluto

Mathews: Pluto - The Renewer

Pluto orbits beyond the orbit of Neptune (usually). It is much smaller than any of the official planets and now classified as a "dwarf planet". Pluto is smaller than seven of the solar system's moons (the Moon, Io, Europa, Ganymede, Callisto, Titan and Triton).

```
orbit:     5,913,520,000 km (39.5 AU) from the Sun (average)
diameter:  2274 km
mass:      1.27e22 kg
```

In Roman mythology, Pluto (Greek: Hades) is the god of the underworld. The planet received this name (after many other suggestions) perhaps because it's so far from the Sun that it is in perpetual darkness and perhaps because "PL" are the initials of Percival Lowell.

SEARCHING TECHNIQUES

Websites such as Google, Yahoo!, and Bing that are specifically designed to help you find other sites are called search engines. Although Google is by far the most popular search engine, you should be aware that there are thousands of others, and you should understand the common features that these search engines share, as well as some of the unique features that distinguish the major ones. Despite the variety of search engines, they all provide a search box in which you can enter your terms and, in return, get a list of links to sites that contain these terms. Search engines often incorporate a variety of resources and services, including web directories, free e-mail, news, chat rooms, and online. Don't be distracted with the opportunities to buy things, chat with people, and check out the latest news. Remember that you have a research paper to write!

Google, which covers billions of pages, has a very sophisticated relevancy-ranking technology that determines order in part by popularity and yields what some users consider the most pertinent results. Although advertising is present in Google results, it is fairly unobtrusive, in the form of links on the right side of the page that are clearly identified as Sponsored Links. Stick to the actual search results for research purposes. And beware—commercial website developers have found ways to work around Google's ranking system to get their websites in the top ten results.

Google's homepage is displayed in Figure 3.2. The main search page is simple and uncluttered. An Advanced Search page is just a click away. In the upper left-hand corner, you can access a search page that limits results to, among other things, images, videos, or news. You can also access maps, shop online, or use Google's free e-mail service, Gmail. Clicking on More brings up a longer list of Google's services which includes Google Books, where you can search for books available to purchase and also view free pages and chapters, and Google Scholar, which provides access to scholarly literature but should not take the place of the databases to which your library subscribes.

Google, however, has not yet completely monopolized the search engine market. Bing (http://www.bing.com), formerly MSN Search, is Microsoft's search engine. With its search results, it offers a selection of suggested "Related Searches," which is a nice feature for people new to searching. Yahoo! (http://www.yahoo.com), one of the oldest directories on the web, yields search results that include "Also try:" suggestions. Meta-search engines simultaneously search multiple search engines including Google, Yahoo!, and

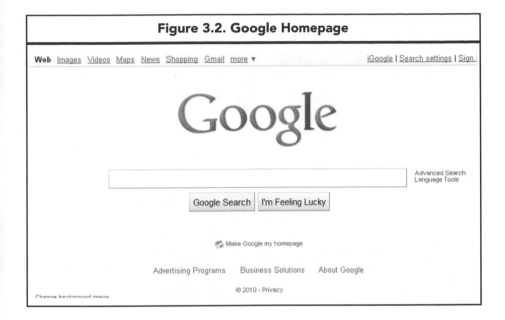

Figure 3.2. Google Homepage

Bing. Although these meta-search tools are not used as much as the search engines they cover, Dogpile (http://dogpile.com) is the most popular in this category.

Other websites can help you find information that the major search engines do not cover. By using these resources you can begin to search the invisible web, which represents a much larger part of the web than is indexed through such search engines as Yahoo! and Google. It can take more effort to find these sources, but they can provide valuable information. The information found in the deep web is stored in databases, in formats that search engines can't collect, and deep within large websites. Many of them enlist the help of volunteers.

- About.com (http://www.about.com)—This site offers in-depth articles on a wide range of topics, all of which are written by the more than 750 expert human site guides and freelance writers who are employed by About.com.
- INFOMINE (http://infomine.ucr.edu)—This web directory covers scholarly resources.
- ipl2 (http://ipl.org)—More than 20,000 sites carefully chosen by librarians are included in this web directory that represents a merger of

the Internet Public Library (IPL) with the Librarians' Internet Index (LII).

- Open Directory Project (http://www.dmoz.org)—More than 4.5 million sites are indexed by this directory compiled by volunteer editors.
- WWW Virtual Library (http://vlib.org)—This is an advertising-free directory of the web compiled by volunteers who are experts in a wide range of subject areas.
- Wolfram|Alpha (http://www.wolframalpha.com)—This website calls itself a "computational knowledge engine: it generates output by doing computations from its own internal knowledge base, instead of searching the web and returning links." It is often listed with invisible web tools as it compiles information that would be hard to collect otherwise.
- CompletePlanet (http://www.completeplanet.com)—This website helps find specialized databases by subject, claiming the most complete list of traditional web search engines and deep web databases.

To provide a way to access sites by subject, search engines often have directories that arrange sites hierarchically into various categories. Thus you can browse if your topic is fairly broad, rather than enter keywords in the search box. Most of the major search engines, including Google, integrate the Open Directory Project (ODP) into their site to provide the directory listings. The Open Directory Project (http://www.dmoz.org) categorizes more than 4.5 million websites under a small number of main headings listed in its directory. The homepage of this directory is displayed in Figure 3.3.

Clicking on one of ODP's main headings will bring you to another page that lists the subheadings for the chosen topic. For example, let's say you wanted to find a list of websites that provide TV theme-song lyrics. Clicking on the first category in the directory Arts brings up the screen displayed in Figure 3.4.

From this screen select Television. The next screen to appear is shown in Figure 3.5, which lists narrower subheadings, including Theme Songs.

Click on Theme Songs and you will see the listing of individual sites, as displayed in Figure 3.6.

What Are You Really Searching?

As mentioned at the beginning of this chapter, no search engine covers the entire web. Even a meta-search engine such as Dogpile, which allows you to

Figure 3.3. Open Directory Project's Homepage

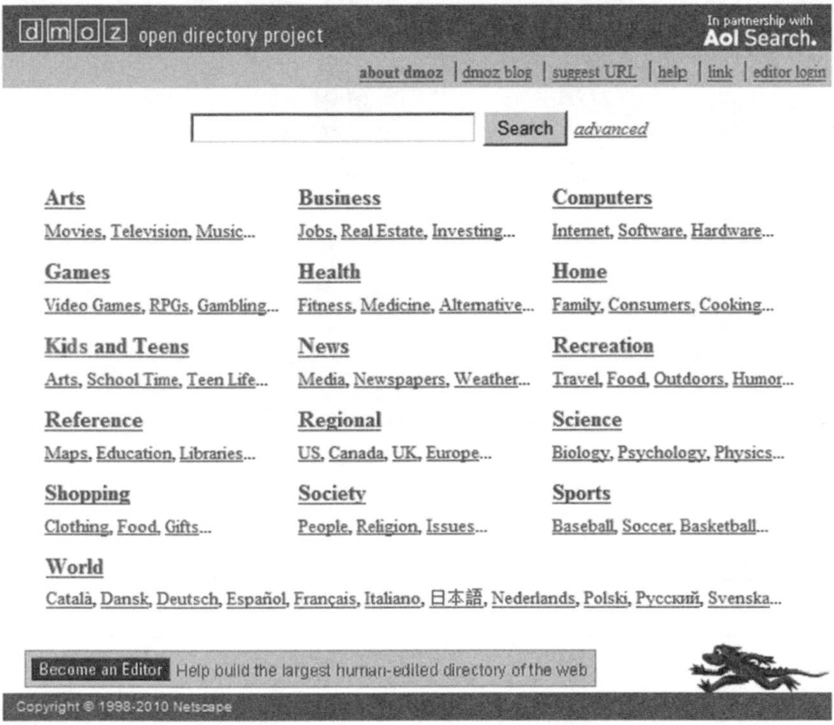

search multiple engines simultaneously, doesn't cover every single page. There are two ways that search engines select the sources to be covered. The first occurs when human beings evaluate sites for inclusion in a directory. Yahoo!, for example, employs a team of people to find acceptable sites and then assign a category to each one. Yahoo! also accepts user submissions, which are also evaluated for inclusion by the Yahoo! team. The second method involves search engines that allow you to search outside the limited scope of a human-compiled subject directory by automating the whole process of selection; they send out electronic "spiders" that "crawl" to sites and add them to the database. The spiders then follow all of the links on the initial sites and add all of those secondary sites, and so on. Some search engines that boast the number of pages they index rely on quantity rather than qual-

---

Figure 3.4. Open Directory Project's Arts Directory

<u>Top</u>: **Arts** *(227,738)*   <u>Description</u>

- <u>Animation</u> *(9,217)*
- <u>Antiques</u>@ *(787)*
- <u>Architecture</u> *(3,041)*
- <u>Art History</u> *(2,168)*
- <u>Bodyart</u> *(779)*
- <u>Classical Studies</u> *(395)*
- <u>Comics</u> *(3,548)*
- <u>Costumes</u> *(32)*
- <u>Crafts</u> *(6,199)*
- <u>Dance</u>@ *(5,298)*
- <u>Design</u> *(1,045)*
- <u>Digital</u> *(233)*
- <u>Entertainment</u> *(478)*
- <u>Graphic Design</u> *(427)*
- <u>Humanities</u> *(229)*
- <u>Illustration</u> *(2,057)*

- <u>Literature</u> *(22,771)*
- <u>Movies</u> *(34,884)*
- <u>Music</u> *(70,339)*
- <u>Myths and Folktales</u>@ *(363)*
- <u>Native and Tribal</u>@ *(418)*
- <u>Online Writing</u> *(3,158)*
- <u>Performing Arts</u> *(21,014)*
- <u>Photography</u> *(3,851)*
- <u>Radio</u> *(2,231)*
- <u>Rhetoric</u>@ *(69)*
- <u>Television</u> *(10,140)*
- <u>Theatre</u>@ *(5,115)*
- <u>Typography</u>@ *(88)*
- <u>Video</u> *(237)*
- <u>Visual Arts</u> *(15,149)*
- <u>Writers Resources</u> *(2,318)*

---

ity. This difference is important when it comes to evaluating the results of your search.

If your topic is somewhat broad, you might want to use a search engine's directory that covers fewer sites and employs some selection criteria. On the other hand, if your topic is a bit more obscure, you may want to start by entering keywords in the search box. To make sure your search is comprehensive, you should use more than one search engine, so that potentially worthwhile materials don't slip through any gaps of a particular search engine's coverage.

Searching Tips

Each search engine is a little different. Most have help pages that provide you with tips and examples to highlight their unique features. There are both basic and advanced ways of using web search engines, but typically the average user never gets beyond entering a string of keywords in the search box

---

Figure 3.5. Open Directory Project's Arts: Television Directory

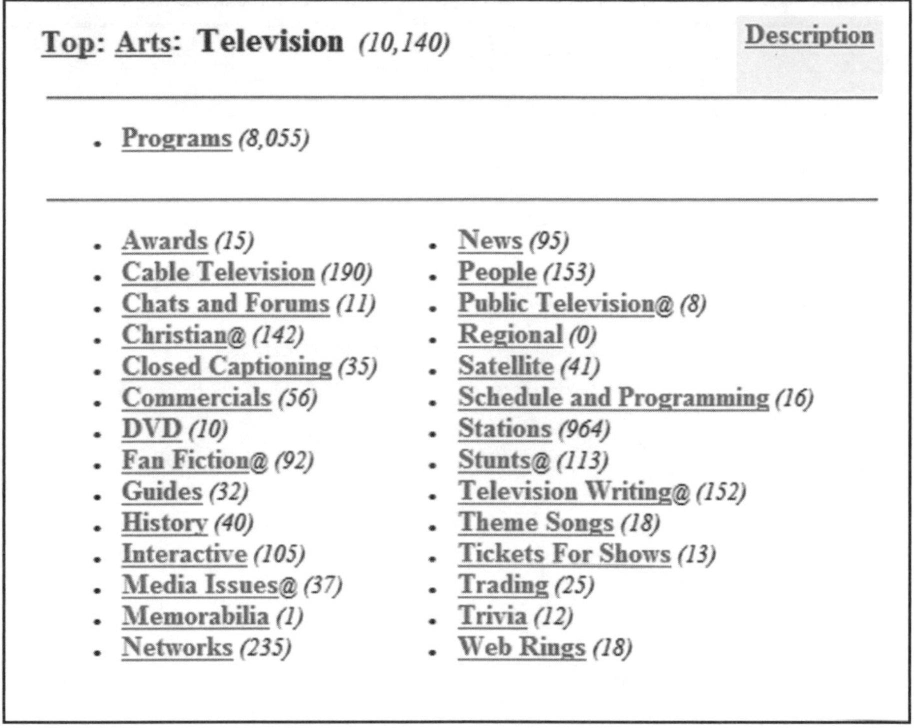

Top: Arts: **Television** *(10,140)*   Description

- Programs *(8,055)*

- Awards *(15)*
- Cable Television *(190)*
- Chats and Forums *(11)*
- Christian@ *(142)*
- Closed Captioning *(35)*
- Commercials *(56)*
- DVD *(10)*
- Fan Fiction@ *(92)*
- Guides *(32)*
- History *(40)*
- Interactive *(105)*
- Media Issues@ *(37)*
- Memorabilia *(1)*
- Networks *(235)*

- News *(95)*
- People *(153)*
- Public Television@ *(8)*
- Regional *(0)*
- Satellite *(41)*
- Schedule and Programming *(16)*
- Stations *(964)*
- Stunts@ *(113)*
- Television Writing@ *(152)*
- Theme Songs *(18)*
- Tickets For Shows *(13)*
- Trading *(25)*
- Trivia *(12)*
- Web Rings *(18)*

---

on the homepage and then browsing through a list of links that can often contain irrelevant sites.

Here are some tips for making the most of search engine capabilities:

- Generally, if you enter a string of keywords, the word **AND** is implied between them in most of the major search engines. **AND** is a special word called a Boolean operator. These words, which also include **OR** and **NOT** will be discussed at length in Chapter 4. So the more keywords you enter, the fewer results you will get and the more precise your search will be.

- Because **AND** is implied, an almost universal rule is that, in order to find an exact phrase, you enter it within quotation marks. If you enter **Faith Hill** in a search engine without quotation marks, you would retrieve all the sites that contain the words **faith** and **hill**, so some of

---

Figure 3.6. Open Directory Project's Arts: Television: Theme Songs Directory

<u>Top</u>: <u>Arts</u>: <u>Television</u>: **Theme Songs** *(18)*   <u>Description</u>

- <u>E-Mail Request</u> *(2)*

- <u>Classic Television Theme Songs and Images</u> - Large collection of themes with their accompanying show logos.
- <u>Classic Themes</u> - Title, composer and publisher information for thousands of classic American TV themes, old-time radio themes and 1950's light music compositions.
- <u>Cowboystars of TV</u> - A collection of theme songs from 1950-60's TV and an interactive trivia quiz.
- <u>Dyla-Vision</u> - Classic TV, theme songs, airing dates, and cast information.
- <u>Mark Little's MyThemes.TV</u> - Includes TV theme tunes alongside jingles, commercials and promos. Also features a mystery theme of the month.
- <u>Matt's TV Theme Songs</u> - Theme tunes in Midi format.
- <u>Midi Database</u> - Collection of TV Themes in midi format.
- <u>Network News Music</u> - Nicely put together site with Real Audio themes to US network newscasts and news magazines. It also features information on each.

---

these sites would be about the singer while others would be irrelevant, including a number relating to mountains and the Bible.

- You can also use the word **OR** between search terms to broaden your search in most search engines. Some search engines consider **OR** a keyword rather than a connecting term unless it is entered in capital letters.
- The minus sign (–) allows you to eliminate a term from your search. For example, if you entered **"Pirates of the Caribbean" –"Johnny Depp"** in just about any of the search engines, you will increase your chances of finding sites concerned with the Disney World attraction rather than Johnny Depp fan club sites and other sites concerned with the swashbuckling movie series.

- Conversely, the plus sign (+) indicates that a term must be found, which is most useful when you need to find words that the search engine usually ignores, such as prepositions (**at, to, from,** and so on) and other short words (including **where, what,** and **that**).

Most search engines have an advanced search page that facilitates the searching process. As you can see in Figure 3.7, Google provides a more detailed search form that simplifies searching by retrieving only sites with "all these words," "this exact wording or phrase," or "one or more of these

Figure 3.7. Google Advanced Search Page

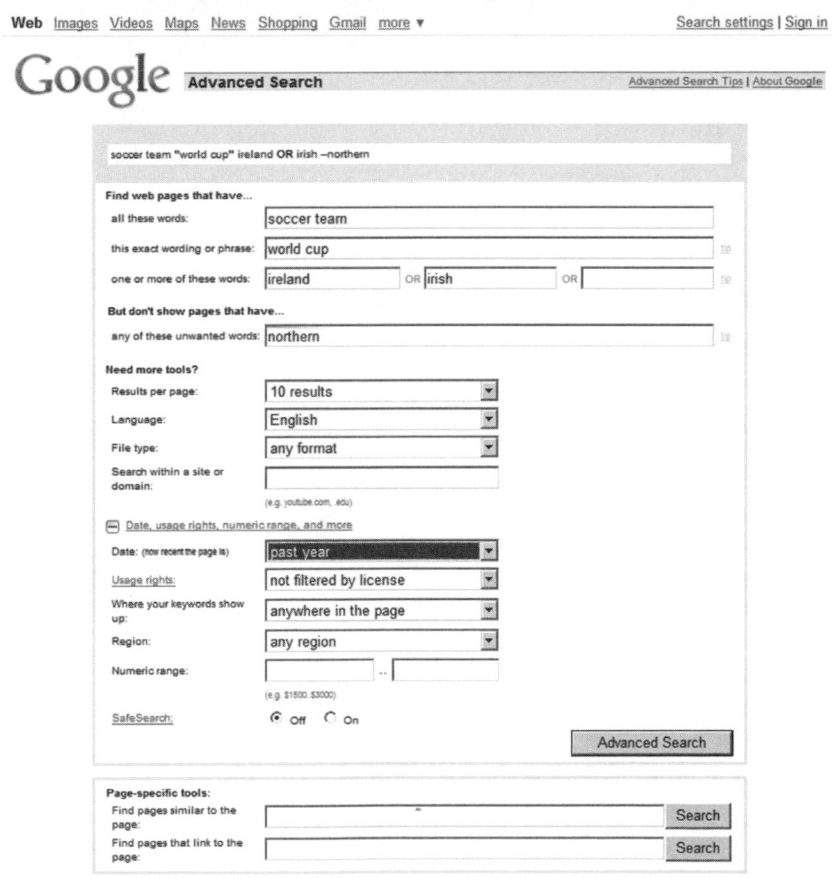

words." You can also specify that you do not want to retrieve sites with "any of these unwanted words." The advanced search screen also lets you limit your search by language and date updated, and allows you to specify where you want the terms to occur (for example, in the title of the webpage, which can help retrieve more relevant sites, or anywhere in the page, which will increase your results). You can also limit your search to certain types of sites, such as educational (*.edu*), nonprofit (*.org*), etc.

The web is an amazing resource that has transformed the way we do research. A lot of the information that is now available literally at our fingertips was previously inaccessible or, at best, very difficult to obtain. It's no surprise, then, that you might think googling your topic is all you need to do to find the sources for your research paper. If that were the case, however, this book would be very short. Read on to discover how much more lies beneath the surface.

EXERCISES

See Appendix A for answers.

1. Which website would be the best choice if you needed to find a few carefully reviewed noncommercial sites about hybrid cars?

    a. Google
    b. Open Directory Project
    c. Yahoo!
    d. About.com

2. Which website would be the best choice if you wanted to search several popular search engines simultaneously?

    a. Ask.com
    b. Google
    c. WWW Virtual Library
    d. Dogpile

3. Which website would be the best choice if you wanted to find the most links to other sites about your topic?

    a. Yahoo!
    b. About.com

    c. Google

    d. Open Directory Project

4. All of the following websites are free from advertising except:

    a. Bing

    b. Open Directory Project

    c. ipl2

    d. WWW Virtual Library

5. Which basic Google search would be the best way to retrieve links to sites about the small tornados that occur in the southwestern United States called dust devils?

    a. **dust devil**

    b. **"dust devil"**

    c. **"dust devil tornado"**

    d. **"dust devil" tornado**

6. What will the advanced Google search displayed in Figure 3.7 do?

    a. Find sites about the Irish World Cup soccer team.

    b. Eliminate sites about the English World Cup soccer team, which includes Northern Ireland.

    c. Both a and b.

    d. Neither a nor b.

7. Google your topic and choose one website from the first page of links retrieved.

    a. What terms did you enter in the search box? _____

    _____

    b. What is the title and address of the site you chose?
        Title: _____
        Address: _____

    c. Evaluate the website using the PACAC method:
        Purpose: _____
        Authority: _____
        Currency: _____
        Accuracy: _____
        Content: _____

Chapter 4

Database Directions: Honing Your Search

So now that you've browsed around the web using Google or another search engine and found a few sites that pertain to your topic, your research is all done and it's time to write your paper. Right? Wrong! Maybe in high school that was enough, but this is college, and the bar has been raised. After reading the previous chapter, it should be clear that you have only seen the tip of the iceberg. Now it is time to delve deeper.

Visit your college library's website where you will be able to access a multitude of resources that will help you find the information you need at any hour of the day or night. These resources, called databases, are collections of information in a computerized format. The databases provided through your library website, which are carefully chosen by your librarians, are gold mines of information.

Your school pays large amounts of money for most of the databases provided on your library website, which is why these resources are often referred to as subscription databases. The databases that your library subscribes to include material which is not available on the free web. Using these databases, you can find articles and other information that is not available through a Google search. Librarians select these databases with you, the student, in mind. No college library has the same combination of resources because each school is unique, with different emphases on certain programs and majors. If your school has a nursing program, for example, the library website should provide access to *The Cumulative Index to Nursing and Allied Health Literature*. If film studies is a popular major, it's likely that your school subscribes to the *Film Literature Index*. Most libraries subscribe to general reference databases, such as *Britannica Online* and *CQ Researcher*.

Appendix B describes many of the subscription databases currently used in academic libraries.

Another reason subscription databases should be used is that human editors have selected the information included in them. These databases are constructed by people who make individual decisions about content and subject coverage. In contrast, web search engine content and coverage are generally automated by computer programs. This human component contributes to the overall superiority of your library's online databases.

A database usually focuses on one particular topic, a fact that is important because as you progress in your studies, your research will require an increasing level of specialization. Using a subject-specific database is a more efficient and time-saving way of doing research than using a web search engine that covers sites on many unrelated subject areas. Another advantage of library subscription databases is that most of them clearly distinguish scholarly from popular material, an essential distinction in college-level research. You can also obtain the full text of many sources by using these databases. In contrast, using Google, you may be directed to a useful site that requires a fee to get the complete text of a source; or if there is no charge for access, you may have to close numerous pop-up ad windows.

Each library website interface is different, and each has a unique collection of databases, but fundamentally they provide the same types of resources. Featured prominently on the homepage should be a link to the online catalog, a large database providing information about all the items that the library owns. While this link may be called Online Catalog, it might be referred to in other ways, such as a Find Books link. On some library websites, a search box is part of the homepage to allow you to enter keywords to search the catalog immediately. Online catalogs do include more than just the books shelved in your library. Many include information about journals and magazines so you can determine whether your library subscribes to a certain periodical. Links to electronic books (e-books) that the library has purchased are also included, as is information about video material, government documents, etc. Your library homepage may also provide an option to search other libraries in your area.

Many academic library websites also have research guides for particular subject areas that suggest appropriate resources to use, including periodical databases, reference sources, and free websites that have been selected by the librarians because they are particularly useful for the needs of the students at a particular school. Because they are free, these sites are often provided by governmental or nonprofit organizations or other educational institutions rather than commercial sources. Among the numerous free websites that are often linked to by college library websites are Purdue University's Purdue Online Writing Lab (OWL) site (http://owl.english.purdue .edu), which was highlighted in Chapter 1; periodical databases that are provided by government agencies such as Education Resources Information Center, or ERIC (http://eric.ed.gov), and MedlinePlus (http://medlineplus .gov); and the United Nations website (http://www.un.org/en/databases), which provides a library of important documents.

Another link on your library homepage should provide direct access to all of the available subscription databases, which are usually categorized alphabetically and sometimes also by subject area if there are a lot of them. Some college libraries have hundreds of databases. Your library website might simply have a link on its homepage—such as Find Articles—that leads you to the databases.

THE STRUCTURE OF DATABASES

One type of database that all libraries have is an online catalog, which is a collection of information about the items owned by a particular library. Each item owned by your library, whether a book, a journal, a DVD, or some other medium, has a record in your library's online catalog. Just as a database is composed of individual records, each record is composed of individual elements called fields. A field is a certain type of information about the item. Figure 4.1 is an example of a record for a book.

Figure 4.1. Example of an Online Catalog Record

AUTHOR:	Tyson, Neil deGrasse.
TITLE:	The Pluto files : the rise and fall of America's favorite planet.
EDITION:	1st ed.
PUBLISHED:	New York: W.W. Norton, c2009
DESCRIPTION:	xii, 194 p.: ill. (chiefly color) ; 22 cm.
CONTENTS:	Pluto in culture -- Pluto in history -- Pluto in science -- Pluto's fall from grace -- Pluto divides the nation -- Pluto's judgment day -- Pluto the dwarf planet -- Pluto in the elementary school classroom -- Plutologue
NOTE:	Includes bibliographical references (p. 181-182), appendices, and index.
SUMMARY:	An exploration of the controversy surrounding Pluto and its planet status from a renowned astrophysicist at the heart of the controversy.
SUBJECTS:	Pluto (Dwarf Planet)
ISBN:	9780393065206 (hardcover)
FORMAT:	Book
LOCATION:	QB701 .T97 2009
AVAILABILITY:	Checked Out. Due: 10/10/10.

Fields for a book record should include the following:

- Author (usually a link you can click to retrieve all items held by the library by the same author)—some books have editors instead of or in addition to authors.
- Title
- Publisher and year of publication
- Physical description—this includes such information as the number of pages and the length of the book's spine (*The Pluto Files* is 194 pages long plus a 12-page introduction; it has mostly color illustrations, and is 22 centimeters long).
- The format of the item—this should indicate whether it is a book or something else.
- Subject headings (which are also links you can click to retrieve all items in the library on the same subject)
- Numbers that identify the book, such as the International Standard Book Number (ISBN) or the Library of Congress Control Number (LCCN)
- The call number, which enables you to find the book on the shelf
- The status, indicating whether the book is available or checked out

A record in the online catalog for a book may also include these elements:

- Table of contents (useful if you are searching for book chapters on your topic)
- Notes indicating the item's special features (for example, if a book has an index or glossary)
- Brief summary
- Edition number (to differentiate item from other editions of the same book)
- The library the item can be found in if the college has multiple library locations, or if the library shares its catalog as part of a consortium

Another type of resource that is commonly available on library websites is the periodical database—a collection of records describing articles in magazines and journals. Figure 4.2 displays a record for a journal article from a periodical database.

Figure 4.2. Example of a Record from EBSCOhost Academic Search Premier

---

What Happened to Pluto?

Authors: Consolmagno, Guy1

Source: Physics Teacher; Jan2007, Vol. 45 Issue 1, p14-19, 6p, 2 Color Photographs

Document Type: Article

Subject Terms: *DWARF planets
*EARTH
*ORBITS
*PLANETS
PLUTO (Dwarf planet)
SOLAR system

Company/Entity: INTERNATIONAL Astronomical Union

Abstract: The article focuses on the demotion of the planet *Pluto* into a dwarf planet status. The planet is a thousand times smaller than Earth and its orbit is highly eccentric and inclined *to* the plane of the other planets' orbits. The International Astronomical Union published resolutions that divided all the objects in the solar system into three classes, namely planet, dwarf planets and small solar system objects. It also noted that *Pluto* was the first of a special class of trans-neptunian dwarf planets.

Author : Vatican Observatory, Vatican City State

A record for an article should include the following fields:

- Article title (or headline, in the case of a newspaper article)
- Author (staff-written articles might not specify an author)
- Periodical title (sometimes referred to as the "source")
- Issue, volume, date, and page numbers needed to locate the article and cite it properly (magazines usually have only a date and page numbers)
- Subject headings or terms (specialized subject headings such as geographic terms or people may also be included)

An article record may also include these elements:

- Descriptive information regarding illustrations
- Abstract—a summary of the article

- Lead paragraph—providing this field is helpful for searching purposes because if your keywords appear in the first paragraph, it is likely that they are not just passing references; therefore, the articles retrieved when searching the lead paragraph will be more relevant than those found searching the entire article.
- Full text—records available through subscription periodical databases often provide the complete text of the articles.

Other databases that may be available on your library website are electronic versions of reference sources, including encyclopedias, dictionaries, and almanacs. Many of these sources will be discussed in Chapter 7.

SEARCHING DATABASES

Databases can be composed of thousands or sometimes even millions of records. How do you find the records that pertain to your topic out of this huge amount of information? By utilizing the searching techniques described in this section, you will save time and frustration. There are two basic ways of finding information on a topic: by keyword and by subject. Keywords are words that appear anywhere in a database record while subjects are standardized terms under which items are categorized. A subject search will locate words in the subject field only. Although it is more precise to find a book or article by subject, keyword searching is a good way to start your search.

Keyword searching allows you to search for single words or phrases, as well as combinations of words and phrases, in just about any field. As a general rule, avoid using common prepositions and articles (such as **the**, **of**, **to**), which are known as stop words, as well as three special terms, **and**, **or**, and **not**, which serve a special function to be discussed shortly. The principles discussed here form the basis of searching any computerized database and of using web search engines more effectively.

Keyword Searching Using AND

Unless you have a very general topic that can be defined by a single word or phrase, you need to know how to do a keyword search for multiple keywords. Keyword searching is invaluable for finding material on multidisciplinary subjects that are difficult if not impossible to define by one single subject. Keyword searching using more than one term or phrase operates according to the principles of Boolean logic, which were developed by George Boole, a nineteenth-century mathematician. The simple rules of Boolean searching can be used to define a topic very specifically, so that from among millions of records in a database you can find the ones that best meet your needs.

Suppose you wanted articles concerning drug abuse among women. To understand Boolean logic, picture two sets of articles: the first contains all those about women, and the second contains all those about drug abuse. The articles that are about both women and drug abuse form a common subset. When the search **women and drug abuse** is entered, records that contain the two terms specified are retrieved, as illustrated in Figure 4.3 in what is called a Venn diagram.

The portion of this diagram in gray is the set representing records that include the terms **women** and **drug abuse**. The more terms you link together, the narrower your search becomes and the fewer records you will retrieve. For instance, a search for **women and drug abuse and treatment** will retrieve a narrower set, as illustrated in Figure 4.4.

The portion of Figure 4.4 that appears black is the set representing records that include the terms **women** and **drug abuse** and **treatment**. The sections in gray indicate where only two of the three sets overlap. Notice that the

Figure 4.3. Venn Diagram Representing a Search for women and drug abuse

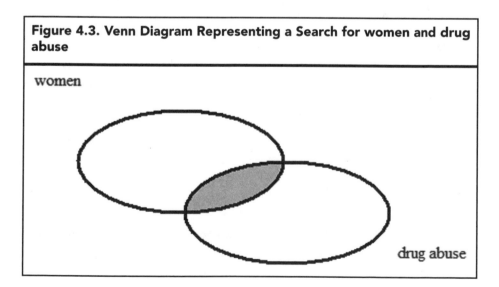

women

drug abuse

Figure 4.4. Venn Diagram Representing a Search for women and drug abuse and treatment

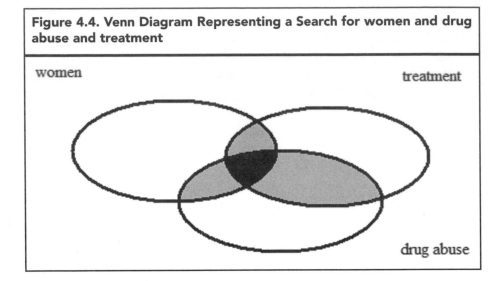

black section in Figure 4.4 is smaller than the gray portion in Figure 4.3 because the number of articles found is smaller.

If you don't find any records, or if you find only a few, you can try removing a search word. This will broaden your search. Or if you get too much, narrow your search by adding a term. You will find that keyword searching can often be a process of trial and error.

Keyword Searching Using OR

You can also use the word **OR** between terms to broaden a keyword search. Picture a set containing all the books about drug usage and another set containing all the books about alcohol usage. Some of these books may certainly overlap in subject material covering both topics. But the set resulting from a search for drug usage or alcohol usage will contain not only the books that address both topics but also those that are about one topic or the other.

In Figure 4.5, the area in dark gray represents those books that address both topics, but the areas in light gray are also included in the resultant set because the connecting term **OR** was used. If you were to add another term to this search using **OR**, the outcome would be even larger because the more terms you link together with **OR**, the broader your search becomes; this is the opposite of what happens when using **AND**.

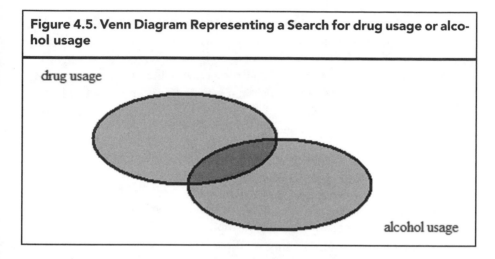

Figure 4.5. Venn Diagram Representing a Search for drug usage or alcohol usage

drug usage

alcohol usage

Truncation

Truncation can serve a purpose similar to that of **OR**. With this technique, available in most databases, you drop the ending of a word and replace it with a truncation symbol. This symbol differs among catalogs and other computerized databases. The question mark (?), asterisk (*), and pound sign (#) are frequently used. For example, you could enter **environment?**, which would retrieve all of the records containing any words beginning with *environment*; in addition to *environment* itself, you would also retrieve *environments, environmental, environmentalists*, and so on. In some databases, no symbol is necessary and truncation is automatic. If you're uncertain, be sure to check the database's online help files regarding truncation (sometimes also called "wild card searching") before you search.

Truncation is helpful when you want to retrieve both the plural and singular forms of a word; just substitute the truncation symbol for the *s*. In some databases you can also use truncation symbols within words. For instance, if you wanted to find either *woman* or *women*, you might be able to enter **wom?n**, which would serve the same purpose as the lengthier **woman OR women**.

Keyword Searching Using NOT

You can use the word **NOT** between terms to eliminate irrelevant items. For example, if you wanted to find all the articles about drug usage in a particular periodical database but weren't interested in those dealing with alcohol usage, you could enter the search as **drug usage not alcohol usage**. This would eliminate all the records in which the word *alcohol* appears, as Figure 4.6 illustrates.

In this figure, the area in gray again represents the resultant set. Now, though, it is a subset not of both original sets, but only of the set of books about drug usage. Although **NOT** is used less often than the other two connecting terms, it can be very helpful in avoiding one of the pitfalls of keyword searching: retrieving irrelevant records.

Combining AND, OR, and NOT

Databases allow you to combine **AND**s, **OR**s, and **NOT**s in one search so that you can more precisely define your topic. Advanced search entry forms simplify this process by providing multiple boxes in which to enter search terms. For example, in Figure 4.7, the upper right corner of the advanced search screen of Academic Search Premier is displayed. Notice the two boxes that say **AND** and **OR**. These are pull-down menus that allow you to select any one of the Boolean operators. By entering terms in the three text entry boxes and specifying which Boolean operators you want to use, you can construct a more precise search of the database. Rows can be added if you need to make your search even more specific.

The example in Figure 4.7 displays a search for articles about obesity among children or adolescents. Literally, the search term set is **obesity and children or adolescents**. So will the set of retrieved articles include ones

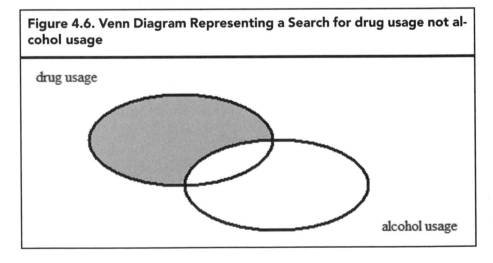

Figure 4.6. Venn Diagram Representing a Search for drug usage not alcohol usage

drug usage

alcohol usage

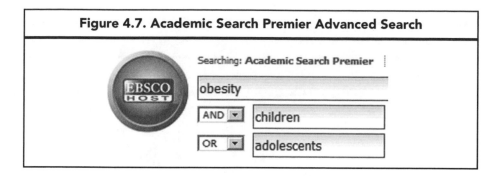

about obesity among children as well as articles just about adolescents in general? That doesn't sound like what you want, but the ambiguous search phrase could be interpreted in that way. These two possible Boolean searches are displayed in Figure 4.8.

Fortunately, in databases that can be searched using Boolean logic, the order in which the operators take effect begins with **OR**. In the previous example, a set would first be formed of all the records containing children or adolescents; then a set containing all the records for obesity would be formed. In the first diagram, the areas where the obesity set overlaps with the set of children *or* the set of adolescents are highlighted in black and gray, and this section forms the set of records you want to retrieve. In contrast, the incorrect diagram below this one includes the set of all records about adolescents, even if they don't overlap with obesity. This set reflects an incorrect ordering of Boolean operators.

In this hierarchy of Boolean operators, **NOT** takes precedence over both **AND** and **OR**, so if **NOT** appears in a search phrase, the term following **NOT** cannot appear in any of the retrieved records. Before any other sets are formed, therefore, any record containing the word following **NOT** is eliminated.

Advanced searching options are also available on most web search engines. Referring back to Figure 3.7 in the last chapter (see p. 49), Google's advanced search simplifies the process by providing the following choices:

- "Find web pages that have . . . all these words" (**AND**)
- "Find web pages that have . . . one or more of these words" (**OR**)
- "But don't show pages that have . . . any of these unwanted words" (**NOT**)

Figure 4.8. Correct and Incorrect Venn Diagrams for the Search obesity and children or adolescents

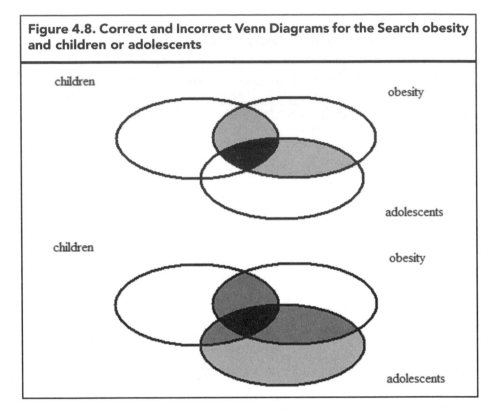

In other search engines, "Include all terms" or "Search must include" boxes allow you to perform a Boolean **AND** search. "Include any term" or "Search must include one of the following" boxes imply that you are using **OR**; and "Do not include term" or "Search must not include" boxes accomplishes the same thing as using **NOT**. To find an exact phrase, either put it in quotation marks or, if available, use an advanced search box that specifies a search for exact phrase as Google does ("Find web pages that have . . . this exact wording or phrase").

Problems with Keyword Searching

Although keyword searching can allow you to search a database with great precision, it does have disadvantages. The first problem is a lack of comprehensiveness. Keyword searching does not necessarily retrieve every record on a subject. For example, if you searched EBSCOhost Academic Search Premier for articles about swine flu and entered **swine flu** as a keyword phrase, you would certainly find a lot of records that contain this phrase. Most of these records will list **H1N1 influenza** as a subject heading. Not every record for an article with the subject heading **H1N1 influenza**, however, will contain the keyword phrase **swine flu**, since that's not the official name of the disease. If you look up **H1N1**, you will retrieve twice as many records for this topic than if you search for **swine flu**. EBSCOhost databases offer assistance with the Thesaurus Term Guide located on the left side of the results page, a tool that can help you identify other search terms. For **swine flu**, it offers **swine influenza, pandemics, H1N1**, and others.

If you rely on keyword searching, it is important to think of all possible synonymous terms. For example, if your topic is the impact of television advertising on teenagers, there are a number of synonyms you need to consider. Teenagers might also be referred to as adolescents, young adults, or simply teens. Advertising, as it relates to TV, could be referred to as commercials.

Another drawback of keyword searching is the retrieval of irrelevant material, which results from words being taken out of context. If you wanted a book about the architecture of Boston, for example, and were to enter **boston and architecture** in the online catalog, in addition to retrieving all the records for books about Boston architecture, you would also retrieve all the books about architecture that were published *in* Boston but not necessarily *about* Boston. Basic keyword searching generally picks up words throughout the record, including the publisher field.

Keyword searching also often retrieves peripheral material. Because keyword searching searches throughout the item record, which might also include summaries for books or even the full text of articles, you might retrieve records that contain only a small amount of information on your topic. For example, articles about Pluto might be found if you searched for the keyword **dwarves** because Pluto is now characterized as a *dwarf* planet. What you are really looking for, however, are articles about "little people" (as they preferred to be called).

Field-Specific Searching

To lessen the possibility of retrieving irrelevant or peripheral material, some databases allow you to limit your keyword searches to particular fields in a record. For example, for books about Boston architecture, you could indicate that you want to find these words only when they are located within the subject headings of records or within the titles. This would eliminate books that were published in Boston but are not about Boston. Limiting keyword searches to subjects and titles is an excellent way to refine your search if you find that you have retrieved too many records or irrelevant records.

You will probably have to use an advanced search screen to access this capability. Figure 4.9 shows the pull-down menu provided in Academic Search Premier that enables you to specify certain fields in which to search. The best fields to use to focus your search are title, subject terms, and abstract. But you may have to find an article in a particular journal, in which case searching the SO (journal name) field would be helpful.

Searching by Subject

Despite the apparent ease of keyword searching, there is no better way to retrieve a complete list of relevant material than by subject searching. Although finding the appropriate subject heading is often a process of trial and error, it's worth the effort. By finding the right subject heading, you eliminate the need to think of all the synonyms for your keywords. While some search engines, such as Yahoo!, do have subject directories, there is not yet a system for subject searching the web as thoroughly as those currently used

Figure 4.9. Field-Selection Pull-Down Menu in Academic Search Premier

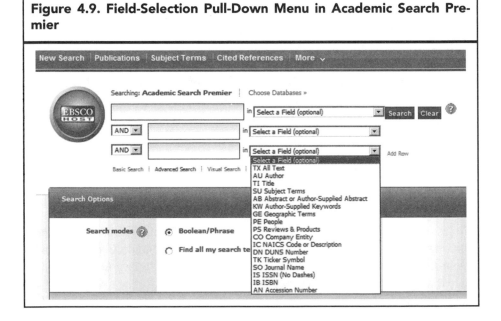

for online catalogs and periodical indexes. Part of the reason you retrieve so much junk when using web search engines is that the web does not rely on subject headings in its overall organization.

Librarians use the phrase *controlled vocabulary* when referring to the standardized set of subject headings used to categorize records in a database. Most database records have a subject field that employs some sort of controlled vocabulary. In the online catalog, for instance, books are assigned Library of Congress (LC) subject headings, a standard set of terminology used by all libraries to categorize their books. Chapter 5 describes in detail how to determine the proper subject headings when searching the online catalog for books.

Unfortunately, no universal subject headings have been established to classify articles as has been done for books. Although some online services have adopted LC headings, many periodical databases have their own terminology. Although there may be a controlled vocabulary within a database, the same terms may not necessarily be used in another database. Many databases have a thesaurus feature to help users determine the proper heading to search. When searching for websites, the lack of controlled vocabulary accounts for most of the irrelevant sites retrieved by search engines.

One way to determine appropriate subject headings both in online catalogs and periodical databases is to do a keyword search first and then look up the subject headings of the pertinent books or articles that you retrieve. This procedure will lead you to all the records categorized under a particular heading. Web-based databases simplify this process because subject headings are usually web links. For example, if you do a keyword search for **athletes and steroids** in an online catalog, you'll probably retrieve some records that list **doping in sports** as a subject heading. Click on this heading to find all the books in the library about this subject. Many databases suggest related terms to search, and clicking on the links provided searches for pertinent material.

To perform a subject search directly, you may need to go to an advanced search screen or select a subject search option from a pull-down menu. Although most databases provide a subject searching option, it may not be on the first screen you see because often the default search method is keyword searching.

OTHER USEFUL DATABASE FEATURES

Databases do have some drawbacks. The time period covered by a database might be restricted. In the case of a periodical database, for example, older or most recent articles might not be included. Another problem is that the automated nature of searching a database sometimes yields irrelevant items. But databases do provide many special features that you can utilize to find exactly what you need. Not every database provides every capability listed below, but some features to look for and take advantage of include the following:

- **Search saving**—create files online in which to save your search results so that you can return to your research later when you have time.
- **Notes**—add your own notes in online files to save for future use.
- **Citation information**—easily compile the necessary documentation for your paper with examples of how to cite a source in several formats including *MLA*, *APA*, and *Chicago* styles.
- **Compatibility with other citation tools**—export records to report-writing tools such as Endnotes, Refworks, or ProCite.
- **E-mailing, printing, and downloading**—obtain a copy of an article and/or share it with classmates.
- **Compatibility with mobile devices**—access information more conveniently.
- **Audio**—listen to an article read aloud or even download the recording to an MP3 player; may be helpful if you are an English as a Second Language (ESL) student building your language skills, or if you are a busy student who wants to multitask and do research while running on a treadmill.
- **Translation**—use an article written in another major language.
- **Dictionary**—look up words in an article that you don't understand.
- **Primary source locator**—limit your search to valuable primary material.

Federated Searching

Some libraries offer federated searching, a function that simplifies the research process by allowing you to enter terms in a single box and search multiple databases simultaneously. Like a meta-search engine for the web, federated search results show how much is found in each database and links you to the material. Although you can find more material in less time, a problem with federated searching is that sometimes the amount of information retrieved is overwhelming. Before proceeding with this type of searching, you should choose particular databases to include rather than doing a general search of all the databases. If you don't narrow down your search in that way, you might waste time plowing through a long list of material.

Another problem with federated searching is that a search term may not work as well in one database as in another. You might get poor results from the best database for your subject just because you use a term that doesn't work well for that particular database. Think of it this way: a fisherman can cast a big net into the sea to catch a lot of fish all at once, but if he doesn't throw the right bait into the water, he won't catch the kind of fish he really wants. In a similar way, search terms are like the bait used to "catch" the information you want.

Although federated searching may not be available at your library because it is very expensive, an increasing number of libraries allow you to search for articles in one database, and if that database provides only a citation for an article, will link you to another database that provides the complete text. The other database it links you to could be your own library's online catalog, so you can find out if your library subscribes to the hard copy of that particular periodical.

The next three chapters focus on specific types of library databases: the online catalog for finding books, periodical databases for finding articles, and online reference sources for finding quick answers to questions as well as background information on your topic.

EXERCISES

See Appendix A for answers.

1. Keyword searching often requires you to think of synonyms. For example, if your topic is about U.S. soldiers stationed in Iraq who maintain blogs, what are other terms for the word *soldiers* that you might include in your search?

    _____

    _____

    _____

2. Insert the Boolean connecting term that is most likely to make the following search phrases find books about Native Americans:

    a.   Indians _____ America
    b.   Indians _____ India

3. What would be the best way to search for articles about the effects on children of watching excessive violence on television and in movies?

    a.

children
OR ▼ violence
AND ▼ motion pictures
AND ▼ television

    b.

children
AND ▼ violence
AND ▼ movies
OR ▼ TV

    c.

children
AND ▼ violence
AND ▼ motion pictures
OR ▼ television

    d.

children
AND ▼ violence
AND ▼ motion pictures
AND ▼ television

4. If you found too many irrelevant articles, what specific field would be the best one to limit your search to?

    a.   all text
    b.   subject
    c.   title
    d.   abstract

Chapter 5

Book Bonanza: Using the Library Catalog

You've heard the familiar old saying, "You can't judge a book by its cover." In other words, don't make assumptions about things based on their outward appearance. These days, you can't possibly judge some books by their physical appearance because the nature of books is evolving. A book can be contained on an audio CD, viewed as a file on an electronic reading device, or accessed as an e-book via the web.

Despite changing times, however, traditional books do still line the shelves of libraries. Although an increasing number of books have been transformed into electronic versions available online, an enormous amount of information is still stored the old-fashioned way. So you need to know how to access this wealth of knowledge. But you should also feel comfortable with finding e-books by using the web and other resources.

When it comes to books, as with all information, format shouldn't be an issue when evaluating the quality and value of the source; what matters is the content provided, whether that information is conveyed in print, audio, or electronic format. What all of these formats have in common is the depth of coverage that only book-length treatment of a topic can provide. When the term *book* is used in this chapter, it refers not only to the traditional book that sits upon a shelf but to all formats of books; when the term *library* is used, it refers not only to a brick-and-mortar building but to the full virtual library that is now accessible via the web.

To find the books that you need from among all of the thousands of books available in your own college library, you need to use the online catalog. You can also use the online catalog to find nonbook material such as periodicals, CDs, DVDs, and videotapes. Searching online catalogs is similar to searching any computerized database. The principles used when searching a periodical database for finding articles or a web search engine for finding websites are the same for using online catalogs.

Because you may need to search the catalogs of other libraries at some time, which can be done on the web, it is useful to understand the basics that underlie all systems. The catalog of another library may be just a click away. There is also the possibility, especially if you're at a small school, that your library is part of a consortium: a group of small libraries that shares its resources and its catalog with other libraries in the same area. By searching this shared catalog, you search the holdings of all the consortium member libraries simultaneously.

A database that you should be familiar with, because most libraries subscribe to it, is called WorldCat. As its name suggests, WorldCat includes the holdings of libraries from around the world, but it can also help you locate sources locally. The free version is available at http://www.worldcat.org (displayed in Figure 5.1), but your library may subscribe to a version with additional features. Search WorldCat as you would any online catalog. Then enter your zip code to see a list of libraries that have the item, with the nearest one listed first.

Figure 5.1. WorldCat Homepage

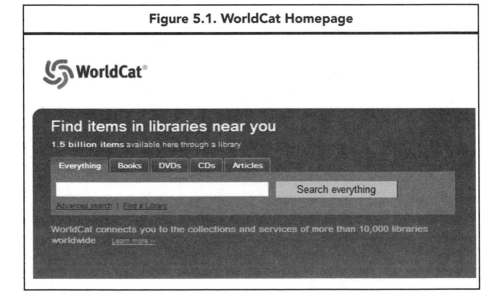

SEARCHING THE ONLINE CATALOG

Although the layout and format of the online catalogs of different libraries may vary, fundamentally they all operate in the same way. There are four basic ways of finding books: by title, by author, by subject, and by keyword. Figure 5.2 displays a sample opening webpage for an online catalog.

By clicking on the link that specifies the type of search you want to do, you will access the appropriate form for entering your search criteria. Many online catalogs, including this one, automatically display the keyword search form. To do another type of search, you must choose an alternative option: subject, author, or title searching (and sometimes a combination author/title search). Aside from these four basic searches, there is usually an option like "Other Searches" that allows you to perform advanced searches or searches by numbers such as call number or ISBN (International Standard Book Number).

Online catalogs often allow you to limit your search in the following ways:

- **location**—the library where items are located if your library is a member of a consortium or has multiple locations on campus
- **format**—books, audiobooks, e-books, CDs, DVDs, journals, etc.
- **language**—most useful for eliminating foreign language works
- **date of publication**

To use these limiters, you may need to access the advanced search form, which provides an area in which to specify limiters, as shown in Figure 5.3.

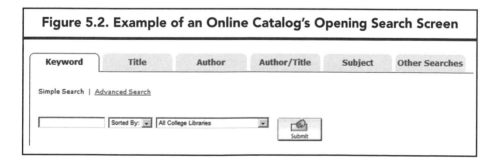

Figure 5.2. Example of an Online Catalog's Opening Search Screen

---

Figure 5.3. Example of an Online Catalog's Limiting Options on the Advanced Search Screen

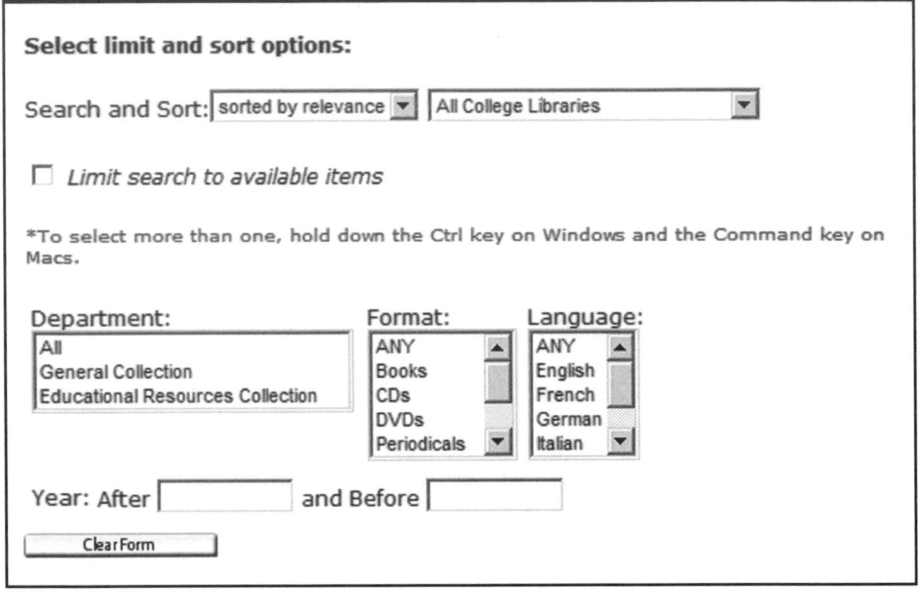

Select limit and sort options:

Search and Sort: [sorted by relevance ▼] [All College Libraries ▼]

☐ *Limit search to available items*

*To select more than one, hold down the Ctrl key on Windows and the Command key on Macs.

Department: Format: Language:

All	ANY ▲	ANY ▲
General Collection	Books	English
Educational Resources Collection	CDs	French
	DVDs	German
	Periodicals ▼	Italian ▼

Year: After [   ] and Before [   ]

[Clear Form]

Searching by Title or Author

It's easy to find a book if you know the author's name or the exact title. Use the following simple rules when searching for books by author or title:

- When looking up an author, use the last name first. For example, a search for Mark Twain should be entered as **twain mark**. Note that usually no comma is necessary and using all lowercase letters is fine.
- When looking up a title, the general rule is to drop any articles (although many catalogs will now just ignore *a*, *an*, and *the*). For example, a search for *The Adventures of Tom Sawyer* should be entered as **Adventures of Tom Sawyer**. Note that capitalization of the title is optional because online catalogs are not case-sensitive.

If you do not find what you're looking for, first make sure that you have followed these two rules. Also, check to make sure that you used the correct spelling and that the author or title you are searching for is valid.

Searching by Subject

As mentioned in the previous chapter, subject searching has certain benefits over keyword searching, but you usually must select the subject search option. If not selected, a keyword search will be done automatically. Let's say you are writing a paper about terrorism, so you enter it as the subject heading **terrorism**. If you do this, you will succeed in finding books if your library has any on the topic. After clicking on the search button, you will see subject headings similar to those listed on the screen displayed in Figure 5.4.

The first subject listed, however, is **Terrorism—5 Related Subjects**. Click on this link to see the page appearing in Figure 5.5. This page provides cross-referencing to such narrow subtopics as **Bioterrorism** and **Cyberterrorism** and the broader term **Political Violence**. Cross-references, which start with "See Also," are often narrower topics that fall under the main subject area, but they can also stand alone. The **Bioterrorism** link takes you to a list of titles pertaining to that subject. Not all library catalogs include the same material, so the list of narrower terms is dependent upon your library's resources. If your library has no books on bioterrorism, for instance, that cross-reference will not appear.

Figure 5.4. Example of a Subject Heading List in an Online Catalog

SUBJECTS (1-12 of 86)

Terrorism -- 5 Related Subjects

Terrorism.

Terrorism -- Addresses, essays, lectures.

Terrorism -- Africa -- Case studies.

Terrorism -- Algeria.

Terrorism and mass media.

Terrorism and mass media -- United States.

Terrorism -- Argentina -- Congresses.

Terrorism -- Bibliography.

Terrorism -- Case studies.

Terrorism -- Congresses.

Terrorism -- Economic aspects.

Figure 5.5. Cross-References for Terrorism

SUBJECTS (1-5 of 5)
Terrorism

1   -- See Also the narrower term Bioterrorism

2   -- See Also the narrower term Cyberterrorism
     Here are entered works on attacks or threats of attack against any portion of an information infrastructure.

3   -- See Also Political violence
     Here are entered general works on acts of violence committed by or against political constituencies.

4   -- See Also the narrower term State-sponsored terrorism

5   -- See Also Terror
     Here are entered works on intense, prolonged fear caused by either recurring frightening imageries or imagined or actual
     present or future dangers. Works on the expression of shock, fear or repulsion caused by an atrocity or a danger directed
     toward oneself or others are entered under Horror.

Returning to Figure 5.4, the main heading **Terrorism** is followed by sub-headings such as **Algeria** and **Economic Aspects**. These are also narrower topics under the main heading, but they subdivide the main heading, and some of them would not be able to be used as subject headings by themselves.

Once you have found the appropriate subject heading, you must delve to the next level to find the individual records by clicking on the heading you want. Clicking on the main heading **Terrorism** brings up a list of the individual books and other items, as shown in Figure 5.6.

This screen simply lists titles, authors, and publication dates. To see a complete record, click on a particular title. Take a look at some of the full records because most items are assigned more than one subject heading. You will notice in Figure 5.7 that one of the books cataloged under **Terrorism**, *Al Qaeda: Brotherhood of Terror* has three other subject headings in addition to **Terrorism**. These subjects may be related to your research topic, so you might be interested in following them further. You can easily do this using a web-based catalog. Simply click on the subject heading. By clicking the link for **Osama Bin Laden**, for example, you will instantly retrieve the records for all the items about this notorious figure. This powerful feature gives you the ability to explore related material with ease.

Subject searching doesn't always work as effortlessly as the previous example might suggest. Although **Terrorism** is a subject heading, many other words will not be. Subject headings, unlike tags used in social networking sites, are determined by the Library of Congress, which puts together the official list of standard, acceptable headings under which all library material is categorized (http://www.loc.gov/catdir/cpso/lcco).

Figure 5.6. Typical Online Catalog Title Display

The age of terrorism Walter Laqueur. Laqueur, Walter, 1921-	c1987 BOOK
Al Qaeda : brotherhood of terror Paul L. Williams. Williams, Paul L., 1944-	c2002 BOOK
The anatomy of terrorism David E. Long. Long, David E.	c1990 BOOK
Communicating terror : the rhetorical dimensions of terrorism Joseph S. Tuman. Tuman, Joseph S.	c2003 BOOK
Creating young martyrs : conditions that make dying in a terrorist attack seem like a good idea Alice LoCicero and Samuel J. Sinclair. LoCicero, Alice, 1945-	2008 BOOK

Figure 5.7. Individual Item Record in an Online Catalog

Author Williams, Paul L., 1944-
Title Al Qaeda : brotherhood of terror / Paul L. Williams.
Publisher [Parsippany, NJ?] : Alpha, c2002.
Description xxvi, 213 p. : ill., ports., maps ; 21 cm.

LOCATION	CALL NUMBER	STATUS
Merrimack College	HV6433.M52 Q35 2002	ON SHELF

[Send via Text Message] [?]

Bibliography Includes bibliographical references (p. [191]-202) and index.
Note Includes glossary (p. 187-190)
ISBN 0028643526 (pbk.) :

Subject Bin Laden, Osama, 1957-
Qaida (Organization)
Terrorism.
Violence -- Religious aspects -- Islam.

If your topic has something to do with Native American tribes, you might just enter the subject heading **Native Americans** to see what items are available. After doing this, however, the following sort of message might appear on the screen: "Native Americans is not used in this library's catalog. **Indians of North America** is used instead." But this is not a major inconvenience because in a web catalog, cross-references are links to other webpages, so you could just click on **Indians of North America** and easily perform the right search.

Language is constantly changing. Because new concepts and new ways of looking at the world emerge while other concepts become obsolete, language must evolve to accommodate these changes. For example, the word *unfriend* was not found in standard dictionaries until the *Oxford American Dictionary* added it in 2009 to refer to the process of deleting friends on social networking sites. Just as dictionaries are revised to reflect changes in language, Library of Congress subject headings are periodically updated to reflect changing times, but sometimes this takes a while. The term **blogs** is now used as a subject heading, replacing the heading **web logs**, a phrase that has become obsolete. For newer words that might not yet be official subjects, it is best to do a keyword search first to determine the relevant subject headings.

Just as it can be in any database, subject searching in the online catalog can sometimes be a process of trial and error. If you entered **war in Iraq**, for example, which is not a valid subject heading, you would be informed that there are no items on this subject. Often just changing the word order or playing around with the phrase a bit will do the trick. For example, you will find that **Iraq war** is a valid heading. Think of synonyms for your heading if the term you enter doesn't work. Perhaps, considering the formality of Library of Congress subject headings, you might enter **daytime dramas** to find items about soap operas, when, in fact, the official heading is the colloquial **soap operas**.

Searching by Keyword

Suppose you are looking for a book that explains the techniques used by headhunters—the kind that recruit people for jobs. Yet a subject search for **headhunters** finds books like *My Friends, the New Guinea Headhunters* and *Off with Their Heads*. If you perform a keyword search for **headhunters**, however, you will find these same titles as well as *Confessions of a Corporate Headhunter* and *Headhunters: Matchmaking in the Labor Market*. A traditional subject search would not have found these more relevant titles because they are categorized under **Executives—Recruiting**.

All of the principles of Boolean logic discussed in Chapter 4 apply to searching the online catalog by keywords. Suppose, for example, you can't remember the title of a particular book or the author's last name, but you do know that the author's first name is Ann and the word *pants* is in the title. By entering the keyword search **ann and pants**, you are easily able to locate *The Sisterhood of the Traveling Pants* by Ann Brashares.

UNDERSTANDING THE CLASSIFICATION SYSTEMS

What would we do without our GPS devices? Before the invention of these handy little gizmos, you may have found your way from one place to another by using a cumbersome paper map. GPS devices direct us to our destinations by giving step-by-step directions in real time as we drive. Similarly, in the library, call numbers provide us with step-by-step directions for finding material—even if we don't yet have a GPS-type device that will lead us through the stacks. As emphasized in the beginning of this chapter, libraries certainly provide access to much more than traditional books, but books still take up the most space. If there are books in your library on your topic, you should find them. The average college library contains hundreds of thousands of books; a large university library contains millions! But even if your library contains millions of books, you can easily find what you need amid this overwhelming amount of material if you understand how everything is organized. With this understanding, you will also be able to locate periodicals, videos, and other materials in those libraries that organize their nonbook collections in the same way as their book collections.

Few libraries existed before the nineteenth century, except for those belonging to a small number of colleges and universities, or those catering to the needs of individuals who could afford to pay dues. Each one of these private libraries organized its books in a different way. But in the 1800s, several factors—all related to the Industrial Revolution—led to the rise of public libraries. A more technologically literate society was needed to support the rise of industry, so public education and literacy became widespread. At the same time, technological advances in printing, which transformed it from a manual to a mechanical process, made the production of books less expensive and less difficult. Finally, Andrew Carnegie and other leaders of industry donated large sums of money to support the building of new libraries.

With more books, more people reading them, and more libraries, there was a greater need for a standardized system of organization. Two systems emerged: Dewey Decimal Classification (DDC), used in many public libraries and some smaller college libraries, and Library of Congress (LC) Classification, the standard in larger public institutions and most academic libraries. To get your hands on the books identified through your search of the online catalog, you need to be familiar with the classification system used in your library.

Libraries assign call numbers to books to classify them by subject and author. This method groups books on similar topics together on library bookshelves. Find a book's call number by looking it up in the library's online catalog. With both standard classification systems, the subject matter and the author's name determine the number a book is given, which in turn determines its location on the shelf.

Although both the Library of Congress and Dewey Decimal Classification systems were developed in the nineteenth century, these two systems still serve to give some order to what could easily be chaos. There are even some web directories that organize websites based on these schemes, including the BUBL LINK Catalogue of Internet Resources (http://bubl.ac.uk/link), which uses DDC categories, and Cyberstacks, which organizes sites by LC call numbers. A growing number of libraries are organizing web resources using the same classification schemes that have been used for years to organize more traditional resources. Norton Grove Public Library's Webrary (http://webrary.org/ref/weblinksmenu.html) and the Ready Reference site provided by the Lakewood Public Library (http://lkwdpl.org/readyref) both provide access to numerous web resources using the DDC system.

Dewey Decimal Classification

Dewey Decimal Classification divides knowledge into ten broad categories, from the 000s through the 900s. Each broad category is subdivided into ten more sections, which are each further subdivided into ten smaller sections and so on, until you get down to the level of individual books that will have call numbers involving decimals. For example, if you are interested in literature, the books you want are located between 800 and 899. More specifically, books of American literature are between 810 and 819. This section is further subdivided into such sections as poetry, drama, and essays, each designated by a whole number. Nineteenth-century American writers are primarily found within the 818 section. Although individual libraries may differ slightly in the exact call numbers they assign to their books, a copy of Henry David Thoreau's classic *Walden* might have the specific call number 818.3.

The part of the number following the decimal point can be a bit confusing. Just remember that decimals don't have the same value as whole numbers. For instance, a copy of *Walden*, as well as books about *Walden*, found at 818.3 will actually be shelved to the right of a book with a number like 818.298, because .3 is greater than .298. When using decimals, zeros get dropped, so .3 is really the same as .30 or .300 and so on. When zeros are added, it's easier to see that .300 is greater than .298.

Dewey Decimal Classification has some inherent weaknesses. Its hierarchical scheme has a strong bias toward Western culture as well as a lack of concern for political correctness. A similar situation is obvious with the emphasis on American, British, and Western European literature. The literature of countries that were considered alien to most people in nineteenth-century America—Asian, African, and Middle Eastern countries, as well as Russia, Poland, and many others—is squeezed between 890 and 899.

Another problem with this system is that, as new subjects arise, they must be shoehorned in somewhere. The original nineteenth-century scheme had no place for such topics as computer programming and television, so computer books are commonly thrown in with encyclopedias, and you'll usually find the books about television along with all the books on movies in the fine arts section, specifically 791.4 (not even a whole number!). Because of this problem, books in these and other unforeseen areas must have longer, more complicated call numbers in order to give each a unique location.

Library of Congress Classification

Library of Congress Classification is more complex than Dewey Decimal Classification. It is used by some larger public libraries, many academic libraries, and, of course, by the Library of Congress, which designed it in the nineteenth century to organize the increasing number of books in its collection. This national library has grown from a one-room legal collection established in the U.S. Capitol in 1802 for the use of Congress to a massive institution that contains more than 100 million items. Such a vast collection requires a more specific scheme of organization than Dewey can provide.

The LC system breaks all of knowledge down into 20 broad categories indicated by letters of the alphabet. You'll find encyclopedias in the A section,

Table 5.1. Dewey Decimal Classification	
Category	Description
000–099	General works, such as encyclopedias, but a lot of other topics have been thrown in over the years ranging from Bigfoot and UFOs to computers and the Internet.
100–199	Philosophy—also psychology, astrology, witchcraft, and related topics.
200–299	Religion—200–289 includes Christianity, while all other world religions are crammed into the 290–299 section.
300–399	Social science—sociology, political science, economics, and related topics.
400–499	Languages—books about individual languages as well as linguistics in general.
500–599	Natural sciences (as opposed to applied sciences, which are covered in the 600s), mathematics, astronomy, chemistry, physics, and life sciences are found here.
600–699	Technology—applied sciences ranging from medicine and engineering to cooking.
700–799	Fine arts—painting, sculpture, music, performing arts, television, games, and the like.
800–899	Literature—classic literary works as well as literary criticism (but does not usually include contemporary fiction and other works not considered "classic" which are generally kept in a separate fiction section arranged by author).
900–999	History—in addition to historical topics, includes biographies, all of which are kept in the 920 section.

atlases in the G section, and literature in the P section. Although it may seem odd that Military and Naval Science are considered top-level categories, the original purpose of the scheme was to serve the needs of the government, which would be concerned with national defense. The basic categories are then subdivided by alphabet. For example, while books of literature are given the letter P, English literature is designated PR and American literature is PS.

The LC system is alphanumeric. Following the initial one-, two-, or occasionally three-letter code are numbers that further divide a particular topic. In many libraries, Ellen Degeneres's *The Funny Thing Is . . .* has the call number PN6165 .D44. How would you actually go about getting your hands on this item? Here are the step-by-step directions:

- First, you have to find out where the P section is located. Libraries usually hang floor diagrams on the walls in convenient locations so you can see on which floor a particular letter is located. These diagrams are also often included on library websites. You may be able to click on the call number to bring up a map that displays the exact location.
- Once you find the general P section, finding the PN area is simply a matter of alphabetical order—it will be between the PM area and the PO area.
- When you find the PN area, follow the call numbers numerically until you get to 6165. Remember these are LC call numbers, not Dewey Decimal, so be sure that the number you look for is six thousand one hundred sixty-five and not six hundred sixteen *point* five. If you try looking for PN616.5, you'll wind up in a totally different section from PN6165, and you'll see books about ancient literature—certainly not what you had in mind.
- Once you have found PN6165, switch back to the alphabet to find D (which stands for the author's last name).
- After finding the D section, look for .44, which will actually be before a book ending in .5, since these are decimal numbers.
- The year of publication is often included at the end of the call number, but I have omitted it here so the numbers appear a bit less daunting. This date is important only in distinguishing one edition of a book from another.

Library of Congress call numbers, however, are not always as simple as in the humor section. As mentioned before, when classification systems were developed in the nineteenth century, many of today's subjects did not yet exist. So when books about such topics as airplanes, television, and space tourism were written, they were added to existing categories. As a result, a lot of books have been crammed into very small call number ranges and therefore must have very long call numbers with lots of digits, letters, and decimals.

There are some big differences between the way a library using DDC is arranged compared to one using LC call numbers. LC libraries don't have a separate fiction section, as do public or high school libraries using the Dewey system. This is because the LC scheme is primarily intended for research rather than for recreational reading. Fiction is most often put in the literature section (designated by call numbers beginning with P), side by side with criticism of the various works. In Dewey libraries, biographies are

Table 5.2. Library of Congress Classification	
Category	Description
A	General Works, such as encyclopedias.
B	Philosophy, religion, and psychology.
C	History—special topics like archaeology, genealogy, and general biography.
D	World history.
E/F	American and Canadian history.
G	Geography (mostly)—in addition to atlases and books about various geographic areas, you'll also find books about such unrelated topics as the environment, dancing, and sports.
H	Social sciences—includes sociology, economics, and business.
J	Political sciences.
K	Law.
L	Education.
M	Music.
N	Fine arts—includes painting, sculpture, and architecture.
P	Literature—also includes theater, movies, and television.
Q	Natural sciences—mathematics, astronomy, chemistry, physics, life sciences, and so on.
R	Medicine.
S	Agriculture.
T	Technology—other applied sciences like engineering, photography, and cooking.
U	Military science.
V	Naval science.
Z	Bibliography—library science as well as bibliographies that list materials on various subjects.

found in the 920 section, whereas LC libraries scatter them throughout the collection, depending on the occupation of the person about whom the book is written. On the shelf where Mark Twain's writings are located, you will also find critical and biographical works on that particular author.

Many items are difficult to classify because they might involve more than one subject. A book about the psychology of women, for example, may be classified in the HQ section rather than BF, which is the primary psychology section, because HQ contains books on women's studies. Such a book could fit in either section. If this book on the psychology of women was of a more medical nature, it could even be placed in the RCs. If there's only one copy of the book, however, it can only have one distinct call number, so the librarian who catalogs the book must make a choice. The same problem can occur when a book is classified with the Dewey Decimal system. This is why it is important to use the online catalog rather than just meandering through the stacks; you may find that books on basically the same subject are cataloged in different call number areas.

Once you get familiar with the system used to organize books, you can do some "educated browsing." Although browsing can be an ineffective way to do research, if you practice educated browsing in certain call number areas, you often find some useful material. Of course, if you're looking for something really narrow, you may have problems. Restrict your browsing to more general information on a topic. To be an educated browser, look up your subject in the online catalog and find a few relevant books and their call numbers. Then, after locating these books in the stacks, take a look at what other books are on the shelf nearby. Since you can also search the catalog by call number, you can browse a shelf of books virtually by viewing a list of titles on the computer in the same order they are shelved.

As a side note, another way to find additional material once you're in the stacks and have found a few books is to look in the back of each of these books for a bibliography of sources. If you come across any titles in the bibliography that look pertinent, look them up in the online catalog to see if your library has them.

E-BOOKS

Subscription E-book Databases

Just as libraries subscribe to databases for finding periodical articles, they can subscribe to databases that provide access to electronic versions of books. Two such databases are ebrary (http://www.ebrary.com) and NetLibrary (http://netlibrary.com), which are accessible through many library websites. Services from ebrary include providing different collections of e-books. The collection chosen by a college is based on its degree programs and also on the subject specialties of the institution. NetLibrary lets libraries buy particular titles rather than subscribe to entire collections.

If your library does subscribe to these resources, you can certainly search them individually to find e-books, but you may also find that the e-books available through ebrary and NetLibrary are actually included in your library's online catalog. This simplifies the research process, because instead of searching the online catalog for books in your library and then searching NetLibrary for e-books, a single search will find both the books that are physically available in your library and the e-books accessed virtually. This convenient one-stop shopping disregards the format of a resource, which should not be considered as an important evaluation criterion anyway, and focuses on the actual content of the item—a process that goes along with the philosophy of this book.

Public Domain Texts on the Web

The full texts of many classic books are available online for free because the copyright is no longer owned by the author, most likely because that author is deceased. These texts are considered public property and are often referred to as being in the public domain. Despite this fact, you can't just cut and paste material from these works into your own writing without giving credit to the author in your paper. To do so is committing plagiarism, which will be discussed in the final chapter of this book.

One of the oldest sources of public domain texts on the web is Project Gutenberg (http://www.gutenberg.org). Records in this database (see an example displayed in Figure 5.8) look like typical online catalog records, but below this bibliographic information is a list of the formats in which the book is available, usually including HTML and PDF files. HTML versions are particularly useful when you want to copy and paste quotes from the source into your paper (with proper credit given to the author, of course).

Google Books (http://books.google.com) is another good source of public domain material (see example displayed in Figure 5.9), and also provides free previews of copyrighted books with the entire text available to purchase. If users need only a bit of information, the free content may provide the needed answers. Google's lofty goal is to someday provide access to every book ever written.

The following are some additional sites where you can access public domain texts:

- Bartleby (http://bartleby.com)
- The Online Books Page (http://onlinebooks.library.upenn.edu)
- PublicLiterature.Org (http://publicliterature.org)

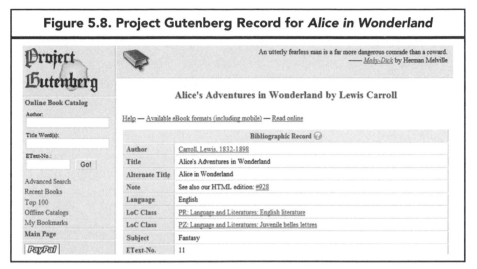

Figure 5.8. Project Gutenberg Record for *Alice in Wonderland*

Figure 5.9. Edition of *Alice in Wonderland* Available via Google Books

Downloading E-books

E-books can be downloaded to computers as well as mobile devices such as cell phones and electronic reading devices. Portable e-reading devices are available to borrow at some libraries, but their use is currently in an experimental stage. Some libraries lend the device and the user purchases the book to download; other libraries download material onto their devices. Most mobile phone apps available for viewing electronic texts charge a fee, but some are available for free.

When a reporter once questioned Mark Twain about a rumor that he had died, Twain responded, "The report of my death was an exaggeration." The impending death of books has also been greatly exaggerated. Their traditional format may be evolving, but the essence of what a book is will never become obsolete. While books will line the shelves of libraries for years to come and be checked out by students thirsting for knowledge, they will also be downloaded to cell phones, read on e-readers, and viewed on the Web by these same students. The format in which someone reads a book doesn't matter; the contents of the book do.

EXERCISES

See Appendix A for answers.

1. List a Library of Congress subject heading that would be a good choice to locate material on the following topics.

   a. Binge drinking among college students: _____
   b. Cyberbullying: _____
   c. TV reality shows: _____

2. Put the following call numbers in the order you would find the corresponding books on a library shelf (1 being the first):

   a. ____ RC514 .A245
      ____ RC514 .A26
      ____ RC514 .A4213
   b. ____ E580 .W66
      ____ E580 .W7
      ____ E580 .W24
   c. ____ 810.2
      ____ 810.02
      ____ 810.122

3. Match each of the following LC call numbers with the book it identifies:

   a. ____ QB701 .W43   A. *Childhood and Adolescent Obesity*
   b. ____ E468.9 H78   B. *How Real Is Reality TV?: Essays*
   c. ____ HD4349 .C6K3   *on Representation and Truth*

d. ___ RJ23 .P4

e. ___ PN1992.8 .R43 H69

f. ___ GV23 .P47

C. *The Naked Olympics: The True Story of the Ancient Games*

D. *Confederates in the Attic: Dispatches from the Unfinished Civil War*

E. *The Big Drink: The Story of Coca-Cola*

F. *Is Pluto a Planet? A Historical Journey through the Solar System*

Chapter 6

Pertinent Periodicals: Searching for Articles

In high school, articles from popular magazines such as *Time* and *People* and similar sources found online via Google were probably acceptable references for some research papers, but your college professors will likely require more academic material in your research. Although you may still find valuable information in popular magazines, you must now generally focus on scholarly sources—articles written by experts in the field for a more educated audience. These articles may be difficult to understand; in fact, some may be downright incomprehensible, but you've come to college to learn, and learning takes effort.

Up until now, you may have just gone to web search engines to find magazine and journal articles, but this is an ineffective means of doing research. Articles are not the same thing as webpages, so your search will retrieve many other things besides what your professor has in mind when requiring periodical sources. You might also retrieve one of the many self-published e-zines that now proliferate on the Internet but these sources require careful evaluation. If you do see a link among your Google results to something that sounds like it might be an article, this site probably won't provide the full text of the article unless you pay a fee. Although some periodicals have their own websites that might provide selected articles for free, to access the full archives usually requires a subscription.

By now, you should not be surprised to learn that your library's website can help you find articles from magazines, journals, and newspapers. A variety of periodical databases—or indexes, as they are sometimes called—can be searched to locate articles. These databases provide records for the contents of publications spanning decades. In addition to helping you determine which periodical issues will contain articles on your topic, these resources often provide the complete text of the articles. Just as with all online databases provided and paid for by your library, periodical databases have been selected to make your research easier. These databases also provide additional features not usually available on free websites.

TYPES OF PERIODICALS

Considering your chosen topic, decide what types of articles you need. Periodicals are published on a regular basis (daily, weekly, monthly, quarterly, etc.) and come in many varieties: scholarly journals, trade journals, general magazines, newspapers, and more. Before proceeding further, you need to understand the differences between types of periodicals since this will determine which databases you search.

When your professors instruct you to find journal articles, they don't have *Reader's Digest* or *Cosmopolitan* in mind. They want you to use scholarly or academic journals in your research. These are periodicals containing articles written by experts in particular fields of study, frequently individuals affiliated with academic institutions. The terms *journal* and *magazine* are often used synonymously, but this can be misleading. You also shouldn't assume a journal is a scholarly journal just because the word *journal* is in the title of the publication. *The Ladies' Home Journal*, for example, is generally not appropriate for academic research. Another type of journal that is useful if you have a business-related topic is the trade journal. Trade journals, such as *Advertising Age* and *Beverage World*, are periodicals written for people working in a specific occupation or industry and should not be confused with scholarly journals.

Scholarly journals tend to be specialized in their subject focus, research oriented, and are more likely to be primary sources of information. Primary sources are those in which scholars report the findings of their own research (as opposed to secondary sources, which report on someone else's activities). Academic journal articles usually have bibliographies at the end citing all the sources referred to by the author. These bibliographies can be helpful, leading to a variety of additional sources that may aid in your research.

Another characteristic of academic journal articles is that they are often peer reviewed, which enhances their authority as informational sources. Before an article is accepted, it must be deemed worthy of publication by an anonymous group of the author's colleagues. If your professor has requested peer-reviewed articles only and you are uncertain about the status of an article you have found, limit your search in a periodical database to peer-reviewed articles; many databases allow you to select only scholarly publications on the search page. Depending on which database you are using, you will check a box labeled Peer-Reviewed, Scholarly Journals, Refereed Publications, or something similar. If this option is not available in the database you are searching, ask a librarian for assistance in determining whether a periodical is peer reviewed.

To fully understand the difference between journal and magazine articles, consider the following list of articles from *The Journal of Popular Culture* (February 2010):

- "Singled Out: Postfeminism's 'New Woman' and the Dilemma of Having It All"
- "From Chick Flicks to Millennial Blockbusters: Spinning Female-Driven Narratives into Franchises"
- "Reading and Composing Indians: Invented Indian Identity through Visual Literacy"
- "From Sport to Business: Evolution of Unlimited Hydroplane Racing 1946–60"
- "Semiotics of Music: Analysis of Cui Jian's 'Nothing to My Name,' the Anthem for the Chinese Youths in the Post-Cultural Revolution Era"

Now take a look at the titles of articles in the March 22, 2010, issue of *People*:

- "A Stun Gun, Police—and a Parrot"
- "The Making of an Oscar Gown"
- "Singer Donna Summer's Daughter Brooklyn—She's a Disco Diva Too"
- "Gilligan's Island: Our Dream Castaways"

While the difference in content reflected in these titles should be obvious, the first list being from a scholarly periodical while the second is from a popular magazine, the physical difference is also apparent. Magazines tend to be glossy publications with eye-catching covers, while journals often look dull—but, just as you should not judge a book by its cover, don't overlook a periodical simply because of its appearance. Magazines are general-interest publications that you would find on a newsstand or in a bookstore, are intended for a general audience, and are designed to encourage an impulse buy. Although they may be more enjoyable to read because they lack the technical depth of scholarly journals, they are usually not as valuable for research, unless your research is focused on contemporary popular culture. Table 6.1 lists some general differences between scholarly journals and popular magazines.

CHOOSING WHICH PERIODICAL DATABASE TO USE

Databases on Your Library Website

A periodical database is essentially an index that often provides access to the articles it catalogs. An index, whether it is a back-of-the-book index that refers to the relevant pages in a nonfiction book or a site map on a website that connects to the appropriate webpages within a site, is a tool that helps you locate the particular information you need. Periodical databases do the same sort of thing by referring you to articles in specific issues of various periodicals. There are many different indexes, each one focusing on periodicals in a particular subject area. See Appendix B for a listing of the databases you are most likely to find on college library websites.

Table 6.1. Journals versus Magazines	
Journal Characteristics	**Magazine Characteristics**
Written for a specialized audience	Written for a general audience
Articles by subject experts	Articles by journalists and generalists
Authors often from academic institutions	Authors are staff writers (often uncredited) or freelancers
Highly focused topics	Generalized topics
Primary research or literature reviews	Secondary sources
Peer reviewed	Edited but not peer reviewed
Include bibliographies	Do not include bibliographies
Covers are usually plain or unremarkable	Glossy covers and eye-catching graphics
Little or no advertising	Often have lots of advertising

Just as you wouldn't rely on a world globe to research the geography of a particular state, you don't use one general periodical database for every research topic. For example, if you are writing a paper about the future of space travel, you would consult a resource like General Science Index. To find articles about the growing interest in space tourism, however, look in a business index like Business and Company Resource Center. If your space travel topic is more historical, Biography Reference Bank will provide citations to material about famous astronauts. You could also use a newspaper index like the *New York Times* 1851–2006 database to find newspaper articles about the Apollo missions and other manned space flights.

Since many topics are interdisciplinary in nature, you can certainly find articles in more than one database. When selecting which resources to use, first become familiar with those available at your library. To find out which periodical databases your library has, click on the link on the library homepage that will bring up the list of available resources. This link has no standard name; it could be called many things, including any of the following: Find Articles, Databases, Electronic Databases, Research Tools, or simply Resources. The databases may be grouped by subject to aid in your selection. There is often an alphabetical listing too.

Consider the following when deciding which periodical database to search:

- What is the subject focus of the database? Choose an index that pertains to the subject area for your topic. You don't have to limit yourself to a single database.
- What type of material does it cover? Does it cover scholarly journals, trade journals, general magazines, newspapers, or a mixture? Your decision to use or not use a particular database will depend on your needs.
- What years are covered? Be aware of what general time period is included in the database. Bear in mind, for example, that you wouldn't want to search a periodical database that includes only citations for journal articles published from 1990 to the present if what you really want are articles published in the 1960s.

Access to most of the indexes and other resources on your library website is restricted. Because the library must pay subscription fees, it doesn't want outsiders who don't pay tuition to use these expensive databases. Sometimes you can use databases only within the library, or you may be able to get to them from the library's homepage in your dorm room or at any computer on campus. Another way of restricting access is to implement passwords so the resources are available from virtually any location on or off campus.

Free Periodical Databases on the Web

Some periodical databases are available freely to anyone with access to the web. A major concern about these tools is that they don't have all the features of subscription databases. They also may have lots of advertising. In addition, some charge fees, so if a fee is required you're better off using your own library's resources. A few sites are worthy of mention, however, including the following:

- Google Scholar (http://scholar.google.com)—a search engine powered by Google technology that can help you find articles, but you may have to pay to view the entire text; there is also no way to limit the results to periodicals, much less scholarly articles, so you will have to sift through many irrelevant citations; because it is not clear how Google Scholar goes about selecting material to include, it should definitely not be your first stop for finding periodicals.
- DOAJ—Directory of Open Access Journals (http://www.doaj.org) —provides free access to more than 5,200 scholarly and scientific peer-reviewed journals.
- MagPortal (http://magportal.com)—offers access to articles in online magazines, mostly well-known publications, many with print versions; although no time frame is mentioned, the oldest articles seem to be from 1999.
- FindArticles at BNET (http://findarticles.com)—a good site to use for finding business-related articles.
- JURN Directory (http://jurn.org/directory)—provides links to 2,300 arts and humanities e-journals, but doesn't allow you to search them as a group, only one at a time.
- PubMed (http://www.ncbi.nlm.nih.gov/pubmed)—sponsored by the National Institutes of Health and the National Library of Medicine, includes more than 19 million citations from biomedical and life science journals; links to the complete text of these articles or to the publisher's website are provided.

- ERIC (http://eric.ed.gov)—Education Resources Information Center, sponsored by the U.S. Department of Education, provides records for journal articles as well as books, conference papers, technical reports, policy papers, and other education-related materials; often include the full text.

Print Indexes

Although articles are usually found these days by using online databases, you may need to refer to print periodical indexes at some point. These resources can occasionally be useful when you need an article from a much older issue of a periodical. Let's say, for example, you are writing a paper about America's justification for dropping atomic bombs on Japan in 1945, which ended World War II. In addition to more recent information, you want to find articles written during the days and weeks following this historic event. If your library does not have a periodical database covering this time period, you could refer to the 1945 volume of *The Readers' Guide to Periodical Literature*, a many-volume set which was once shelved in a prominent place and used frequently in pre-computer days. Since these books may no longer be kept in a public area, ask a librarian for help with locating and using print indexes.

PERIODICAL DATABASE RECORDS

If you wanted to find articles about the reality show *The Biggest Loser*, you could search for **biggest loser** and **reality television** in Academic Search Premier (searching for **biggest loser** by itself brings up many irrelevant articles about unsuccessful people). Some of the results for this search are displayed in Figure 6.1. These citations provide all the information you need about these articles including their titles, the titles of the periodicals in which they appear, the dates of the issues containing the articles, and the page numbers. The authors' names are also included because these articles had bylines. These citations also include volume and issue numbers, which are required for journals but are not mandatory for magazines. The volume number generally refers to the year of publication. Volume 22 of *Journal of Media and Cultural Studies*, for example, refers to the twenty-second year the journal was published. Issue 4 is the fourth issue that appeared in 2008.

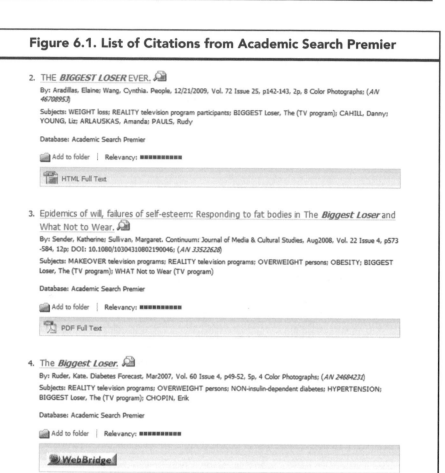

Figure 6.1. List of Citations from Academic Search Premier

You can click on any of the titles displayed in Figure 6.1 to view the full citations. An example of a complete record is shown in Figure 6.2. This full record provides an abstract of the article and links that you can click to find related articles. You need to view the full citation to click on the authors' names and find other articles by those authors or to click on the subject headings to find related material. At this level of the database, you can also use tools to print, e-mail, or download the citations or use other helpful features. Another important piece of information often given is the author's affiliation, which will help you to establish the authority of the article.

Figure 6.2. Full Record for an Article in Academic Search Premier

Epidemics of will, failures *of* self-esteem: Responding to fat bodies in The Biggest Loser and What Not to Wear.

Authors:	Sender, Katherine1
	Sullivan, Margaret1
Source:	Continuum: Journal of Media & Cultural Studies; Aug2008, Vol. 22 Issue 4, p573-584, 12p
Document Type:	Article
Subject Terms:	*MAKEOVER television programs
	*REALITY television programs
	*OVERWEIGHT persons
	*OBESITY
Reviews & Products:	BIGGEST Loser, The (TV program)
	WHAT Not to Wear (TV program)
Abstract:	In this article the authors examine aspects *of* makeover television programs, reality television shows that seek to cause significant personal or material change in the lives *of* participants. The authors focus on the participation *of* obese individuals in the weight loss and exercise program "The Biggest Loser" and a fashion makeover show "What Not to Wear." They discovered that audience reaction to the depiction *of* the overweight on both shows was largely negative and that viewers condemned the humiliating treatment *of* the obese and did not trust the authority *of* the advice provided by the experts on the programs.
Author	1Annenberg School for Communication, University *of* Pennsylvania, Philadelphia, USA

SEARCHING PERIODICAL DATABASES

Subject versus Keyword Searching

As explained in Chapter 5, there are no universally standardized subject headings used to classify articles the way there are in the Library of Congress subject headings for books. Each database has its own standard terminology. For example, let's say you were researching the topic of binge drinking on college campuses and found the article "Beer Pong's Big Splash" by Rebecca W. Keegan and Meaghan Haire that appeared in *Time* magazine in August 2008. The subject headings assigned by EBSCOhost's Academic Search Premier to this article about a drinking game involving beer cups and Ping-Pong balls are:

- drinking games
- binge drinking
- beer
- drinking of alcoholic beverages
- college students

The same article in InfoTrac's Student Resource Center uses the following headings:

- alcoholic beverages—usage
- liquor
- malt beverages

Besides bearing little resemblance to EBSCOhost's subject headings, the InfoTrac headings don't even reflect your topic that well because they don't relate to the abuse of alcohol by college students.

As with searching for books, determining the appropriate subject headings is still the best way to get a comprehensive listing of very relevant articles. Keyword searching poses the problems of finding irrelevant material or not finding all the relevant material. To help you find the best subject headings, many databases provide a thesaurus that suggests synonymous terms for your subject. If you look up **adolescents** in EBSCOhost's Subject Terms, for example, you will be instructed to use **teenagers** instead, since this is the official heading.

Another way to find appropriate subject headings is similar to something you can do in any online catalog. If you find just one relevant article through keyword searching, you can take a look at the subject headings given to the article and backtrack, clicking on an appropriate heading. Notice the subject headings for the citation displayed in Figure 6.2. One of them is **makeover television programs**, so you can click on this heading to retrieve all results on this subject, which includes articles about *Extreme Makeover* and *Queer Eye for the Straight Guy*. By doing this, you come up with a more focused set of articles. You could also click on the link to a TV program you may not know about, called *What Not to Wear*. In this way, subject heading links can lead you unexpectedly to a gold mine of related information.

Broadening Your Search by Searching the Full Text

If you haven't found many articles and need more information, you can broaden your search in many databases by searching the complete text of available articles. Most databases automatically limit their searches to the citation and abstract. On the opening search screen for EBSCOhost databases, you can click on the option Search Within Full Text Articles, while in other databases this might be phrased differently. On the advanced search screen displayed in Chapter 4 (Figure 4.9, p. 66), you can specify that certain terms be located anywhere in the article by selecting TX All Text in the pull-down menu. Be forewarned, however, that full-text searching increases your chances of finding irrelevant material much more so than when only the abstract is searched. You may want articles about the dwarf planet Pluto, but searching the full text will likely also retrieve some articles about Mickey Mouse's dog.

Narrowing Your Search

Limiters

You can also limit your search in very specific ways if you have found too much. Figure 6.3 displays the Academic Search Premier Search Options form, providing numerous ways to limit your search which are common in many databases including:

- **publication name**—limits search to one specific periodical
- **date**—limits search to a certain date or date range
- **full text**—finds only those citations that also contain the complete text
- **type of publication**—allows you to specify whether you want newspapers, journals, magazines, etc.
- **type of material**—allows you to specify whether you want articles, book chapters, interviews, editorials, etc.
- **length**—limits results to items that are within a specified range of pages
- **special features**—allows you to specify that you want items with additional material such as bibliographies, illustrations, etc.
- **peer-reviewed journals**—finds only those articles in refereed scholarly journals

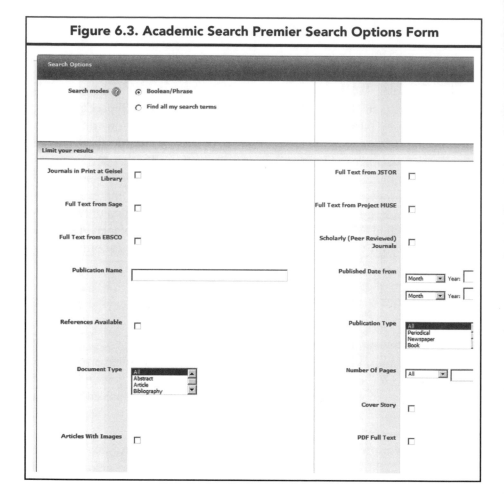

Figure 6.3. Academic Search Premier Search Options Form

Proximity Operators

In addition to Boolean connectors, you may be able to use something called a proximity operator in certain databases. This method allows you to narrow your search by specifying that two or more words appear within a certain number of words of each other. Proximity operators are usually composed of the letter *N* for *near* or *W* for *within* followed by a number to specify how many other words can separate your search terms. You place the proximity operator between the words that are to be searched. For example, **television N5 violence** in EBSCOhost will find **television violence** as well as **violence in movies and television** because the *N* proximity operator disregards the order in which you put the specified words. The proximity operator *W*, however, finds the words only in the order you entered them—so **drug W3 abuse** would find **drug abuse** as well as **drug and alcohol abuse**, but not **abuse of alcohol**.

Field-Specific Searching

Generally, when you do a basic keyword search, the entire citation including the abstract for each record in the database is searched automatically, even though the chances of retrieving irrelevant articles are increased if the abstracts are searched. Limiting your search to certain fields, as discussed in Chapter 4, can be very effective in focusing your search and reducing the number of irrelevant articles you find.

Take a look again at Figure 4.9 in Chapter 4, which displays a form that includes several pull-down menus. The menu lets you choose which fields to search. You can choose nothing, which will do a Default Fields search for your term in the citations and abstracts, or TI Title, which searches only the article titles, narrowing your search substantially. Other fields that narrow your search include SU Subject Terms, AB Abstract, and SO Journal Name. Be aware that if you select the field TX All Text, however, you will probably broaden rather than narrow your search, because records will be retrieved that contain your terms anywhere in the article. Since you can add rows to the search screen, you can combine as many field-specific searches as necessary in this database to really home in on your subject. The more boxes you fill in on this form, the narrower your search will be.

GETTING YOUR HANDS ON THE ARTICLES

Once you find relevant citations, you need to get the articles themselves. Online indexes often eliminate the need to locate a hard copy of the periodical containing the article because they provide the text for many of the articles cited. If you see an article title that looks helpful, however, don't pass it if only the citation is available. Instead, check to see if your library subscribes to the periodical cited or if the full text is available through another subscription database.

Formats

You will find articles in three basic formats: electronic, hard copy, or microfilm. While hard copies are the actual physical magazines, newspapers, or journals, microfilm provides a space-saving copy on film that can be read and reproduced using a microfilm machine. At one time, microfilm was considered the latest in information technology, since a whole month's worth of newspapers or a year's worth of periodical issues could fit on one roll of film. Today, microfilm may seem outdated and awkward to use, but it is still common in libraries and will be around for the foreseeable future.

The full text of articles is available online in either PDF or HTML format. In Academic Search Premier (displayed in Figure 6.1), for example, the available format is indicated by the last link in the citation. If you click on PDF Full Text in the first citation shown, an exact replica of the article as it appeared in the print journal version will appear, complete with illustrations. Acrobat Reader (available online as a free download) or a similar program is required to open PDF files. The second citation displayed in Figure 6.1 indicates that the HTML Full Text is also available. Clicking this link will bring up the article as web-based text. Advantages of an HTML version include the ability to copy and paste text or, if you choose to print the article, it will usually require fewer print pages. The disadvantage is that you won't get the illustrations and it will be difficult to cite the correct page numbers in your bibliography. Some databases include articles in a hybrid format; these contain the text in HTML and include the article's images. In most databases, files can be printed, e-mailed, or downloaded regardless of the format.

A growing number of libraries now subscribe to individual journals in electronic format. Through such services as JSTOR, Project Muse, and EBSCOhost's Electronic Journal Service (EJS), articles can often be obtained in PDF. Many libraries that subscribe to e-journals include a record for these titles in their online catalog; when you look up the journal title, you will be provided with a web link rather than a call number. Click the link and you will be taken to the journal directly.

Suppose you have searched a database such as EBSCOhost Academic Search Premier and found a citation that has neither the HTML nor PDF file of the article. In some libraries, you will see the WebBridge icon like the one seen in third citation in Figure 6.1. Others use the Find It link or something similar. If you click on this link, you will be directed to the following options, if they are available:

- Another database available through your library website that will provide the article
- The record for the appropriate journal in your library's online catalog, if your library subscribes to it
- Your library's interlibrary loan form, which allows you to order the article from another library

Generally, full-text periodical databases are more recent in their focus. While EBSCOhost Academic Search Premier goes back to the 1970s, Readers' Guide Retrospective provides coverage all the way back to 1890s. There are a growing number of databases that have an historical focus. Accessible Archives provides access to the full text of numerous publications from the eighteenth and nineteenth centuries through such databases as The Civil War: A Newspaper Perspective, *Godey's Lady's Book*, and American County Histories to 1900. ProQuest Historical Newspapers is a database that provides the digitized full images of every page of the *New York Times* and the *Wall Street Journal* back to their beginnings in the nineteenth century. Other newspapers available through this database include the *Washington Post* and the *Christian Science Monitor.* Keep in mind that for many topics, the latest information may not be the most appropriate, so these resources may be useful.

You may be tempted to use only those articles that are readily available online so that you can avoid using microfilm or having to track down the hard copy in the periodical room. While some periodicals are available online from their very first issues, others are not. And while you can access the most recent issues of many publications online, some publishers do not provide the current issues in order to promote sales of the printed publication. By disregarding any citations that might send you to the microfilm or periodical room, therefore, you may miss out on the most helpful information for your paper.

While many periodicals appear in both print and electronic formats, a growing number of periodicals are published only online. Some of these are free, while others require a fee; some are scholarly, and some are not; some are self-published, while others have been peer reviewed. Be very careful in evaluating these sources.

Periodical Organization

While the nonelectronic copies of older magazines and newspapers (also referred to as *paper*, *print*, or *hard copy*) are generally stored on microfilm, past issues of scholarly journals are often in book form, with a year's worth of issues bound into a single volume. Not all libraries organize their periodicals in the same way. In some libraries, periodicals (both hard copy and microfilm) are arranged alphabetically by. title. In other libraries, each periodical is assigned a call number, depending on its subject focus. The same rules of Library of Congress or Dewey Decimal call numbers apply. Bound volumes of journals arranged by call number may be shelved in the periodical room or in the same stacks where circulating books are found. You can find out where all the journals in a particular discipline are located by doing a subject search on the online catalog such as **biology—periodicals** or **American history—periodicals**. If your library has closed stacks so that you must request the material, you don't have to worry about how periodicals are arranged.

What If Your Library Doesn't Have It?

Tens of thousands of magazines and journals are published in the world today, along with thousands of newspapers. With so many periodicals available, a single library can't subscribe to each one, so academic libraries generally subscribe to what are known as the core (or most important) journals in those fields in which the college specializes. They may also get some of the peripheral (or less essential) journals in these same fields, as well as many general magazines, major newspapers like the *New York Times*, and the local papers for the area in which the library is located.

You can usually search for a periodical title in the same way you look for a book title in the online catalog. If your library doesn't subscribe to the periodical you need to complete your paper or doesn't have it available in electronic format, don't lose hope. If you have allotted yourself sufficient time for obstacles along the way, you can take advantage of the resources of other libraries.

Your library website may provide links to the other libraries in your area, and you can determine if another library has a particular periodical by searching its online catalog. If your library is part of a consortium, there may be an electronic list of periodicals so you can search many libraries at once. When you have determined the location of the periodical you need, you can either go to the library yourself to copy the article or have a copy sent to your own library, if such a delivery service is available. Sometimes requests for articles can even be submitted through your library website and e-mailed to you as a PDF attachment.

If the periodical cannot be located in the immediate vicinity, your library can obtain it through interlibrary loan (ILL). Even if the article you need is in an obscure scholarly journal held by only a handful of libraries in the country, your library's ILL department can request this article and usually get it to you in about a week, or sooner if the article can be e-mailed or faxed. The time factor involved here is the main drawback of ILL and the reason that many students, starting their papers too late, cannot take advantage of this valuable free service.

Finding articles is an essential part of college research, particularly ones from scholarly journals. For some narrow or very recent topics, articles may provide you with the only information you will be able to find. Your professors expect you to delve much deeper into periodical sources than you ever had to do in high school. The periodical databases provided on your library's website will enable you to do this.

EXERCISES

See Appendix A for answers.

1. Judging from the title alone, identify each of the following periodicals as a popular magazine (M) or a scholarly journal (J):
    a. ___ *Child Development*
    b. ___ *U.S. News & World Report*
    c. ___ *Yankee*
    d. ___ *Sex Roles*
    e. ___ *Public Relations Review*
    f. ___ *The New Yorker*
    g. ___ *The Saturday Evening Post*
    h. ___ *Popular Mechanics*
    i. ___ *Studies in Latin American Popular Culture*
    j. ___ *Journal of Popular Film and Television*

2. A search for articles can usually be limited by all of the following except:

    a.   Publication date

    b.   Academic affiliation of author

    c.   Full text availability

    d.   Type of publication

3.   Which of the following searches using proximity operators would locate more records?

    a.   Mars W5 water

    b.   Mars N5 water

    c.   Mars N8 water

    d.   Mars W8 water

4.   Referring to Appendix B, "Common Subscription Databases," choose two databases that would be good choices to search for articles on each of the following topics:

    a.   The acceptable uses of graffiti

    b.   The environmental effects of the 2010 oil spill in the Gulf of Mexico

    c.   The banning of books from the *Twilight* series in public schools and libraries

    d.   The economic effects of rising gas prices

    e.   The constitutionality of school vouchers

    f.   Former athletes who became politicians

    g.   Physical implications of excessive Wii video game usage

    h.   The benefits of "attending" an online university

    i.   The Tea Party movement

    j.   Depression among Iraq War veterans

Chapter 7

Ready Reference: Getting Answers

REFERENCE AND THE WEB

You may think that *Wikipedia* can now quickly find the answers to all those questions that students previously used *Encyclopedia Britannica*, *Webster's Dictionary*, and *The World Almanac* to answer. So you may be asking yourself why this chapter is even necessary. Aren't more traditional reference sources obsolete? Absolutely not! You must go way beyond *Wikipedia* and its ilk to find the reliable information you need. If you use the authoritative resources highlighted in this chapter, you can be confident that the information provided is reliable and accurate. These resources include subscription databases often provided on college library websites as well as selected free web resources and the traditional print reference books upon which many of these sites are based.

Many of the free reference sources on the web include advertising because revenue from this advertising allows these sites to provide information for free. Often, the information provided is only a tease; to get more complete information, you must either subscribe or pay a fee. Many online encyclopedias, like *Britannica Online*, for example, allow you to access some information for free, but only after you have had to view a number of advertisements; you can view complete entries only if you are a paying subscriber. Free web resources may also be of questionable authority, as explained in Chapter 2. Often, the purpose of these sites is to sell something. Be cautious when searching the web for reference sources, and be extremely skeptical if you feel the urge to simply use a web search engine to find the answer to your question—you will probably retrieve a lot of irrelevant and inaccurate information.

In addition to its subscription databases, however, your library's website may provide links to free web-based reference sources. These sources have already been thoroughly evaluated by librarians and were selected because of their quality and applicability to your college's unique combination of academic programs, so they are preferable to the sources retrieved by an automated search engine. When it comes to evaluating free web-based reference sources yourself, use the same PACAC criteria as you would for evaluating websites and informational sources in general. Numerous free websites are suggested in this chapter. You can either go directly to these sites and search them individually or google terms from your reference question; if any of these sources come up in the list of results, you know you have found a reliable source.

TOPIC SELECTION AND BACKGROUND INFORMATION

Encyclopedias

If your question requires more than a brief answer, an encyclopedia is a good resource to use. Although encyclopedias can certainly answer questions that ask *who, what, where,* or *when,* they are ideal resources for answering more complex questions that begin with *why* or *how*—the kinds of questions that lead to stronger thesis statements and better research papers.

Whether electronic or in their traditional place on the bookshelves, encyclopedias are good places to start your research because they provide concise, factual overviews on a vast number of subjects. They are also good sources to use for choosing topics because browsing through them can facilitate the initial brainstorming process. They can also help you identify keywords and concepts related to your research topic, which is important in developing your search strategies for more in-depth material.

Once you have selected a topic, educate yourself about it so that your writing reflects confidence and knowledge. The best way to begin this process is to read overviews on your chosen topic in encyclopedias and other general reference sources. Go to the sources described in this section and find the appropriate entries to read.

Among the free encyclopedias available on the web are Encyclopedia.com (http://www.encyclopedia.com) and Infoplease.com (http://www.infoplease

.com/encyclopedia). Unlike *Wikipedia*, both of these resources provide access to encyclopedia articles that have appeared in reputable published sources like the *Columbia Encyclopedia*. Unfortunately, both also contain advertising, including banner and pop-up ads, making these sources less preferable to the encyclopedia subscriptions of your library.

Britannica Online

The general encyclopedia that is most often available through college library websites is *Britannica Online*, considered the most scholarly resource in this category. This subscription database offers much more content and added features than the free version. While based on the print source published for well over two centuries, the *Britannica* site also provides access to other reference tools such as timelines, maps, and quotations.

You can browse *Britannica* to help in the process of topic selection by clicking on links within a hierarchically arranged subject list, and later read articles more closely for background information on your chosen topic. *Britannica*'s subject directory, which allows you to home in on a specific topic, is similar to the hierarchically arranged directories that are incorporated into many search engines such as the Open Directory Project described in Chapter 3.

A Word about Wikipedia

You don't have to completely avoid *Wikipedia*. While it's okay to take a look at *Wikipedia* entries to get overviews of topics, don't cite it as an authoritative source in your paper. The problem with *Wikipedia* is that any user can edit the information. You could go to *Wikipedia* right now, look up the entry for "Apollo 11," and enter the sentence, "The Apollo 11 moon landing was a hoax perpetrated by NASA to convince the Soviet Union that the United States had a superior space program." Eventually, another *Wikipedia* user would read this sentence, realize it was nonsense, and delete it. In the meantime, the inaccuracy would remain for the world to see. Messages often appear on *Wikipedia* pages such as "This article is incomplete and may require expansion or cleanup" or "This article does not cite any references or sources"—statements you would never see in *Britannica*. *Wikipedia*, however, can certainly be useful in the process of homing in on a topic.

As you browse *Wikipedia* you may find that you start by looking at one topic and end up with a completely different one. You might begin with the entry for "Martians" then click on a link to Ray Bradbury, author of *The Martian Chronicles*. On that biographical page, you would see a number of links to other websites about Bradbury. *Wikipedia* can be useful in directing you to related information on the web that might be more authoritative and appropriate for your research.

Subject-Specific Encyclopedias

Specialized encyclopedias focus on topics that may not be covered in depth in general encyclopedias. Some of the more common specialized encyclopedias include the *Encyclopedia of Philosophy*, the *Encyclopedia of Religion*, and the *Encyclopedia of Popular Music*. For every major subject area there's probably an encyclopedia that focuses on it. There are also encyclopedias that focus on even narrower subjects, some of them quite offbeat, such as *The Encyclopedia of Bad Taste*, *The Star Trek Encyclopedia*, and *The Encyclopedia of Unbelief*.

Although many subject-specific sources like these line the shelves of college library reference rooms, an increasing number are becoming available online. Your library probably subscribes to one of the following databases: Gale Virtual Reference Library, Oxford Reference Online, Credo Reference, or a similar database that provides access to a wide variety of reference e-books. For example, click on the link to encyclopedias in Credo Reference and a list of more than 40 encyclopedias categorized by subject appears. Glancing at this list, the science encyclopedias might catch your eye, and then a particular title, like *Encyclopedia of the Solar System*, with such intriguing entries as "Astrobiology" and "The Origin of the Solar System." Since the first rule of topic selection is to choose a topic that interests you, browse by clicking the links that interest you.

Many subject-specific encyclopedias are still only available in print and shelved in the reference room of your library. You locate these helpful sources by keyword searching since these reference books are included in the online catalog. For example, to find out if your library has an encyclopedia about sleep, enter the keyword search **encyclopedias and sleep** in the online catalog. Find a subject-specific encyclopedia that looks interesting and browse through it. Topic selection is where browsing serves a purpose. Once you have homed in on your topic, however, browsing is not an efficient means of finding the specific information that you require.

Sometimes it's just as easy to pick up a volume of a general encyclopedia as it is to look up the information online. Although many questions can be answered by online reference sources, don't overlook your library's print reference collection. Simply browsing through the print reference sources often accomplishes the same purposes as using the online versions. The reference collection also includes books that have no electronic equivalent, including subject-specific encyclopedias that are not available in an electronic format.

CQ Researcher: An Encyclopedic Guide to "Hot Topics"

A common assignment given to students in college writing classes is to write an argumentative essay on a controversial issue. An excellent source to use to help you select an issue for this type of paper is *CQ Researcher*, published by Congressional Quarterly. This resource, subscribed to by many libraries and available both in print and online (see Figure 7.1), provides unbiased, in-depth, well- researched lengthy reports on social, political, and economic issues. These reports provide concise background information as well as timelines, maps, statistics, and bibliographies.

Figure 7.1. The *CQ Researcher* Homepage

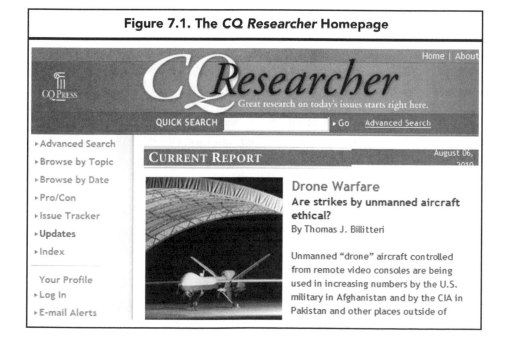

Exercises

The exercises in this chapter will appear in the form of sample reference questions at the end of each section. Try to answer the questions but, more important for the purpose of this chapter, identify where you could find the answers. See Appendix A for suggested sources.

1. When did the Emancipation Proclamation freeing the slaves become law in the United States?
2. How did the slave narratives written by former or fugitive slaves contribute to the eventual abolition of slavery?
3. What is the Electoral College?
4. Why was George W. Bush elected president in 2000 even though Al Gore received more votes?
5. Who founded the organization Mothers Against Drunk Driving (MADD)?
6. How have the activities of MADD led to fewer deadly car accidents involving alcohol?

USING REFERENCE SOURCES TO UNDERSTAND YOUR OTHER SOURCES

Let's imagine that you've searched the web for some authoritative sites on your topic, you've found some books, and you've printed out a few articles. Now you sit down to read these sources and find that questions arise. Most of the material you've collected is written for an educated audience. Many academic journal articles and scholarly books can be difficult to comprehend. Don't be discouraged if you don't understand the author at first. Reference sources can help.

Consider an article that appeared in the Spring 2010 issue of the *Journal of Popular Film and Television,* titled "Hollywood and the Rhetoric of Panic: The Popular Genres of Action and Fantasy in the Wake of the 9/11 Attacks." In the first sentence, the author refers to the "attack at the Munich Olympics in 1972, transmitted by television via satellite to the world." If you don't know what he's talking about, you could ignore this sentence; a better choice would be to find out what the attack at the Munich Olympics was all about. You could go to Google and search for **attack munich olympics,** and the first site in the list of results is a link to the *Wikipedia* entry for the Munich massacre in which members of the Israeli Olympic team were held hostage, and 11 athletes and coaches were eventually murdered by Palestinian terrorists. Using Google and *Wikipedia* to answer questions in order to comprehend the material you are reading is an appropriate use of these resources. If you eventually choose to include this information in your paper, you must confirm that any facts obtained through these sites are accurate by verifying them through a more authoritative source.

Dictionaries

The second paragraph of the article referred to in the previous section begins, "On September 11, 2001, this symbiosis between terrorism and visual spectacle was reproduced . . ." Symbiosis? That's a term you might vaguely remember from high school biology, but what does it mean in the context of this sentence? A simple Google search will retrieve a number of web-based dictionaries, including Dictionary.com, which will define symbiosis as a close association between two unrelated entities. Ideally, you should look up the meaning of every word with which you are unfamiliar in a book or article. Not only will this help you better understand the writing but also improve your vocabulary.

Among the many free dictionaries available via the web is *Wiktionary* (http://www.wiktionary.org), which works along the same principles as *Wikipedia* and so has the same shortcomings. A user could go to this site right now and change the definition of any word or invent a new word. Instead of this nonauthoritative source, use YourDictionary.com (http://www.yourdictionary.com), which draws on the definitions included in *Webster's New World College Dictionary*, or try *Merriam-Webster Online* (http://www.merriam-webster.com). To find specialized dictionaries, google your subject area keyword plus the word **dictionary** (for example, **art dictionary**). An excellent subscription resource available on many library websites is the *Oxford English Dictionary*, often referred to as the *OED*. Not only does this dictionary provide current definitions for words; it also gives the complete history of a word from when it was first introduced into the English language.

Exercises

7. What shape is a trapezoid?

8.   If a person is described as obstreperous, would you want to sit next to him in the library?
9.   When did the word *Internet* first appear in a published source?

USING REFERENCE SOURCES TO FIND SUPPORTING INFORMATION

As you write your paper, you may find some gaps that need to be filled with information. To write an effective argumentative essay, for example, you will need to find convincing facts and information that support your argument. In the case of a topic such as lowering the drinking age, you would need to find statistics that show that lowering the drinking age in the past did not lead to more motor vehicle deaths. You may want to find a biography of Candy Lightner, the founder of Mothers Against Drunk Driving, or a timeline indicating when drinking ages were changed in various states before the standard age of 21 was adopted nationwide. In addition to the resources available via such subscription databases as Credo, Oxford Reference, and Gale Virtual Library, a number of free websites may be useful in providing the supporting information you need to complete your paper:

- **Best Online Reference Sites** (http://rcls.org/deskref)—Ramapo Catskill Library System's site provides links to a wide variety of free but surprisingly useful online reference sources from encyclopedias and dictionaries to shoe-size conversion charts and used-car price guides.
- **Virtual Reference Shelf** (http://loc.gov/rr/askalib/virtualref.html) —compiled by the Library of Congress to provide links to reliable web resources, links are arranged by category, which makes it easy to find dictionaries, directories, statistical sources, maps, and other resources for all major subject areas.
- **RefDesk.com** (http://refdesk.com)—claiming to be the "Fact Checker for the Internet," this site offers links to a variety of practical resources including calculators, weather forecasts, stock quotes, headline news, and legal information, as well as links to most subject areas and reference sources like encyclopedias and dictionaries.

Finding Statistical and Geographical Information

While you do your research, you may have questions such as: "How far away from the sun is Pluto?" or "How many gallons of soda does the average American child drink in a year?" A reference source that provides statistics is the tool that is required to answer such questions. The most popular statistical source that can be found in any library as well as in many homes is *The World Almanac and Book of Facts*. A new edition of this book, which has no online equivalent, is published every year and, in addition to statistical information, provides basic facts on geography, current events, history, sports, and more. *Statistical Abstract* (http://www.census.gov/compendia/statab), an annual collection of statistics derived from the U.S. Census as well as from private sources, is an excellent site to check for any sort of national statistical information (see Figure 7.2). Among the many categories of statistics provided are vital statistics such as births, deaths, and life expectancy; consumer expenditures; food consumption; crime rates; and household income.

One site that should come in handy is USA.gov, which claims, "whatever you want or need from the U.S. government, it's here on USA.gov. You'll find a rich treasure of online information, services, and resources." On the homepage, the Explore Topics link will allow you to select Reference and General Government as a destination. This page provides a trove of useful

Figure 7.2. *Statistical Abstract* Homepage

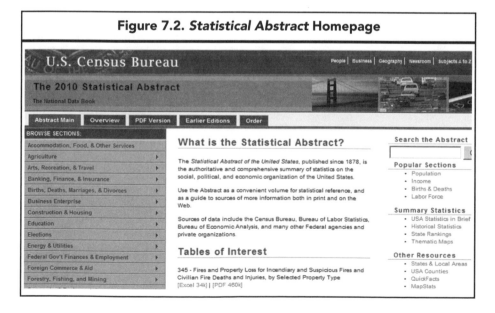

reference sources, as shown in Figure 7.3, including statistics, contact information, historical documents, maps, and many other government publications.

Another valuable government resource, FedStats, accessible through the USA.gov site or directly at http://www.fedstats.gov, is described as a "statistical gateway," enabling you to find the government statistics without knowing what agency publishes the information. The homepage for FedStats is shown in Figure 7.4.

Aside from free sources provided by the government, there are a variety of databases to which libraries can subscribe. For example, Social Explorer

Figure 7.3. The Reference Center and General Government Page on the USA.gov Website

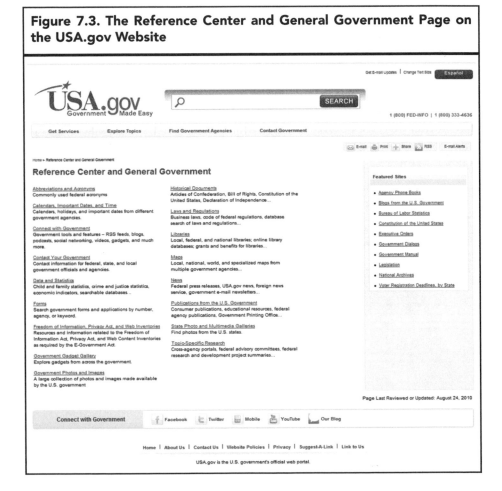

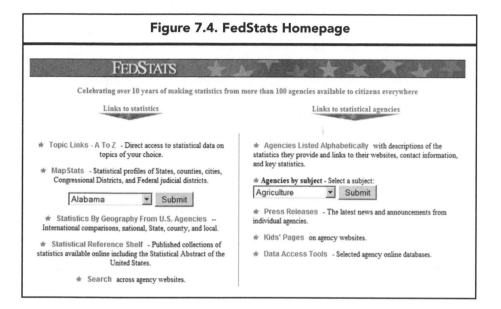

Figure 7.4. FedStats Homepage

provides demographic information taken from the U.S. Census from 1790 to the present. What differentiates it from the free government sources it draws upon is its interactive features that allow you to create maps and reports. A limited amount of the material on this site (http://socialexplorer.com) is available for free to the public. Lexis-Nexis Statistical offers access to statistics produced by not only the U.S. government and state agencies but also major international intergovernmental organizations.

Since geographical and statistical questions are often interrelated, many geographical sources answer statistical questions, and many statistical sources answer geographical questions. When you need to find the answer to a question that asks "where," geographical reference sources are the place to turn. Atlases are probably the first thing that comes to mind when you think of geography and reference. These compilations of maps are used to find out where a place is, how to get to it, what its geographic features are, and so on. They are handy for many research purposes, and most students are familiar with the standard atlases that are basically books containing maps of physical places. But atlases can also highlight historical eras, population growth, industry, and other developments.

Among the notable geographical reference sources available online are:

- **Google Earth** (http://www.earth.google.com)—allows you to view satellite images of any location on earth. The latest edition features historical imagery. Aside from its helpfulness as a reference tool, it's also pretty cool to view your college campus, your home, or Disney World from the perspective of a satellite.
- *Country Studies* (http://lcweb2.loc.gov/frd/cs/cshome.html)—book-length overviews provided by the Library of Congress which contain authoritative information about major foreign countries including history, geography, economy, and culture.
- *The World Factbook* (https://www.cia.gov/cia/publications/factbook/index.html)—produced by the Central Intelligence Agency, this site provides comprehensive information on every recognized country in the world, complete with maps.
- *Statesman's Yearbook* (http://www.statesmansyearbook.com)—privately published and available as a subscription database only. If your library subscribes to this authoritative source that has been in print since 1864 and is now also available online, it can provide you with "reliable, concise information on any country in the world," as its website claims.

Exercises

10. What type of animal is the most popular pet in the United States?
11. Has vehicular homicide decreased since the implementation of a nationwide drinking age of 21 years?
12. How many U.S. citizens under the age of 25 voted in the presidential election of 2008? Of 2000?
13. Through which states would runaway slaves from Kentucky pass on their way to Canada?
14. What countries compose the area once occupied by the former Soviet Union?
15. What has been the increase in the illegal immigrant population of U.S. states bordering Mexico?

Finding Chronological Information

It is often necessary to answer a question that asks "when," or what else happened at the same time as another important event. For information such as this, you refer to chronological sources, which are often called timelines.

For free on the web, you can use:

- **Timelines of History** (http://timelines.ws)—maintained by independent researcher and compiler Algis Ratnikas, who cites his information meticulously, this timeline comprehensively covers world history from the origins of the universe to the present.
- **InfoPlease Year by Year 1900 to 2010** (http://www.infoplease.com/yearbyyear.html)

If your library subscribes to the Oxford Reference collection of resources or *Britannica Online*, you can access some useful timelines. The Timelines link on the Oxford Reference homepage leads you to a variety of timelines arranged thematically and geographically. Select the Timelines link on the *Britannica* homepage and a pop-up window containing the interactive timelines will appear. You can then click on a subject area, such as Daily Life, Exploration, Literature, Religion, Sports, etc., and then enter a date to see what was going on at that time. Your library might also subscribe to *Facts On File World News Digest*, a news service that provides summaries of world events. This is an excellent source for finding not only dates but also more descriptive information about events.

Exercises

16.   Where were the first and last battles of the Civil War fought?
17.   What other events happened in Europe at about the same time that Columbus discovered America?

Finding Biographical Information

Many reference sources can answer simple "who" questions, as well as more complex questions that require you to find out about people. A good free source of biographical information on the web is Biography.com (http://biography.com), but this site sponsored by the Biography Channel has a commercial purpose and tends to focus on celebrities and iconic historical figures. Still, you can view entire episodes of its well-researched documentaries on famous people. Your library might subscribe to biographical databases such as Biography Reference Bank or *Marquis Who's Who Biographies*. Other useful biographical reference sources include *Current Biography*, the *Dictionary of American Biography*, and the *Encyclopedia of World Biography*, which may be available through a subscription reference service like Gale Virtual Reference Library or as a print resource in your library's reference room.

A common assignment that requires biographical information is the literary analysis, which may need to include information about an author's life. There are many good reference sources for literary biographies; some of these also provide good critical analysis. In general, the web sources that come up when you search Google are inferior ones such as *CliffsNotes* or *SparkNotes*. Better choices, which have been available in print format for many years and may now be available through subscription reference databases, include:

- *Concise Dictionary of American Literary Biography*
- *Concise Dictionary of British Literary Biography*
- *Contemporary Authors*
- *Dictionary of Literary Biography*

Exercises

18. Who was the world's first "space tourist?"
19. Who founded the Special Olympics?
20. To what extent was Louisa May Alcott's novel *Little Women* autobiographical?

Finding People and Organizations

The web has certainly simplified the process of locating contact information for people and organizations. But if you have difficulty finding the contact information you need via googling the person or organization name, a number of directories are useful. *The U.S. Government Manual* provides contact information for government agencies and officials, in print and online (http://gpoaccess.gov/gmanual/index.html). A number of subscription reference databases include *Associations Unlimited*, the online version of *Encyclopedia of Associations*, and *Who's Who in America*, which functions both as a directory and a source of biographical information. If your library doesn't subscribe to the online version, however, these two should be available in print since they are such standard reference books.

Exercises

21. What specific functions does the Department of Homeland Security perform?
22. Who is the founder of STARFLEET: The International Star Trek Fan Association?
23. What organizations are involved in environmental causes?

Finding Quotations

As you are writing your paper, you may want to add a general quote in the introduction or conclusion. Maybe you remember a quote but don't know who said it and need to identify the quote in order to use it; maybe you have a particular person in mind whom you want to quote and you need to find particular quotations attributed to that person. Or maybe you want to find quotations on a particular theme, regardless of who said the words. In a paper about lowering the drinking age, for example, you might want to include a quote about the use or abuse of alcohol.

You should be careful if you think that Google will provide you with your quotation needs. The famous Mark Twain line, "The report of my death was an exaggeration," previously quoted in Chapter 5, has been misquoted many ways on websites, including:

- "The reports of my death are greatly exaggerated."
- "Rumors of my death are greatly exaggerated."
- "Rumors of my demise have been greatly exaggerated."

Attempts to find the exact wording of this quote with Google searches will retrieve these and other inaccurate sites. Instead of Google, use specialized reference sources that cover quotations. In addition to quotation sources provided by subscription databases like Credo and Oxford Reference, two good free websites are *Bartlett's* (http://bartleby.com/100), which provides the content of previous editions of *Bartlett's Familiar Quotations*, and The Quotations Page (http://quotationspage.com).

Exercises

24. Who wrote "The mass of men lead lives of quiet desperation"?
25. Find some quotes attributed to Albert Einstein.
26. Find some quotes about abstaining from drinking alcohol.

USING REFERENCE SOURCES TO FIND ADDITIONAL SOURCES

Although you might think of a bibliography simply as the list of sources at the end of a book or journal article, or as the list you must compile for your own research paper, there are also reference sources that provide bibliographic information that will help you find more sources to use for your research. While bibliographies are often found at the end of encyclopedia articles and other sources, such as in *CQ Researcher* reports, there are also book-length bibliographies that can be enormously helpful because they are focused on one particular subject and provide a comprehensive list of citations for books, periodical articles, websites, audiovisual material, and rare unpublished works relating to the subject. To find these sources, do an advanced search in the online catalog for the term **bibliographies** in the subject field and then insert the subject area in which you are interested.

USING REFERENCE SOURCES TO WRITE AND CITE

When the time comes to write your paper, a number of reference sources can help you with this process. Of course, the dictionaries previously highlighted can help you with spelling. The other basic writing source you should use is a thesaurus, which provides synonyms, adding variety to your writing. A decent free resource despite the presence of advertising is Thesaurus.com, which extols itself as "the world's largest and most authoritative online thesaurus." A subscription resource, *Oxford American Thesaurus of Current English*, is available via Oxford Reference. Any old-fashioned print version of *Roget's Thesaurus* will also do.

In addition to the basic dictionary and thesaurus you should always have by your side while writing a paper, you also need a good grammar guide to answer all those annoying questions that come up, such as "Does a comma go before or after closing quotation marks?"; "Should this word be hyphenated?"; or "When is *that* used instead of *which*?" Refer to the "Guide to Grammar and Style" (http://andromeda.rutgers.edu/~jlynch/Writing/contents .html), *The Elements of Style* by Strunk and White (4th ed., 2000), or one of the following sources that provides not only grammatical guidance but also guidelines on how to cite your sources, a topic that will be explained in detail in the next chapter:

- *The Chicago Manual of Style* (16th ed., 2010)
- *A Manual for Writers of Research Papers, Theses, and Dissertations* by Kate Turabian (7th ed., 2007)
- *MLA Handbook for Writers of Research Papers* (7th ed., 2009)

Exercises

27. Using WorldCat (http://worldcat.org) find some book-length bibli-ographies about unidentified flying objects (UFOs).
28. Shouldn't *UFOs* in the preceding question have an apostrophe?

Reference sources are handy tools to use throughout the research process. They can provide a general introduction on a subject when you are choosing a paper topic or background information to give you familiarity with your chosen topic. They can answer those numerous minor questions that come up as you write your paper or provide the data needed to reinforce your the-sis. Research can sometimes seem like an intellectual scavenger hunt to find the answers to very specific questions; the place you can find these answers is in reference sources.

Chapter 8

Integrated Information: Using Sources

Perhaps you're now sitting in the library or in your dorm room with a stack of books and copies of articles in front of you, and a list of bookmarked websites on your laptop. You've done everything that this book has told you to do. You've found lots of information. . . . You sigh. . . . Then you wonder, *Now what do I do?* At this point, you have evaluated your sources and scanned through them to a certain degree, so you probably feel that some might be better than others or address your topic more fully. Prioritize your sources, and begin with those that are higher on your list.

TAKING NOTES: QUOTING, PARAPHRASING, AND SUMMARIZING

You must actively work with your sources by taking notes rather than just passively reading them. Note taking is the process of recording the information that will be useful in your paper. There are three basic ways to take notes: quoting, paraphrasing, and summarizing.

Quoting Your Sources

The following quote is the familiar opening line of the Gettysburg Address delivered by Abraham Lincoln on November 19, 1863, at a ceremony dedicating a cemetery for the soldiers who died in the decisive Battle of Gettysburg.

> *"Four score and seven years ago our fathers brought forth on this continent a new nation, conceived in liberty, and dedicated to the proposition that all men are created equal."*

If you were to quote this line in your paper, however, you would need to integrate it into your text. You might write:

> *In the first line of his most famous speech, Lincoln asserts, "Four score and seven years ago our fathers brought forth on this continent a new nation, conceived in liberty, and dedicated to the proposition that all men are created equal."*

The phrase "Lincoln asserts" is called a signal phrase and indicates that someone else's idea is about to be used. In its most basic form, a signal phrase includes the author's name or a pronoun that clearly identifies the author followed by a verb that indicates expression. Some examples of signal verbs, which are usually written in the present tense, are *says*, *argues*, *concludes*, *declares*, *observes*, etc. You should never have a quotation in your paper that is not introduced by some sort of a signal phrase. This is often referred to as a "dropped quote" and is a research paper no-no.

Brackets

Brackets are used to clarify a quotation by identifying a word, often a pronoun, that may be ambiguous due to its context. For example, in the sentence "American schoolchildren have learned its cadences by heart for decades," what does *its* refer to? If the meaning is not made clear by a signal phrase or other information in the paragraph, a word or phrase in brackets should be inserted to add clarity. The revised sentence, "American schoolchildren have learned its [the Gettysburg Address's] cadences by heart for decades," leaves no doubt what *it* is.

Ellipses

Sometimes you don't want to use an entire quote. Maybe it just seems too long, and you can cut some words out without changing its essential meaning. In order to do this, you use ellipses. Let's say you thought the idea contained in the following passage that includes the previous example was worth quoting, but you'd like to shorten it a bit:

> *"American schoolchildren have learned its cadences by heart for decades; many of us, young and nervous, recited it at patriotic ceremonies as our parents, proud and nervous, looked on. But the venerated address was not universally admired at the time" (Owen 32).*

If you wanted to shorten this quote, you could do so by cutting out the middle part without changing the author's meaning:

> *"American schoolchildren have learned its cadences by heart for decades. . . . But the venerated address was not universally admired at the time" (Owen 32).*

You could not, however, use ellipses in this way:

> *"American schoolchildren have learned its cadences by heart for decades; many of us, young and nervous, recited . . . the venerated address . . ." (Owen 32).*

The omission of the phrase "was not universally admired at the time" changes the meaning because the author believes that the Gettysburg Address was not always venerated, but your revision makes it sound like it was.

Ellipses consist of three periods with a space between each period. If you are cutting out the end of a sentence, add an additional period to the ellipses.

Paraphrasing

> *The founding fathers of the United States of America created a new kind of country based on the universal freedom derived from the inherent equality of all citizens.*

This sentence probably sounds familiar because it is a paraphrased version of the first line of the Gettysburg Address. A paraphrased version, rather than being word for word what the author said, is in your own words and should be about the same length. If the original source is written in the first person (using the pronouns *I*, *me*, *my*, *we*, *us*, and *our*), a paraphrased version needs to be put in the third person (using *he*, *him*, *his*, *they*, *them*, and *their*) to reflect your perspective, not the author's. Similarly, a source written in the present tense would have to be paraphrased in the past tense. There are many ways to paraphrase the same thing. You could also write:

> *Those who founded the United States of America implemented unique ideas about freedom based on the belief that all citizens were equal.*

This statement means the same thing as the previous one. If Lincoln spoke the paraphrased lines instead of his famous words, however, the world would, as he ironically stated, "little note, nor long remember" his speech. The important thing to remember when paraphrasing is to use not only your own words but also your own structure. Consider the following:

> *Eighty-seven years ago, the founding fathers created on this land, a new country, conceived in freedom, and dedicated to the idea that everyone is born equal.*

This paraphrased version borders on plagiarism because it retains too much of the original author's style, replacing a few words and phrases with synonyms but keeping the same rhythm and structure. To avoid this problem, read the material you need to paraphrase; then set it aside and try to write down the same ideas. The ideas should remain the same, but the phrasing should be different.

To Quote or to Paraphrase? That Is the Question

Sometimes an author writes something that is expressed so perfectly that you can't paraphrase it without it sounding inferior. The Gettysburg Address is a perfect example of something you should quote directly. On the other hand, if you can express the thoughts of an author in your own words while still conveying the information effectively, then paraphrase. You can't have an entire paper full of quotes. This is boring to read and doesn't show much of your own analysis. Paraphrase when you can, and quote when the wording of the quotation reflects exactly the idea you are trying to convey. No one would paraphrase the Gettysburg Address because it sounds so mediocre compared to Lincoln's words, but it does provide a good example of the differences between paraphrasing and quoting.

The following passage is the second paragraph of Lincoln's speech in its original form:

> *"Now we are engaged in a great civil war, testing whether that nation, or any nation so conceived and so dedicated, can long endure. We are met on a great battlefield of that war. We have come to dedicate a portion of that field, as a final resting place for those who here gave their*

lives that that nation might live. It is altogether fitting and proper that we should do this."

A paraphrased version could be written as follows:

The large-scale war being fought within the country was threatening both the survival of the United States and any other country like it. The people who came together at Gettysburg were setting aside part of the battlefield as an appropriate and respectful memorial for the soldiers who died for the cause of the Union.

If Lincoln had delivered the second version (in a first-person, present-tense format, of course), it is doubtful that his words would now be inscribed on one of the marble walls of the Lincoln Memorial.

Most of the material you will be using in your paper will not be as eloquent as the Gettysburg Address, so you will be paraphrasing a lot in your notes. The important thing to remember when paraphrasing is that although you are changing the words, you are not changing the meaning. Therefore, the idea you intend to express is not your own and you must cite the source of the idea.

Summarizing

Another way of dealing with information is to summarize it. This is different from paraphrasing because a summary is shorter than the original material and focuses on the main points in a general way. If you are writing a paper arguing that the Gettysburg Address is the most eloquent speech ever written, you might want to give a brief summary of what Lincoln said. In your notes you could list the points that Lincoln makes:

- United States founded 1776—unique country based on liberty/equality
- Civil War threatens existence of country
- Battlefield dedicated at Gettysburg as final resting place for soldiers killed
- Soldiers had already dedicated it by fighting
- To really honor soldiers who died, living must win war so democracy doesn't end

Here is a summary that could appear in your paper based on these notes:

> *Lincoln acknowledges that the United States is a unique country, but its existence has been threatened by a civil war. Although it is appropriate to honor the soldiers who died at Gettysburg by dedicating the battlefield as a memorial, he asserts that the soldiers themselves have already sanctified this place by their actions. To truly honor those who sacrificed their lives, those still living must fight on and win the war, which will allow democracy to continue.*

Notice that this summary is shorter than the original speech (79 words versus 268). Summaries can be of varying lengths and levels of detail, depending on your purpose in using them. Summaries should have signal phrases in your final paper to clarify that the ideas are not your own. In the example above, "Lincoln acknowledges" and "he asserts" are signal phrases.

Composing Summaries for Annotated Bibliographies

No matter what length a source is, you can summarize it in a few sentences, which is what you need to do when you write an annotated bibliography, a common assignment that prepares you to write your research paper. This differs from the bibliography that should accompany your final paper in that you need to provide a brief summary for each source in a paragraph following each citation. This paragraph should also include an evaluation of the source, addressing the basic criteria outlined in the PACAC method, particularly authority. You should also explain why the source is particularly appropriate for your paper. Here is an example of an annotated citation:

> Wills, Garry. *Lincoln at Gettysburg: The Words That Remade America*. New York: Simon and Schuster: 1992. Print.
> This book by Garry Wills, an adjunct professor of history at Northwestern University and prolific writer of works on American history, won a Pulitzer Prize in 1993. Wills provides both a close analysis of Lincoln's speech and the historical background within which it was delivered. He addresses some of the myths and misconceptions surrounding the speech and explains its significance and its effects on history, politics, and society. Because this book emphasizes the rhetorical excellence of the speech and gives the reader a thorough understanding

of its meaning and impact, it is a valuable source for explaining why the Gettysburg Address is among the greatest speeches ever written.

- The first sentence of the annotation establishes the author's credibility.
- The next two sentences briefly summarize the book.
- The final sentence indicates why the source is a good choice.

Noting Source Information

When taking notes, it is very important to distinguish quotations from paraphrased information. If you don't, you will have trouble later when you can't tell the difference between your own words and those of someone else. Make sure you enclose all quotations in quotation marks. You could also highlight quotes so they don't get mixed up with your own words. Whether you are putting the quotes and information in a notebook, in a word-processed document, or on traditional index cards as some instructors still advise, it is important to identify the information's source. Your notes should clearly indicate the author's last name or the title of the source if no author is identified. The page numbers should also be included if the source has pagination so you can cite the source later and, if necessary, locate the information again to double-check its accuracy. Maintain a "working bibliography" in which you record the information listed in Table 8.1 for all the sources on which you take notes. You may not use all of these sources in your paper, so your final bibliography will probably be shorter than your working bibliography. Later in this chapter and in Appendix C, examples are provided to show how to format this information properly in your final bibliography.

AVOIDING PLAGIARISM

There are two kinds of plagiarism: intentional and unintentional. To understand the difference, consider a criminal who deliberately shoots and kills his victim as opposed to a driver who accidentally hits and fatally injures a pedestrian. While premeditated murder is the most serious crime that could ever be committed, vehicular homicide is also considered a criminal offense. In the same way, intentional plagiarism is considered more heinous than unintentional plagiarism, but both types are wrong and need to be avoided.

Table 8.1. Noteworthy Source Information			
Authored Book	**Edited Book**	**Periodical**	**Website**
Author	Chapter author	Author	Author
Title	Chapter title	Article title	Title
Year published	Book editor	Periodical title	Date last updated
Publisher: Location	Book title	Volume number	Organization name
Publisher: Name	Year published	Issue number	Date accessed
Page of quote	Publisher: Location	Date	
	Publisher: Name	Page numbers	
	Page range of chapter	Database retrieved from (if applicable)	
	Page of quote		

When you knowingly take the words or thoughts of another person and present them as your own, you are committing intentional plagiarism. Copying and pasting information from a website or copying entire sentences or paragraphs word for word from an article or book without giving credit to the source is obviously plagiarism. Worse yet is buying a research paper on one of those notorious websites that sells such things. In these cases, you are deliberately passing off someone else's ideas as your own.

Intentional plagiarism is a serious offense because you are stealing something; in the case of presenting an author's work as your own, you are stealing someone's intellectual property. But aside from the issue of morality, plagiarism is simply a foolish thing to do. Teachers become familiar with your writing style and can easily tell when something you have written doesn't sound like you wrote it. You are also more likely to be caught these days because, if you are suspected of plagiarizing, phrases from your paper can be searched online and easily found. Some colleges also use Turnitin (http://turnitin.com), an online plagiarism-detection service, and require their students to submit their papers to this service, which then checks them for plagiarism.

If you are caught intentionally plagiarizing, the ramifications are certainly serious, including a failing grade and, in some cases, getting kicked out of school. But perhaps even more significantly, you will have violated the trust of someone in a position of authority; trust, as we all know, is a very hard thing to regain. You will also have cheated yourself out of an education because you will have learned nothing and, ultimately, wasted your tuition. You will have also contributed to creating an atmosphere of suspicion, which is antithetical to the goals of academic institutions and jeopardizes learning for all students.

Unintentional plagiarism should also be avoided. Although you might not get kicked out of school for it, your paper may get a bad grade. This type of plagiarism often occurs because your notes are messy and disorganized. Notes should clearly distinguish between quoted and paraphrased material, and paraphrasing should be done following the guidelines previously discussed in this chapter. Perhaps you think your paraphrasing is just fine, but remember that if you make only minimal changes in word choices, or retain too much of the author's original style, you are committing plagiarism even if you cite the source properly. Unintentional plagiarism can also result from confusion over what types of information need to be cited. The next section will explain when a citation is required as well as the difference between facts and general information which do not need to be cited and ideas or opinions that do require citations.

Two good sites that provide further information about plagiarism and how to avoid it are:

- Valdosta State University's "Plagiarism: A Student's Guide to Recognizing It and Avoiding It" (http://www.valdosta.edu/~cbarnbau/personal/teaching_MISC/plagiarism.htm)
- Long Island University's "Students' Guide to Preventing and Avoiding Plagiarism" (http://www2.liu.edu/CWIS/CWP/library/exhibits/plagstudent.htm)

CITING YOUR SOURCES

The end product of all your research is the paper that you complete for your class. An important component of your paper is the documentation that gives credit to the sources you used to write it. Without this documentation, you are essentially committing plagiarism. Citing your sources has three purposes:

- To give credit where credit is due, thus avoiding any allegations of plagiarism

- To enable any reader of your paper to locate the sources used in the paper
- To give credibility to the facts you state in your paper

Statements that reflect an opinion must always be cited unless the opinion is your own. When you state factual information, however, you do not always have to cite your source. If the majority of people know the fact, or it could easily be found in multiple sources, it is considered common knowledge and does not need to be cited.

- An example of a fact that you should cite:
  Contrary to what many people have been told, Lincoln did not actually write the Gettysburg Address on the back of an envelope.
- An example of a fact that would not have to be cited:
  There were more than 51,000 casualties in the Battle of Gettysburg.

When in doubt, cite. There's nothing wrong with citing the sources of information that are considered common knowledge, except perhaps a paper that is a bit cluttered with unnecessary notes. But failure to provide the necessary citation of a source is an act of plagiarism.

Citation Styles

There is no one standard way to cite a source. The variety of documentation styles reflects the diversity and sheer amount of information available today and the specific needs that researchers in different fields have. Legal documents are much different from scientific articles, and the way they are documented has to reflect this. No matter which style you have to use, the important thing is to be consistent. In other words, if you use *MLA* style for one citation, you must use *MLA* for all.

Each style has a handbook, some of which are listed in the previous chapter. *MLA* style is most often used for English papers, in freshman composition, and in some humanities courses. The Modern Language Association publishes *MLA Handbook for Writers of Research Papers* (7th ed., 2009) and an abridged version can be found at http://www.mla.org/style. If you are told to use *Chicago* style, which is often used for humanities papers, refer to Chapters 14 and 15 in *The Chicago Manual of Style* (16th ed., 2010), which also has an abridged version at http://www.chicagomanualofstyle.org/tools _citationguide.html. *A Manual for Writers of Research Papers, Theses, and*

Dissertations, by Kate Turabian (7th ed., 2007) is also helpful if you need to use *Chicago* style.

APA and *CSE* styles are not likely to be used in composition classes, but you may need to familiarize yourself with them for science and social science courses. If so, *Publication Manual of the American Psychological Association* (6th ed., 2009) and *Scientific Style and Format: The CSE [Council of Science Editors] Manual for Authors, Editors, and Publishers* (7th ed., 2006) are the guides to use. There are other specific styles used for music, law, engineering, geology, and business, and many other disciplines. The examples in this chapter will highlight *MLA* documentation since that is most often used in freshman composition courses. Appendix C offers basic examples for other common styles.

Your library website probably provides links to reputable guides for all the major documentation styles which offer examples of how to cite various sources. Your librarians may even have developed their own style guides for your use. There are many places where you can find examples of how to cite your sources. The important thing to consider in evaluating these sites is currency; check to see when the site was updated. *MLA* style changed significantly with the publication of the Seventh Edition of the *MLA Handbook*, so don't use a style guide from 2008 or one that follows the rules found in the *MLA Handbook*'s Sixth Edition. If you do, your bibliography will be incomplete and incorrect because one of the major changes is that each source must now be identified as either Print or Web.

Some websites that provide excellent guidelines on citations include:

- *Research and Documentation Online* by renowned style handbook author Diana Hacker and Barbara Fister (http://bcs.bedfordstmartins .com/resdoc5e/)
- Duke University Libraries, "Citing Sources" (http://library.duke .edu/research/citing)
- Texas A&M University Libraries, "Citation Style Guides" (http:// library.tamu.edu/help/help-yourself/citing-sources/citation-styles# subject-specific-style-guidelines)
- University of Arizona Libraries, "Citation Guide" (http://library .arizona.edu/search/reference/citation-subj.html)
- Long Island University, "Citation Style for Research Papers" (http:// www2.liu.edu/cwis/cwp/library/workshop/citation.htm)

- The Writing Center at the University of Wisconsin-Madison (http://writing.wisc.edu/Handbook/Documentation.html)
- Purdue Online Writing Lab (OWL) (http://owl.english.purdue.edu/owl/section/2)—displayed in Figure 8.1

Some websites and computer programs actually generate citations for you based on information you enter about the source. Citation Machine (http://citationmachine.net) and EasyBib (http://easybib.com) are two interactive sites that create *MLA*, *Chicago*, and *APA* citations after you enter the required information. Although they will format the citations correctly, if you enter erroneous information the resulting citations will be incorrect.

Figure 8.1. Purdue OWL's "Research and Citation Resources"

OWL Purdue Online Writing Lab

| Purdue OWL | Writing Lab | OWL News | Engagement | Research | Contact | Site Map |

General Writing • Research and Citation • Teaching and Tutoring • Subject Specific Writing • Job Search Writing • ESL

OWL Family of Sites > OWL > Research and Citation

Search the OWL   GO

Research and Citation
Conducting Research
Using Research
APA Style
MLA Style
Chicago Manual

Suggested Resources

-2009 MLA Guide
-2009 APA Guide
-Purdue OWL Flash Movies
-Purdue OWL Podcasts
-How to Navigate the New OWL
-Workshop and PowerPoint Index
-Owl Exercises

Research and Citation Resources

If you are having trouble locating a specific resource please visit the search page or the Site Map.

Conducting Research
These OWL resources will help you conduct research using primary source methods, such as interviews and observations, and secondary source methods, such as books, journals, and the Internet. This area also includes materials on evaluating research sources.

Using Research
These OWL resources will help you use the research you have conducted in your documents. This area includes material on quoting and paraphrasing your research sources, as well as material on how to avoid plagiarism.

APA Style
These OWL resources will help you learn how to use the American Psychological Association (APA) citation and format style. This section contains resources on in-text citation and the References page, as well as APA sample papers, slide presentations, and the APA classroom poster.

MLA Style
These OWL resources will help you learn how to use the Modern Language Association (MLA) citation and format style. This section contains resources on in-text citation and the Works Cited page, as well as MLA sample papers, slide presentations, and the MLA classroom poster.

Chicago Manual of Style
These OWL resources will help you learn how to use the Chicago Manual citation and format style. This section contains resources on in-text citation and the Bibliography.

Colleges often provide citation aids that can help, like RefWorks and EndNote. These tools can also work with databases to import citations and are set to deal with all kinds of formats.

The list of sources that you include at the end of your paper is generically referred to as a bibliography and, using *Chicago* style, that's exactly what it is called: "Bibliography." *MLA* style requires the heading "Works Cited" at the top of the page instead, while an *APA* paper would require "References"

Figure 8.2. EasyBib Form for Generating an *MLA* Book Citation

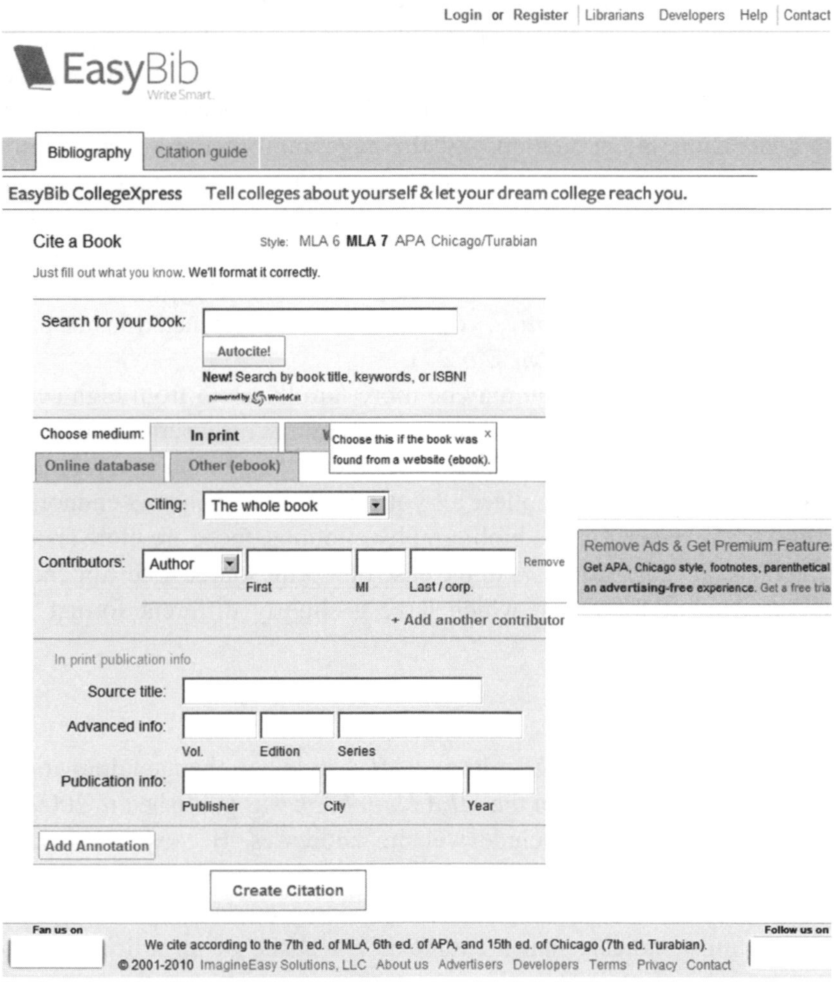

as the section header. The other important format issue is alphabetical order: Your bibliography should be alphabetized according to the authors' last names.

Incorporating Notes into Your Paper

In addition to providing a bibliography, you need to incorporate notes into your paper. Immediately after you use a direct quote or paraphrase the idea of someone else, you must give credit to the source. If your professor tells you to use *MLA* style, you will use parenthetical citations to provide notes. For example, if you quoted what Shelby Foote wrote on page 27 of his book *The Civil War: A Narrative*, you would insert (Foote 27) immediately after the closing quotation mark, followed by a period. If you introduce a quote with a signal phrase such as "Foote writes," you don't need to include the author's last name in the citation, just the page number. For a web resource, which doesn't have a page number, cite the author's name; if that is not available, a shortened version of the title will suffice. You also need to use a shortened title to differentiate among multiple sources by the same author. For example, if you used two books by Shelby Foote in your paper, one of which was *The Civil War: A Narrative*, you could use the shortened title in a parenthetical citation: (Foote, *Civil War* 27).

Chicago style, which you may be more familiar with from high school, requires footnotes or endnotes. A superscript number is inserted at the end of the passage you want to cite. Then either include a citation as a footnote at the bottom of the page or collect all your citations together as endnotes, at the end of the paper. Unlike bibliography citations, these are more specific, citing the exact page numbers in the case of a print source. See Appendix C for examples of footnotes, which have a slightly different format from endnotes.

Citing Websites

The way to cite websites according to *MLA* style has changed dramatically since the Seventh Edition of the *MLA Handbook* was published in 2009. It's no longer necessary to include website addresses. Because these URLs change so often, and developments in search engine technology have made it easier to locate web sources, you don't need to provide the URLs anymore. You also must indicate that a source is a website or an article obtained through a periodical database by including the word *Web* in the citation.

Here's how to cite the Pluto page from Bill Arnett's The Nine Planets website:

Arnett, Bill. "Pluto." *The Nine Planets*. 12 February 2010. Web. 26 May 2010.

The following information should be included in website citations:

- **author's name**—basically, whoever is responsible for the content; this could be an individual or an organization. If no author is indicated, you'll just have to leave it out.
- **title of webpage**
- **title of website**
- **date**—when the page was created (or date of most recent update)
- **date visited**—when you accessed it

Citing Periodical Articles

By now you should be familiar with the basic components of a periodical article citation since they are included in all periodical database citations: the author, the title of the article, the title of the periodical in which the article is published, the date of the issue, the page numbers, and, in the case of a journal, the volume and issue numbers. If you accessed the article through a periodical database, you should also indicate which one.

The format for your citations, however, is a bit different from what you've seen in indexes. Here is a sample *MLA* citation for an article in a popular magazine:

Loria, Leonard. "Disney without the Mouse." *Yankee*, April 2005, 128–133. Print.

If you are citing an article from a scholarly journal, you must also include the volume and issue numbers before the date and page numbers, so the format would follow this example:

Wright, Chris. "Natural and Social Order at Walt Disney World." *Sociological Review* 54: 2 (2006): 303–317. Print.

If you got the article from a periodical database, the citation format has to reflect this. Let's say you found the *Yankee* article by Leonard Loria online on EBSCOhost's Academic Search Premier. Here's how you would cite it using *MLA* style:

> Loria, Leonard. "Disney without the Mouse." *Yankee*, April 2005, 128–133. EBSCOhost Academic Search Premier. Web. 11 May 2010.

Some periodical databases have Help screens that indicate how to cite the material contained in them. Be careful, however, because this information is sometimes improperly formatted. In addition to the citation of the original print source of the article, you must indicate what online service you used and the date you accessed it. Page numbers are irrelevant when it comes to web versions of articles, but a citation for the online version of an article that originally appeared in print should indicate the numbers for the print version. If the exact range of pages is not known, give the first page followed by a plus sign.

Citing Books

The basic components of a book citation are the author, the title, the publisher, and the place and date of publication. For example, here is a typical *MLA* citation for a book:

> Wills, Garry. *Lincoln at Gettysburg: The Words That Remade America*. New York: Simon and Schuster: 1992. Print.

If this same book were accessed as an e-book, you would omit *Print* and add:

- The name of the e-book service (NetLibrary, ebrary, Google Books, etc.)
- The word *Web* (instead of *Print*)
- The date you accessed the e-book

So an e-book version of the book cited above would be:

> Wills, Garry. *Lincoln at Gettysburg: The Words That Remade America*. New York: Simon and Schuster: 1992. Google Books. Web. 27 May 2010.

There are many variations for citing books: Your book may have two, three, or more authors, or it may have no author but an editor instead, as in the case of many reference works. It could be a multivolume work or a specific edition. Maybe you're using only one chapter. In each of these cases, the citation is a little different, so refer to Appendix C for examples of the most common citations, or refer to the style manuals and websites listed in the beginning of this section for guidance on specific types of sources. There are also many variations in the way other types of sources are cited. Because the variety of resources available has expanded so rapidly and documentation styles have been revised to reflect new information, even librarians find themselves referring to style guides.

Once you've read through all of the sources you found by using the research techniques explained in this book, taken copious and meticulous notes, and compiled a working bibliography, it's time to start writing your paper. Although this book has been limited to explaining the research aspects of research papers, the research process doesn't end when you start to write your first rough draft. You may find that your thesis evolves into something that raises new questions requiring additional information. Even as you proofread your final draft the night before the paper is due, you may need to check a fact or find a statistic to support your argument. If you have thoroughly researched your topic in the way this book has explained, you should feel confident when you hand in your paper that, regardless of how well it is written, it is based on excellent informational sources that your professor will appreciate.

EXERCISES

See answers in Appendix A.

1. Paraphrase the final paragraph of the Gettysburg Address

    "But, in a larger sense, we cannot dedicate—we cannot consecrate—we cannot hallow—this ground. The brave men, living and dead, who struggled here, have consecrated it, far above our poor power to add or detract. The world will little note, nor long remember what we say here, but it can never forget what they did here. It is for us the living, rather, to be dedicated here to the unfinished work which they who fought here have thus far so nobly advanced. It is rather for us to be here dedicated to the great task remaining before us—that from these honored dead we take increased devotion to that cause for which they gave the last full measure of devotion—that we here highly resolve that these dead shall not have died in vain—that this nation, under God, shall have a new birth of freedom— and that government of the people, by the people, for the people, shall not perish from the earth."

2. Indicate which of the following factual statements should be cited by writing Y (yes) or N (no) before each statement:

   a. _____ The solar system consists of eight major planets because Pluto is now considered a dwarf planet.
   b. _____ Walt Disney World is the most popular tourist destination in the world.
   c. _____ The tallest trees in the United States grow in California.
   d   _____ Grover Cleveland was the only U.S. president to serve two nonconsecutive terms.
   e. _____ Animals feel pain in the same way that humans do.
   f. _____ The Magic Kingdom in Disney World was established in 1971.
   g. _____ Pluto follows the same orbit as other objects in the Kuiper Belt.
   h. _____ President Andrew Johnson's impeachment trial was politically motivated by those politicians who objected to his policies.

3. Rewrite the following sentence in three different ways that show how you could integrate it into your own paper:

   "If attendance figures and repeat visits are our guide, it would certainly seem that Disney has made good on its claim to have built 'the happiest place on earth . . . '" (Van Maanen 5).

   a. _____
       _____
   b. _____
       _____
   c. _____
       _____

A Review of the Research Process

- Define your topic. Pick a topic that interests you.
- Determine what types of sources you need, how you will find them, and roughly how much time it will take you. Don't procrastinate!
- Use the PACAC method for evaluating your sources; consider purpose, authority, currency, accuracy, and content.
- Use web resources recommended in this book or by your library's website, or search the web using Google or another search engine.
- Determine what databases are available at your library; then select the most appropriate ones for your topic. Locate periodical articles on your topic using periodical databases. If you find too much information when searching a database, narrow your search. If you don't find enough information, broaden your search utilizing the principles outlined in Chapter 4.
- Search the online catalog for books. If you have problems with subject searching, try keyword searching using the basic principles of Boolean logic. Go to the stacks and locate the books cited in the records you found on the computer. If you need more books, do some educated browsing or consider using the collections of other libraries.
- Consult some basic reference sources if you need to check a fact or get some background information.
- Take meticulous notes to avoid unintentional plagiarism and cite your sources accurately.

Answers to Exercises

CHAPTER 2

1a. L: Statistics are facts, and, as we all know, "facts are facts," and "facts don't lie." Statistics, therefore, are helpful in supporting a logical argument.

1b. C: Olivia Munn is a celebrity, not an expert. Using her name to lend support to the cause of animal cruelty is an ethical appeal, but it is not the sort of ethical appeal that establishes the level of credibility necessary for a source that will be used in an academic research paper.

1c. C: This is also an ethical appeal, but it shows a very inappropriate bias. By associating one candidate with a popular figure while associating the opponent with an unpopular figure, the author is using a specific ethical appeal called "guilt by association," which is inappropriate.

1d. E: This author is appealing to the readers' fear that something bad will happen if they don't do what he suggests.

1e. L: Although this article suggests that something bad will happen, the author is not appealing to emotions; however radical his view seems, he is using evidence from primary research to support it.

1f. C: This is a more appropriate use of an ethical appeal. Citing legal precedents is an excellent way for authors to support their own arguments.

1g. E: Beginning a book or article with a story of an individual helps the reader relate to the issue being discussed. This sort of anecdotal evidence appeals to emotions because the reader tends to sympathize with the individual. This technique is acceptable as long as it doesn't go too far in playing on the readers' emotions.

2. There is no one correct answer for this question. Judging only from the information given, the ranking of these authors could be argued as follows:

    (c)   The college professor's previous publications indicate a high level of expertise, and the academic degrees he has been required to obtain for the job, including probably a doctorate, add to his stature.

(e)   The award-winning journalist might not have the academic credentials of a college professor, but the fact that this writer has won awards and written articles that have had a huge impact contribute to his status as an expert.

(a)   The owner of a Fortune 500 company has had real-life experiences as well as recognition from an academic institution as an expert.

(b)   A former U.S. governor who ran for president doesn't necessarily have the experience and knowledge required of an expert.

(d)   The founder of an organization that supports the legalization of marijuana doesn't necessarily have any qualifications that indicate expertise, and the intentions of this individual are questionable.

3a.   S: The author who wrote this book did not actually write the primary source that was written about.

3b.   P: Interviews are always considered primary sources whether you conduct the interview yourself or use a source in which someone else does the interviewing.

3c.   P: The author has written about research that he himself conducted.

3d.   S: While the films themselves might be considered primary sources, an article about these films is not.

3e.   P: A diary is a firsthand account of someone's experience.

3f.   S: The author was not present at the actual event that was written about.

CHAPTER 3

1.   Open Directory Project (b) would be the best choice because it utilizes human editors and is a noncommercial site, as indicated by the *.org* top-level domain. Google (a) would find many commercial sources. Yahoo! (c) would find fewer sites but mostly commercial ones, and About.com (d), although it has human editors and would be a good second choice, is a commercial rather than nonprofit site.

2.   Dogpile (d) is the only meta-search engine listed.

3.   Google (c), although it certainly doesn't cover the entire web, is unrivaled in the number of websites it retrieves compared to the other choices.

4.   Bing (a), although it has an advertising-free homepage, incorporates unobtrusive ads and sponsored sites into its search results.

5.   **"dust devil" tornado** (d); by a simple process of elimination you can disregard **"dust devil"** (b) which will retrieve sites containing this phrase, many of which are about sports teams. **Dust devil** (a) retrieves these sports-related

sites and more because a search without quotation marks is broader, including both the phrase and sites containing both words. Conversely, the third answer is too specific; although it will eliminate the sports sites, it will also eliminate sites that do not include the exact phrase, which includes **tornado.**

6.   (c). The advanced Google search displayed in Figure 3.7 (p. 49) is very specific. It must find the words **soccer** and **team**, not necessarily in that order; it must also contain the phrase **world cup** and either **irish** or **ireland**, so it will find sites about the Irish World Cup soccer team (a). The retrieved sites, however, cannot contain the word **northern.** Because Northern Ireland is part of the United Kingdom, this search will also eliminate sites about the English World Cup soccer team (b).

CHAPTER 4

1.   Other terms you should enter include **troops, military, army,** and **armed forces**.

2a.   **Indians AND America**
2b.   **Indians NOT India**

3.   The search strategy in answer (c) would be the best to find articles on the topic because it indicates that the terms **children** and **violence** must be found in the resulting records, and either the word **television** or **motion pictures,** so some of the records will be about children watching violent movies, some will be about them viewing violent TV shows, and some will be about them watching both.
Here are the problems with the other answers:
(a)   The results might retrieve sources about children watching nonviolent motion pictures and television or about adults watching violent films and programs.
(b)   The problem with this answer is not the way the Boolean search is constructed but in the use of the terms **movies** and **TV;** a search of the subject list will show that **motion pictures** and **television** are the appropriate subject terms.
(d)   This search is too narrow because all of the terms would have to be found, so sources about children only watching TV or only watching movies would be eliminated.

4.   To find the most relevant articles, limit your search to the subject field (b). Limiting it to the title field (c) may retrieve relevant records but not as many; limiting it to the full text (a) will still retrieve many irrelevant records because your terms might be taken out of context; limiting it to the abstract (d) may

make the search more relevant, but if synonyms for your terms are used in the abstract instead of the terms you enter, not all pertinent records will be found.

CHAPTER 5

1a.   **College students—Alcohol use**
1b.   **Internet—Safety measures; Computers and families; Computer Crimes**
1c.   **Reality television programs**

2a.   1, 2, 3
2b.   2, 3, 1
2c.   3, 1, 2

3a.   F
3b.   D
3c.   E
3d.   A
3e.   B
3f.   C

CHAPTER 6

1a.   J
1b.   M
1c.   M
1d.   J
1e.   J
1f.   M
1g.   M
1h.   M
1i.   J
1j.   J

2.   b

3.   c. You can eliminate the answers that use the **W** proximity operator, (a) and (d), since the terms have to be found in the order entered; (b) will only find **Mars** within five words of **water**, while (c) will find **Mars** either within eight words before **water** or eight words after **water**, and so will retrieve the most records

4.   Articles about most, if not all, of the topics listed in this question could be found using one of the general periodical databases (Academic Search, Aca-

demic OneFile, Expanded Academic ASAP, or *Reader's Guide* Full Text). The databases suggested below are two other periodical databases considered most likely to provide articles on the subject, but other databases could certainly be used depending on the specific thesis of the research paper.

4a. Art Full Text; Social Sciences Full Text
4b. General Sciences Full Text; LexisNexis Academic
4c. ERIC, LexisNexis Academic
4d. Business Source; Social Sciences Full Text
4e. ERIC; JSTOR
4f. Biography Reference Bank; LexisNexis Academic
4g. Health Reference Center Academic; MedlinePlus
4h. ERIC; JSTOR
4i. LexisNexis Academic; Social Science Full Text
4j. PsycArticles; Social Sciences Full Text

CHAPTER 7

1. January 1, 1863. This is an easy, straightforward factual question that could be answered by many sources, including the chronological ones to be discussed later in this chapter, general encyclopedias such as *Britannica Online*, Encyclopedia.com, and Infoplease Encyclopedia, or reference databases like Gale Virtual Library, Credo Reference, and Oxford Reference. Just don't use *Wikipedia* because a user might have just edited the entry for Emancipation Proclamation to say it was issued by President Clinton in 1996 to free consumers from high credit card interest!

2. In a nutshell, by writing about their harsh treatment, former and fugitive slaves elicited the sympathy and support of Northerners, many of whom were unaware of the horrible conditions of slavery. This question is more complex but could also be answered by most general encyclopedias or subscription reference databases. The only challenge here is to choose the right term to search; using **slave narratives** brings up many entries.

3. In U.S. government, the Electoral College is the group that actually chooses the president and vice president; when voters go to the polls, they are voting for electors rather than the actual candidate. This is a basic question requiring a definition that could be found in most general encyclopedias or subscription reference databases.

4. Even though Bush lost the popular vote, he won the electoral vote, which is the one that matters, and went on to become president. Unlike the previous question, this is a much more complex one which involves understanding the difference between the popular vote and the electoral vote and analyzing the

results of this particular election. In addition to answers that many of the ency-clopedias already cited in the previous questions provide, *CQ Researcher* gives an in-depth report explaining this issue.

5.   Candy Lightner. This is a straightforward question that could be answered by most general encyclopedic sources and subscription reference databases.

6.   Between 1980, the year that MADD was founded, and 1997, traffic fatalities attributed to alcohol were reduced from 60 percent to 40 percent, which corre-sponded with the organization's "20 by 2000" program described in an entry in Gale Virtual Reference Library from *The Encyclopedia of Drugs, Alcohol & Addictive Behavior.*

7.   A trapezoid is a four-sided shape that has two parallel sides and two that are not parallel. YourDictionary.com is just one of the many dictionaries that could answer this question.

8.   Since an obstreperous person is noisy and unruly, you would probably prefer a different seat. This definition is easily found in any decent dictionary includ-ing Dictionary.com.

9.   1974. Since this question pertains to the history of a word, it is a perfect exam-ple of a question that can be answered by the *Oxford English Dictionary.*

10.   This is a tricky question because it depends on how you define popularity. Al-though there are more cats than dogs owned in the United States, cat owners are more likely to own multiple cats, so dogs are actually owned by more households. This is a perfect question to answer with *Statistical Abstract of the United States* (see Table 1204).

11.   According to Table 1067 in *Statistical Abstract of the United States* (2010), the number of motor vehicle fatalities resulting from a collision with another automobile was 23,000 in 1980 and 17,200 in 2007. Since the National Mini-mum Drinking Age Act was passed in 1984, vehicular homicide has de-creased since the implementation of a nationwide drinking age of 21 years. This would be an extremely persuasive fact to use in an essay arguing that the legal drinking age should not be lowered.

12.   According to Table 406, "Voting Age Population—Reported Registration and Voting by Selected Characteristics: 1996 to 2008" in *Statistical Abstract of the United States*, 28.4 percent of 18- to 20-year-olds and 35.4 percent of 21- to 24-year-olds voted in 2000; in 2008, the percentages had increased dramati-cally to 41 percent and 46.6 percent. What accounted for this increased inter-est in voting goes far beyond the scope of statistical tables.

13. The most direct route between Kentucky and Canada would pass through either Indiana or Ohio, depending on the exact point of departure, and then through Michigan. Any basic atlas will answer this question; Google Maps is particularly helpful.

14. If you're the average-aged college student, you weren't even born yet when the Soviet Union was the arch nemesis of the United States. Now, the area that used to be this superpower is occupied by 15 independent countries. If you look up **Soviet Union** in the index of the *World Almanac*, which is not available online and provides more than just statistics, you'll see a subheading for "break-up." Turning to the page indicated, you'll see that Lithuania, Latvia, and Estonia declared independence first in August 1991, followed shortly thereafter by Russia, Ukraine, and Belarus, countries that further declared the death of the Soviet Union. These are the only countries specifically mentioned, but the entry says that most of the newly formed nations formed the Commonwealth of Independent States. If you look up the CIS in the *World Almanac*, you'll find that Armenia, Azerbaijan, Georgia, Kazakhstan, Kyrgyzstan, Moldova. Tajikistan, Turkmenistan, and Uzbekistan also joined this alliance. Other sources may answer this question, but it's amazing what you can find out in this one little indispensable book.

15. This question is somewhat ambiguous, as many of your questions may be. *Statistical Abstracs* provides Table 47: "Estimated Unauthorized Immigrants by Selected States and Countries of Birth: 2000 and 2008," which sounds like it would provide some statistical evidence that would be useful in your paper. According to this table, the estimated increase in the illegal immigrant population from 2000 to 2008 was more than 1.1 million. If you didn't know what states border Mexico, you could look at any U.S. map and see that they are California, Arizona, New Mexico, and Texas. Even though New Mexico is not specifically included in the table, the estimated answer is close enough to make your point.

16. Although the Civil War officially began when the South fired on Fort Sumter, the first actual battle was at Bull Run in Manassas, Virginia, and the last significant battle was at Five Forks near Petersburg, Virginia. InfoPlease.com provides these answers.

17. According to Timelines of History, lead pencils were first used in 1492, the same year that "Columbus sailed the ocean blue." Leonardo da Vinci also drew a flying machine (but whether he did so with a lead pencil is not specified), and a meteorite landed in Ensisheim, Germany, prompting a visit from Emperor Maximilian.

18. *Facts on File* reports that on April 28, 2001, Dennis Tito, age 60, took off on a Russian Soyuz capsule with two cosmonauts to visit the International Space Station. The American businessman and former aerospace engineer paid $20 million to the Russian space agency.

19. If you enter **special olympics** in the Gale Virtual Reference Library search page, an entry about Eunice Kennedy Shriver from *Women in World History: A Biographical Encyclopedia* comes up as the second item retrieved. She is indeed the founder of the Special Olympics, and this entry provides a concise biographical essay about her.

20. Louisa May Alcott was one of four sisters that lived in Concord, Massachusetts (just like Jo March, the main character in the classic children's book). One of Alcott's sisters died (just like in *Little Women*), but it happened before the Civil War, not after. These and other similarities can be drawn from the entry for Alcott in the *Dictionary of Literary Biography* and other biographical sources.

21. *The United States Government Manual* states, "The Department of Homeland Security leads the unified national effort to secure America. It will prevent and deter terrorist attacks and protect against and respond to threats and hazards to the Nation. The Department will ensure safe and secure borders, welcome lawful immigrants and visitors, and promote the free-flow of commerce."

22. Aside from the organization's website, either *Associations Unlimited* or its print version *Encyclopedia of Associations* will get you in touch with this group, and you won't even need to use a tricorder or get beamed up by Scotty.

23. Because just about every organization or association has a website, most people now just go to Google to find contact information like that required in the previous question. *Associations Unlimited* (or *Encyclopedia of Associations*) still comes in handy when identifying organizations according to their mission. So if you wanted to find a detailed list of environmental groups, this would be a better source to go to than Google.

24. Henry David Thoreau wrote this famous quote in his masterpiece *Walden*. You could use Oxford Reference, among other sources, to determine this if you didn't know it already.

25. Among Einstein's noteworthy observations are: "Imagination is more important than knowledge," and "Science without religion is lame, religion without science is blind." These two quotations attributed to Einstein can be found on *Britannica Online*, a resource that provides more than just the text of the *Encyclopedia Britannica*. One of its added features is a quotations database.

26. British politician Nancy Astor once explained, "One reason I don't drink is that I want to know when I am having a good time," while nineteenth-century American writer Henry David Thoreau asserted, "[Water is] the only drink for a wise man." These quotations can be found at The Quotations Page.

27. The first two items listed in WorldCat following a search for **UFOs and bibliographies** are *UFOs and the Extraterrestrial Contact Movement: A Bibliography* and *UFOs and Related Subjects: An Annotated Bibliography*.

28. No apostrophe is required since the acronym *UFOs* is plural rather than possessive. Any decent style guide will make this distinction.

CHAPTER 8

1. A suggested paraphrased version of the Gettysburg Address:
   Those who gathered to dedicate the battlefield could not make the site any more holy than the soldiers who fought there, many of whom sacrificed their lives, had already done. Lincoln believed the things that were said at the dedication would soon be forgotten, but he hoped the brave deeds of the soldiers would always be remembered. He suggested that all of those still alive focus on winning the war and committing themselves to the principles that so many soldiers had died for. Inspired by the memory of the deceased, the living must carry on with the mission that others had died for, and commit themselves to assuring that the United States would continue and that the principles of democratic government would endure forever. By doing this, all of the deaths at Gettysburg would have had a purpose.

2a. N: When Pluto's reclassification was first announced in 2006, it elicited a lot of heated debate. Since then, most standard reference sources clearly indicate that Pluto is a dwarf; therefore, this statement need not be cited.

2b. Y: This statement needs to be cited because the definition of "popular" is ambiguous. How is popularity measured? By the number of people who enter each of the four major theme parks at Disney World? By the number who enter the Magic Kingdom alone? By the number of people who stay at a Disney World Resort?

2c. N: This fact is easily found in such standard reference sources as the *World Almanac*.

2d. N: This fact is easily found in any standard general reference source that provides a list of presidents.

2e. Y: This statement is debatable rather than factual.

2f. N: Basic date questions such as this do not require documentation.

2g. Y: This statement about Pluto is a bit more complicated, and so it should be cited.

2h.   Y: This statement reflects a judgment rather than a simple fact, such as "Johnson was the first president to be impeached."

3.   Some of the ways you could integrate this sentence into your paper include the following:
   a.   Van Maanen contends, "If attendance figures and repeat visits are our guide, it would certainly seem that Disney has made good on its claim to have built 'the happiest place on earth'" (5).
   b.   "If attendance figures and repeat visits are our guide," according to Maanen, "it would certainly seem that Disney has made good on its claim to have built 'the happiest place on earth'" (5).
   c.   One expert contends, "If attendance figures and repeat visits are our guide, it would certainly seem that Disney has made good on its claim to have built 'the happiest place on earth'" (Maanen 5).

Common Subscription Databases

Your college library will probably not have every resource listed here because that would be repetitive and expensive. But these are the most popular databases in use as of 2010, so you should be able to access some of them at your school. At the same time, while some of the more popular subject databases are listed in this appendix, this is not a comprehensive list by any means; some university websites provide literally hundreds of databases. The ones chosen for inclusion here are most useful for undergraduate research.

GENERAL REFERENCE DATABASES

- *Britannica Online*: Based on the renowned print encyclopedia published for more than two centuries, this online version also provides access to other reference tools such as timelines, maps, and quotations.
- *Encyclopedia Americana*: You may have used this online version of the popular print resource in high school, but it is also suitable for college-level research.
- Each of the following databases allows you to search its specific collection of reference e-books:
  - Credo Reference
  - Oxford Reference
  - Gale Virtual Reference
- Biography Reference Bank: Produced by H.W. Wilson, this database provides the full text of such reference sources as *Current Biography*, Wilson Biographies Plus Illustrated, and *World Authors*, as well as all of the periodicals and books covered by Biography Index since 1984.

- Opposing Viewpoints Resource Center: Addressing all sides of important controversial topics, this database is a good place to start when writing a persuasive essay that must consider both the pros and the cons of your chosen subject.
- *CQ Researcher*: Providing unbiased, in-depth, well-researched reports on social, political, and economic issues, this resource gives concise background information as well as timelines, maps, statistics, and bibliographies.

PERIODICAL DATABASES

General

- Academic Search (Complete, Elite, or Premier editions, depending on the number of periodicals included): Produced by EBSCOhost, these general periodical databases cover most subjects and offer a selection of scholarly journals, magazines, and a few major newspapers, most in full text. This resource is a great place to start your research!
- Academic OneFile or Expanded Academic ASAP: These databases, produced by Gale Cengage Learning, are similar to the EBSCOhost general databases. Sometimes referred to as InfoTrac, they provide a good place to begin your search for articles in both magazines and scholarly journals.
- *Reader's Guide* Full Text: Based on the once-popular print index *The Reader's Guide to Periodical Literature*, this WilsonWeb database published by H.W. Wilson offers another good starting point for research on most subjects. Although its title suggests that all citations provide full text, this is actually true for selected titles only.
- JSTOR: This database, with a title that is short for "journal storage," is a good place to find the full text of the scholarly journal articles you are expected to use in your college-level research—although the articles published in the most recent two years are never included. Because it provides only scholarly content, JSTOR may not sufficiently cover topics related to popular culture, controversial issues, and current events in comparison to the databases previously mentioned.
- Project Muse: This full-text database, often found on academic library websites, provides access to scholarly publications covering most subjects.

Subject-Specific Periodical Databases

Business

- Business Source (Complete, Elite, or Premier editions, depending on the number of periodicals included): This EBSCOhost database covers all business topics and, like its "cousin," Academic Search, offers a selection of scholarly journals, magazines, and a few major newspapers, most in full text.

- Business and Company Resource Center: In addition to articles, this database also provides company profiles, histories, and industry reports.
- ABI/Inform: This database, published by ProQuest, covers business magazines and online news sources as well as scholarly business journals.
- Business and Company ASAP: This Gale database includes business and management journals, trade journals, newspapers, and business directories.

Education

- Education Full Text: This WilsonWeb database covers all topics relating to educational policy and teaching.
- ERIC (Educational Resources Information Center): Although this government-sponsored database can be found for free on the web, it is also available for a fee from such major database producers as EBSCOhost; these paid versions include features not available in the free versions.

Health

- Health Reference Center—Academic: This Gale database covers nursing and health journals, as well as a wide variety of other personal health periodical sources.
- Health Source—Nursing Academic: This EBSCOhost database also covers nursing and health journals and other periodicals dealing with health-related topics.
- CINAHL—The Cumulative Index to Nursing and Allied Health Literature: This database is available via EBSCOhost because it is owned by ESBCO Publishing. This database is considered the most comprehensive resource for nursing and allied health literature.
- MedlinePlus: Like ERIC, this government-sponsored database is available for free on the web but is also available from such major database producers as EBSCOhost. The paid versions include added features not available in the free versions.

Humanities and Literature

- Humanities Full Text: This WilsonWeb database covers art, music, philosophy, folklore, linguistics, communication, theater, religion, dance, and much more.

- Art Full Text: Periodicals concerned with fine, decorative, and commercial arts, as well as photography, folk art, film, architecture, and much more are covered by this WilsonWeb database.
- Religion and Philosophy Collection: This EBSCOhost database provides access to hundreds of periodicals covering topics such as world religions, religious denominations, biblical studies, religious history, political philosophy, philosophy of language, moral philosophy, and the history of philosophy.
- Literature Resource Center. This Gale database offers access to author biographies, literacy criticism from books and journals, information on literary movements, and timelines.

Sciences

- General Science Full Text: This WilsonWeb database covers periodicals in all major science areas.
- AccessScience: Based on the *McGraw-Hill Encyclopedia of Science & Technology,* this database is a starting point to learn about any scientific subject.
- Applied Science and Technology Full Text: This WilsonWeb database covers trade journals, technical society journals, specialized subject periodicals, and conference proceedings to provide information on a wide variety of technological topics.

Social Sciences

- Social Sciences Full Text: This WilsonWeb database provides coverage of periodicals in subject areas including but not limited to anthropology, criminal justice, economics, environmental studies, geography, law, political science, public welfare, and social work.
- History Reference Center: Suitable for undergraduate historical research, this EBSCOhost database provides information from books and major history periodicals, as well as historical documents and visual material.
- PsycArticles: Produced by the American Psychological Association, this database provides the full text of peer-reviewed scholarly journals on topics in psychology.

Newspaper Databases

- LexisNexis Academic: This database covers national and international newspapers, trade publications, and newsmagazines.
- *New York Times* Historical, 1851 to 2006: This database provides full-text access to more than 150 years of America's most respected newspaper that has always strived to publish "all the news that's fit to print."

Citation Style Guide

This appendix provides sample citations of the most commonly used types of sources in *MLA*, *Chicago*, and *APA* styles. If you do not find an example of the type of source you need to cite, refer to the following style guides:

- *MLA Handbook for Writers of Research Papers* (7th ed., 2009)
- *The Chicago Manual of Style* (16th ed., 2010)
- *Publication Manual of the American Psychological Association* (6th ed., 2009)

Following this list are brief instructions about how to do the citations within the text of your paper to identify your sources in all three major styles.

BOOKS

A Book by One Author

MLA

Author's Last Name, First Name. *Book Title in Italics*. Place of Publication: Publisher, year. Print.

> Gunn, Angus M. *Unnatural Disasters: Case Studies of Human-Induced Environmental Catastrophes*. Westport, CT: Greenwood Press, 2003. Print.

Chicago

Author's Last Name, First Name. *Book Title in Italics*. Place of Publication: Publisher, year.

> Gunn, Angus M. *Unnatural Disasters: Case Studies of Human-Induced Environmental Catastrophes*. Westport, CT: Greenwood Press, 2003.

APA

Author's Last Name, Initials. (year). *Book title in italics*. [Capitalize only first letter of first word of title and first word of subtitle]. Place: Publisher.

> Gunn, A. M. (2003). *Unnatural disasters: Case studies of human-induced environmental catastrophes*. Westport, CT: Greenwood Press.

A Book with Two or More Authors

MLA

First listed author's Last Name, First Name and second listed author's First Name Last Name. *Book Title in Italics*. Place of Publication: Publisher, year. Print.

> Geraci, Joseph R. and David J. St. Aubin. *Sea Mammals and Oil: Confronting the Risks*. San Diego: Academic Press, 1990. Print.

If there are three authors, the author whose name appears first will again be listed as Last Name, First Name, the second author's First Name Last Name, and the third author's First Name Last Name.

If there are four authors or more, then only the first author's name need be given followed by et al., as shown here: Author's Last Name, First Name, et al. The rest of the citation format remains the same.

Chicago

First-named author's Last Name, First Name, and second author's First Name Last Name. *Book Title in Italics*. Place of Publication: Publisher, year.

> Geraci, Joseph R., and David J. St. Aubin. *Sea Mammals and Oil: Confronting the Risks*. San Diego: Academic Press, 1990.

If there are three or more authors, all names should be cited.

APA

First author's Last Name, Initials, & second author's Last Name, Initials. (year). *Book title in italics*. Place of Publication: Publisher.

> Geraci, J. R., & St. Aubin, D. J. (1990). *Sea mammals and oil: Confronting the risks*. San Diego, CA: Academic Press.

If there are three or more authors, list all names with a comma between each author's last and first names, and use an ampersand (&) between last two listed authors.

A Book with an Editor but No Author

MLA

Editor's Last Name, First Name, ed. *Book Title in Italics*. Place of Publication: Publisher, year. Print.

> Oliver-Smith, Anthony and Suzannah M. Hoffman, eds. *The Angry Earth: Disaster in Anthropological Perspective*. New York: Routledge, 1999. Print.

If there is more than one editor, the first editor's name is listed Last Name, First Name and the second editor's is listed First Name Last Name followed by "eds."

Chicago

Editor's Last Name, First Name, ed. *Book Title in Italics*. Place of Publication: Publisher, year.

> Oliver-Smith, Anthony, and Suzannah M. Hoffman, eds. *The Angry Earth: Disaster in Anthropological Perspective*. New York: Routledge, 1999.

APA

Editor's Last Name, Initials. (Ed.) (year). *Book title in italics*. Place of Publication: Publisher.

> Oliver-Smith, A., & Hoffman, S. M. (Eds.) (1999). *The angry earth: Disaster in anthropological perspective*. New York, NY: Routledge.

If there is more than one editor, the names are joined by an ampersand (&), as they are when there is more than one author.

An Edited Book with an Author

MLA

Author's Last Name, First Name. *Book Title in Italics*. Ed. Editor's First Name Last Name. Place of Publication: Publisher, year. Print.

> Fingas, Mervin. *Basics of Oil Spill Cleanup*. Ed. Jennifer Charles. New York: CRC Press LLC, 2001. Print.

Chicago

Author's Last Name, First Name. *Book Title in Italics*. Edited by Editor's First Name Last Name. Place of Publication: Publisher, year.

> Fingas, Mervin. *Basics of Oil Spill Cleanup*. Edited by Jennifer Charles. New York: CRC Press, 2001.

APA

Author's Last Name, First Initial. (year). *Book title in italics.* Editor's First Initial Last Name (ed.). Place of Publication: Publisher.

> Fingas, M. (2001). *Basics of oil spill cleanup.* J. Charles (ed.). New York, NY: CRC Press LLC.

A Book Chapter

MLA

Chapter author's Last Name, First Name. "Title of the Chapter in Quotes." *Book Title in Italics.* Ed. Editor's First Name Last Name. Place of Publication: Publisher, year. Chapter pages. Print.

> Testa, Stephen M. and James A. Jacobs. "Oil Spills and Leaks." *Handbook of Complex Environmental Remediation Problems.* Ed. Jay H. Lehr. New York: McGraw-Hill, 2002. 9.1–9.85. Print.

Chicago

Chapter author's Last Name, First Name. "Chapter Title in Quotes." In *Book Title in Italics*, edited by Editor's First Name Last Name, chapter pages. Place of Publication: Publisher, year.

> Testa, Stephen M., and James A. Jacobs. "Oil Spills and Leaks." In *Handbook of Complex Environmental Remediation Problems*, edited by Jay H. Lehr, 9.1–9.85. New York: McGraw-Hill, 2002.

APA

Chapter author's Last Name, Initials. (year). Chapter title. In Editor's Initials Last Name (Ed.). *Book title in italics* (chapter pages). Place of Publication: Publisher.

> Testa, S., &. Jacobs, J. A. (2002). Oil spills and leaks. In J. H. Lehr (Ed.). *Handbook of complex environmental remediation problems* (9.1–9.85). New York, NY: McGraw-Hill.

An Entry from an Encyclopedia or Other Reference Book

MLA

"Article Title in Quotes." *Book Title in Italics.* Year. Print.

> "Oil Spills." *Encyclopedia of Environment and Society.* 2007. Print.

If the article is signed, begin with the author's Last Name, First Name.

Chicago

Entry author's Last Name, First Name (if provided). "Entry Title in Quotes." In *Reference Book Title in Italics*, edited by Editor's First Name Last Name, entry pages. Place of Publication: Publisher, year.

> "Oil Spills." In *Encyclopedia of Environment and Society*, edited by Paul Robbins, 1294–1296. Thousand Oaks, CA: Sage, 2007.

APA

Author's Last Name, Initials (if provided). (year). Article title. In *Book title in italics*. (Vol. number, page numbers). Place of publication: Publisher.

> Oil spills. (2007). In *Encyclopedia of environment and society*. (Vol. 4, 1294-1296). Thousand Oaks, CA: Sage.

If the article has no author, as in the example above, begin the citation with the entry title followed by the year and then the book title.

An E-book

MLA

Author's Last Name, First Name. Full Title of Book in Italics. Place of Publication: Publisher, Date. Title of Database or Online Collection in Italics. Web. Date of access written day month year.

> Tamminen, Terry. *Lives Per Gallon: The True Cost of Our Oil Addiction*. Washington, D.C.: Shearwater Books, 2006. *ebrary*. Web. 28 May 2010.

Chicago

Author's Last Name, First Name. *Full Title of Book in Italics*. Place of publication: Publisher, Date. Access date. URL.

> Tamminen, Terry. *Lives Per Gallon: The True Cost of Our Oil Addiction*. Washington, DC: Shearwater Books, 2006. Accessed February 28, 2010. http://shearwaterbooks.com/lives_per_gallon.

If the electronic version is not web-based (e.g., a Kindle edition), indicate the version after the publication date.

APA

Cite using a print book format.

> Tamminen, T. (2006). *Lives per gallon: The true cost of our oil addiction*. Washington, DC: Shearwater Books.

ARTICLES

A Scholarly Journal Article

MLA

Author's Last Name, First Name. "Article Title in Quotes." *Journal Name in Italics* volume number. issue number (year): pages. Print.

> Priest, Tyler. "Extraction Not Creation: The History of Offshore Petroleum in the Gulf of Mexico." *Enterprise and Society* 8.2 (2007): 227–267. Print.

Chicago

Author's Last Name, First Name. "Article Title in Quotes." *Journal Name in Italics* volume number, issue no. [must use "no."] (year): pages.

> Priest, Tyler. "Extraction Not Creation: The History of Offshore Petroleum in the Gulf of Mexico." *Enterprise and Society* 8, no. 2 (2007): 227–267.

APA

Author's Last Name, Initials. (year). Title of article. [Capitalize only first letter of first word in title and subtitle] *Journal name in italics*, *volume number in italics*, issue number [only used if pagination is not continuous from one issue to another], pages.

> Priest, T. (2007). Extraction not creation: The history of offshore petroleum in the gulf of Mexico. *Enterprise and Society 8*, 227–267.

A Magazine Article

MLA

Author's Last Name, First Name. "Article Title in Quotes." *Magazine Name in Italics.* Day month year: pages. Print.

> Walsh, Bryan and Steven Gray. "The Meaning of the Mess." *Time.* 17 May 2010: 28–35. Print.

Chicago

Author's Last Name, First Name. "Article Title in Quotes." *Magazine Name in Italics,* Date: pages.

> Walsh, Bryan and Steven Gray. "The Meaning of the Mess." *Time,* May 17, 2010: 28–35.

APA

Author's Last Name, Initials. (year, month day). Title of article. [Capitalize only first letter of first word] *Magazine Name in Italics, volume number in italics*, pages.

> Walsh, B., & Gray, S. (2010, May 17). The meaning of the mess. *Time, 175,* 28–35.

A Newspaper Article

MLA

Author's Last Name, First Name. "Article Title in Quotes." *Newspaper Name in Italics* Day month year: pages. Print.

> Gillis, Justin. "Scientists Fault Lack of Studies Over Oil Spills." *New York Times* 20 May 2010: A1. Print.

If there is no author cited, begin citation with article title.

Chicago

Author's Last Name, First Name. "Article Title in Quotes." *Newspaper Name in Italics*, Month day, year.

> Gillis, Justin. "Scientists Fault Lack of Studies over Oil Spills." *New York Times*, May 20, 2010.

APA

Author's Last Name, Initials (ycar, month day). Article title. *Newspaper Name in Italics,* pages.

> Gillis, J. (2010, May 20). Scientists fault lack of studies over oil spills. *New York Times,* A1.

An Article Obtained through a Periodical Database

MLA

Author's Last Name, First Name. "Article Title in Quotes." *Journal Name in Italics.* Vol. number. Issue number (year): article pages. *Database Name in Italics.* Web. Date of access written day month year.

> Cima, Greg. "Responders Prepared for Oil, but Impact Unclear." *Journal of the American Veterinary Medical Association.* 236.11 (2010): 1142–1164. *Academic Search Complete.* Web. 4 June 2010.

Chicago

Author's Last Name, First Name. "Article Title in Quotes." *Journal Name in Italics* volume number, issue no. (year): pages. Accessed Month, day, year. URL.

Cima, Greg. "Responders Prepared for Oil, but Impact Unclear." *Journal of the American Veterinary Medical Association* 236, no. 11 (2010): 1142–1164. Accessed June 4, 2010. http://rpa.laguardia.edu:2048/login?url=http://search.ebscohost.com/login.aspx?direct=true&db=a9h&AN=51188191&site=ehost-live.

APA

Author's Last Name, Initials. (year). Title of article. [Capitalize only first letter of first word in title and subtitle] *Journal name in italics, volume number in italics*, issue number [only used if pagination is not continuous from one issue to another], pages.

Cima, G. (2010). Responders prepared for oil, but impact unclear. *Journal of the American Veterinary Medical Association, 236,* 1142–1164.

The same format is used whether the article is retrieved online or in print.

WEB SOURCES

Webpage

MLA

Author's Last Name, First Name. "Title of webpage or work in quotes." *Title of the Overall Website in Italics.* Publisher or sponsor, day month year last updated. Web. Day month year of access.

"Gulf of Mexico Response." *BP Global.* BP, 28 May 2010. Web. 28 May 2010.

URLs are no longer required since they change so frequently and most sites can be found through Google. If no author is listed, begin the citation with the webpage title. Use n.p. if no publisher information is given and n.d. if no publishing date is given.

Chicago

Author's Last Name, First Name. "Title of Webpage in Quotes." Sponsoring Organization or Overall Website Name. Revised/Modified/Accessed Month day, year. URL.

"Gulf of Mexico Response." BP Global. Accessed September 9, 2010. http://www.bp.com/extendedsectiongenericarticle.do?categoryId=40&contentId=7061813.

If no author is given, begin the citation with the webpage title.

APA

Author's Last Name, Initials. (year, date). *Title of webpage in italics*. Retrieved from URL.

> *Gulf of Mexico response* (2009). Retrieved from http://www.bp.com/ extendedsectiongenericarticle.do?categoryId=40&contentId=7061813.

If no author is listed, start with *Title* (year, date). and continue as above.

Website

MLA

Author's Last Name, First Name. *Title of Website in Italics*. Publisher or sponsor, Day month year last updated. Web. Day month year of access.

> *Emergency.Louisiana.gov*. Louisiana State. 6 June 2010. Web. 6 June 2010.

If no author is listed, begin the citation with the webpage title. Use n.p. if no publisher information is given and n.d. if no publishing date is given.

Chicago

Author's Last Name, First Name. Title of Website. Sponsoring organization. Revised/Modified/Accessed Month day, year. URL.

> Emergency.Louisiana.gov. State of Louisiana. Accessed June 6, 2010. http://emergency.Louisiana.gov.

If no author is listed, begin citation with website title and continue.

APA

Author's Last Name, Initials. (year, date). *Title of website in italics*. Retrieved from URL.

> *Emergency.Louisiana.gov*. (2010). Retrieved from http://emergency.Louisiana .gov.

If no author is listed, start citation with website *Title* (year, date) and continue as above.

OTHER SOURCES

A Film or Videorecording

MLA

Film Title in Italics. Dir. Director's First Name Last Name. Other information that distinguishes the film, such as performer or writer. Distributor. Year. Specify format as film, DVD, or videocassette.

Valdez after the Spill: Sea of Oil. Dir. M. R. Katzke. Affinityfilms. 1990. Videocassette.

Chicago

Title of Film in Italics. Format. Directed by First Name Last Name. Place of Publication: Publisher, year.

Valdez after the Spill: Sea of Oil. Videocassette. Directed by M. R. Katzke. New York: Affinityfilms, 1990.

APA

Producer's Last Name, Initials. (Producer), & Director's Last Name, Initials (Director). (year). *Film title in italics.* [specify format]. Place: Production Company Name.

Katzke, M. R. (Director). (1990). *Valdez after the spill: Sea of oil.* [Videocassette]. New York: Affinityfilms.

An Interview

MLA

Last Name of person interviewed, First Name. Personal Interview. Date of interview day month year.

Smith, John. Personal Interview. 4 June 2010.

If the interview is published in a book or periodical, use the citation format for that type of source.

Chicago

Personal interviews should be mentioned in the text of the paper with all appropriate information given. There is no need to include this source in the bibliography. If the interview is published in a journal or magazine, then it is cited as an article.

APA

Personal interviews should not be included in reference list. All the appropriate information should be listed in the text of your report. If the interview appeared in a journal or magazine, then it is treated as an article citation.

IN-TEXT CITATION

MLA

In-text citation requires two facts: the last name of the author and the page being referenced. This information appears in parentheses after the last word of the sentence but before the period. If the author's name has been introduced in the sentence, then only the page number is needed in the parentheses. If the author is unknown, use a short form of the title in the parentheses or, in the case of a website, the sponsor.

Chicago

In-text citation is indicated by using a footnote or a number at the end of a sentence. The complete information on the source is then identified by that number either at the bottom of the page or as an endnote at the end of the paper. A footnote or endnote for a book should give the following information:

1. Author's First and Last Names, *Source Title in Italics* (Place of Publication: Publisher, year), page number.

1. Angus M. Gunn, *Unnatural Disasters: Case Studies of Human-Induced Environmental Catastrophes* (Westport, CT: Greenwood Press, 2003), 25.

Note that the style for footnotes and endnotes varies from the style used for bibliography entries in these ways: the author names are presented in normal order, rather than inverted; the different elements of the source are separated by commas, rather than periods; the facts of publication appear in parentheses; and only the first line of the citation is indented.

Further references to a source already cited in the text need only include the author's Last Name, *Title in Italics*, and page number. You may also use a shortened version of the title.

2. Gunn, *Unnatural Disasters*, 28.

See *The Chicago Manual of Style* for examples of how to footnote journals, websites, and other sources.

APA

In-text citation requires that information be introduced in the sentence presenting an author's ideas. The sentence should include the author's name immediately followed by the year of the source in parentheses. A page number is given in parentheses at the end of the sentence before the period and is introduced with the letter (p.).

Index

Page numbers followed by the letter "f" indicate figures; those followed by the letter "t" indicate tables.

About the Authors

Arlene R. Quaratiello received an MA in English literature from the University of New Hampshire, an MLS from Simmons College, and a BA in English from the College of the Holy Cross. She wrote the first edition of *The College Student's Research Companion* while she was Coordinator of Library Instruction at Emerson College in Boston. In 2010 Prometheus Books released a paperback edition of her book *Rachel Carson: A Biography,* first published by Greenwood Press in 2004. She is currently an adjunct instructor of English at Saint Anselm College in Manchester, New Hampshire, and has also taught freshman composition at the University of New Hampshire.

Jane Devine has been the Chief Librarian and Department Chair for LaGuardia Community College, part of the City University of New York, since 2004. Previously she served as LaGuardia's Periodicals/Government Documents/Electronic Resources librarian. Before joining the LaGuardia faculty she worked for the New York Public Library. She received both her MLS and master's in English from St. John's University in New York. She has co-authored the book *Going Beyond Google: The Invisible Web in Learning and Teaching*, published in 2009, and articles that have appeared in the *Journal of Academic Librarianship* and the *Internet Reference Services Quarterly*. Her writing reflects her strong interest in the research process.

WALTER DEAN MYERS

SCHOLASTIC INC.
New York Toronto London Auckland Sydney
Mexico City New Delhi Hong Kong Buenos Aires

FOR CHRIS

This book was originally published by Scholastic Press in 2003.

ISBN 0-439-36842-1

1 2 3 4 5 6 7 8 9 10 11 12
5 6 7 8 9 10/0

Printed in the U.S.A. 23 • First paperback printing, May 2005
The text type was set in 11-pt Sabon. • Book design by David A. Caplan

THE BEAST,

HALF HUMAN, HALF BULL, ROAMED THE ENDLESS CORRIDORS OF THE LABYRINTH, WAITING FOR THE YOUTH UPON WHICH IT WOULD FEED.

— *ADAPTED FROM* THESEUS AND THE MINOTAUR

PROLOGUE

L*a misma ola vagabunda que te lleva te devuelva.'*
'May the same waters that take you bring you
back to me.'" Gabi kissed my hand twice.

"Are we supposed to make promises to each other
now?" I asked.

"What kind of promises are you going to make to me?"

"I promise to be true to you, and that our first child will
have eyes as dark as the winter sky," I said.

"I'm sure our first child will have dark eyes," Gabi said.
"But I've heard those white girls are easy, so I'm not too

sure of how faithful you're going to be. But remember this, a woman can always tell."

"You know what I was thinking?" An old man passed with two small children who were harnessed together. I thought they were probably his grandchildren. "I was thinking that if I get into a good school —"

"Have you heard anything?"

"No, but say I do. I mean, that's the main reason I'm going up to Wallingford, right? Anyway, I was thinking that if I did get accepted at a good school, we wouldn't have to wait until I graduated before we were married."

"How did you figure that?"

"Well, I was reading this piece on the Internet the other day, and they were saying that an Ivy League education is worth a hundred and some thousand dollars a year. So, if I got into one of the Ivies we could get married, borrow the money to live on, and then pay it back later."

"You're sixteen, right?"

"I'll be seventeen in October."

"So two years from now you'll be eighteen."

"You said that people get married at sixteen in the Dominican Republic."

"I said that *girls* get married at sixteen in the Dominican Republic," Gabi said. "And boys if the girl is pregnant."

2

"It'll work," I said.

"It could work," she answered. She bent over my hand and kissed it again. "It could work."

"You nervous about me going?"

"A little," she said.

Gabi leaned back against the bench and put her long legs out in front of her, crossing them at the ankles. She still had her hand on mine. Her hand was the color of golden sand and mine as dark as newly turned earth. That's what she had said on the day we had first admitted to loving one another.

"Do you really think I would start chasing after some blonde just because I was away from the city?" I asked.

"When I was very young, maybe eight or nine, my parents took me to the DR to see some relatives," Gabi said. "In the little town my father was from they had a fortune-teller. She told everyone's fortune and you gave her a dollar.

"When she came to me she said I was very pretty —"

"You're really not that pretty," I said, touching the gentle curve of her cheek. She pushed aside a wisp of wavy hair, then looked up quickly and captured me with eyes so hugely dark and deep that I was once again swimming in the mystery of them. I knew she could sense my heart racing.

"And she said I would always be remembered well.

Later, I asked my mother what that meant, and she told me there was a saying that when a man leaves you he'll come back if he remembers you well." Gabi turned her head toward me. "I hope you will remember me well."

"What did you say about the waters taking me away?" I asked.

"May they bring you back to me," Gabi said. "It's from my poet-saint."

"Well, I'll remember where to come and who to come to," I said. "That's my promise to you."

I put my arm around her and Gabi drew close to me. She was small and fit so easily in the curve of my arm. I was nervous about leaving the city, and about the school, but I wasn't concerned with my feelings about Gabi. I knew that I loved her, and that I always would. I don't know how I knew it, but I did.

WALLINGFORD ACADEMY

The rain was beating fiercely against the windows of Hill Dining Hall. A far window was open and the curtains flapped wildly. A dining room worker started toward it. A student, small enough to be a fourth former, beat her to it and closed it. In the corner I saw Brand, his chair tilted away from the round table, his hands clasped behind his neck. Chanelle saw me at the same time and waved me over.

I signaled I would be over in a minute and went for a cup of coffee. An image floated through my mind. My first day at the Academy and Miss Mathews inviting me to have a cup of coffee with her in the dining room. I had never seen a dining room that large before, or floors that nicely cleaned and polished. The sunlight slanting through the windows seemed somehow more subdued than I had ever seen it in Harlem, and the soft lights on the walls and the chandeliers had intimidated me that day and for weeks later.

"The Academy is a place you'll have to get used to," Miss Mathews had said. She had looked closely at me, never mentioning that I was from Harlem, or that her warm tones were meant to suggest a bridge between a black counselor and a black student. I felt good about her. "But the wonderful part of it is that you will get used to it. Students have a way of absorbing the traditions of this school and transforming them into something that resonates with their own lives."

She had been right or, at least, the comfort I began to feel over the next weeks seemed genuine. I noticed that so many of the kids laughed at the idea of tradition, but all of them knew the history of the Academy.

Breakfast had been over for a half hour and the coffee was barely warm in the paper container as I put it down across from Brand. Brand, a face without character, dirty blond hair that would look in place on the six o'clock news in Milwaukee. Chanelle and Julie were sitting with him.

"Here's the deal." Chanelle made her usual parallel hand gestures as she spoke. "Brand is driving down to New York, and so is Julie. Brand has two people going with him and Julie has one, so far. They want us to go but my dad is coming up to take me home and I am absolutely desperate for someone to come with me so I don't have to talk to my father the whole way to New York. So I want you to come with me and my dad."

"I'll be in the city in two hours," Brand said. "Julie is going to crawl in after about two and a half hours. Chanelle's dad is going to take three hours."

"Which is why I need you to come with me!" Chanelle added.

"Okay, I'll go with you," I said.

"What did you think about that math test?" Brand asked.

Chanelle's eyes rolled to the ceiling.

"About halfway through I said a small prayer to the calculus god," I said. "Then I added another one at the end of the test. If I passed it's because one of those prayers got through."

"The problem with your prayers, brother man, is that the calculus god is Asian," Brand said. "He don't want to hear no prayers from no white dudes or no black dudes."

"I think the theory is to give you a math test that's going

to shake you up just before you go on Christmas break," Julie said. "That gives you something to worry about, especially while you wait to hear from your college choice."

The conversation continued about the exams with Brand talking about how the Asians had it made because they were natural test takers and Julie agreeing with everything he said. Julie lived in Fort Lee, New Jersey, just across the George Washington Bridge. She was friends with Chanelle, although I didn't know why Chanelle liked her, and she made sure she kept her distance from me. I was fine with that. I didn't think that Julie wanted to be anywhere near another black person.

There were only a handful of blacks — we called ourselves African Americans at the Academy — in the sixth form. The guys were cool. Some of them thought they were a little special, but I could deal with them. The girls were something else. There were only nine in the sixth and three of them were completely standoffish. The others, except for Julie, were all right but came from a different kind of life than I knew. They were kids, like Chanelle, whose parents had summer homes in Sag Harbor or took them Christmas shopping in London. I thought that maybe one day I would fit in with them, but it would take a while.

Julie, on the other hand, was a trip. She was like an old-time white minstrel dressing up in blackface and woolen

8

wig. Except that under her green eye shadow, auburn wig, and "Oh, my golly!" accent, she *was* black. I told myself that one day I would like to see her naked, no wig, no crazy makeup, no accent, and no exaggerated talk about how she just *loved* baroque music.

We broke up with Brand, actually James Brand, still on a search for riders into the city. Julie took off to gather her laundry to take home.

"You want to walk over to the pond?" Chanelle asked.

The pond. During my first days at the Academy I walked along the path that went around it and tried to ignore it pushing into my consciousness. I made myself think about math and English, and not the differences that Wallingford laid out in this secluded place. Later, as the weather cooled, and the knit pastel scarves and bulky sweaters circled it, I tried not to think of the pond as representing a world I hadn't touched before. It wasn't supposed to feel like home. It was, after all, only water.

"When's your father coming?"

"How much of a hurry are you in?" she asked.

"I haven't been home since I got here in August," I said. We were at the door and I saw that the rain had eased up. There was still a bank of clouds overhead, gray and threatening, but they were moving fairly swiftly toward the west.

"You haven't gone home at all?"

"You know I've been having trouble," I said. "I haven't flunked anything but my grades need all the work I can give them."

She had forgotten I worked in New Haven on weekends. If I could have gotten off from the sneaker store I would have gone home for Thanksgiving, at least.

We started walking across campus. There was still a light rain, but we ignored it. There were cars in the distance, and I imagined that the entire campus would be empty by nightfall. It had been that way at Thanksgiving. I had eaten in the Hall and hung out with some Thai students and the kitchen help until nine. Later I had called home and spoken to Mom and Dad. I didn't get an answer at Gabi's house and that had depressed me. I didn't know if she had received the letter I sent her or not.

"So the truth is" — Chanelle took my arm — "that my father isn't coming, and I bought two tickets for us on the 3:20 Amtrak to Penn Station."

I tried to stop and she pulled me along. Chanelle had been a friend from the time I reached the Academy. Perhaps not so much a friend as the most completely honest person I had met so far at Wallingford. Maybe they were the same thing.

"I was supposed to stay with my dad because I've been doing the switching bit — one holiday with my mom, and one with him — since they've been divorced."

"The courts made that arrangement?"

"No, they were being what they called civilized, only I'm the one who's being split up and I'm the one who has to jump back and forth and understand who's sleeping with who and why it's not really anyone's fault that they're not together," Chanelle said. "I've tried to be understanding of them both and now I'm just tired of it. I'm staying with my mom over the holidays because I feel like it."

"And you want somebody to ride the train with you."

"Spoon, how did you guess?"

"And you blow my chance for a ride without even asking?"

"You don't like Brand, and you don't want to ride all the way down to New York with Julie," Chanelle said. "Case closed. We go over to the chapel, pick up my music, pick up our bags, and then we take the shuttle over to the train station. Right?"

"I guess."

Chanelle was walking next to me, pushing against me even when weren't touching. She was pretty. She moved well, her legs were strong, and sometimes I knew, even when I wasn't around, she thought about me. But I didn't know that.

Chanelle sang hymns and went to the candlelight service on Sunday evenings. It was a simple service, and beautiful. The light in the chapel varied quite a bit. In August, when I first arrived at the Academy, there was an open, warm feeling to the blend of the evening sun and the chapel lights. Later, as the days shortened and the lights dimmed, the flicker of candlelight across the tapestry could lift the spirit and make it soar.

She got her music and showed it to me.

"The music pleases you," I said.

She nodded. Yes, it did.

THE TRAIN TO NEW YORK

I like trains. As opposed to airplanes — there is a sameness about flying, the gray seats in the waiting areas, the identical people checking tickets behind the identical desks. On the plane everyone sits upright, strapped in, facing the same way. The train moves sometimes smoothly, sometimes in fits and jerks. You can feel the curves, the stilted rhythm of the rails. People relax on trains, they sprawl across the seats, some read while others sleep. They face in different directions.

I once took a trip to Savannah with my parents for

Thanksgiving. Two hours into the trip my father was complaining, telling my mother how he would never go by train again. But I loved it. The train was impossibly crowded with people headed south for the holiday. There were suitcases everywhere, not the kind you see on planes — smart, nearly new bags of synthetic fibers — but duffel bags and old suitcases with duct tape holding them together. I imagined these same people, perhaps their parents, coming up from the south thirty years earlier. I knew my father, with his Strivers Row mentality, wouldn't like it, but I did.

"I'll get home by six, and the first thing my mother will want to do is to go out to a fancy grocery store and buy something expensive and barely edible," Chanelle said. "She'll go into her usual shock that I'm still a vegetarian. After that it's the Significant Sit Down where she asks me to tell her all about school. She won't listen to a word, but I'll be up until midnight talking to her."

"It's what parents do," I said. "They have lists in their heads and check off things as you talk. In ten years we'll be doing the same thing."

"You just going to hang out, or do you have plans?"

"I'll have to see what's going on," I said. "Brand said he was going to try to get a game up with some guys he knows. Other than that I don't know."

"What's your girl like?"

What's my girl like? Do I frame Gabi? Do I defend her? Why does my mind race for answers to such a simple question? What is my girl like?

"You'd like her," I finally answered. "She's smart, cool. She wants to be a media specialist on the college level but I think she could make it as a writer."

"If I give a party, do you think she'd come?" Chanelle asked.

"I guess so. Why not? Are you giving a party?"

"I might. I have to do something to keep my sanity."

I'd lost Chanelle's thoughts. Did I ever have them? We sat for twenty minutes in New Haven, changing engines, and Chanelle opened the novel she had brought along. I was thinking about Gabi. At first we had communicated by phone, excited calls with me telling her about the Academy and her telling me how proud she was of me, but how much she missed me. Then her phone had been cut off. I wrote to her and she had answered, a beautiful letter, handwritten, rich with her feelings about what was going on in the neighborhood. She told me that her grandfather, nearly blind, had come to live with them, and that it was a good thing. She apologized for her phone. "*Habla* poverty?" she had asked.

I worked hard on my letter to her, trying to describe what life was like at the Academy, trying to put down on paper what I felt about it. I didn't want to make it seem too good, I knew. The kids weren't any smarter than at our high school in Harlem, but they had already been so many places. Their parents were doctors, or lawyers, or business executives, people who had done all the right things and made the right decisions. Chanelle's father was an editor at a financial newspaper. All the kids, even the ones who complained the most about how phony the Academy was, or how out of touch their parents were, expected to follow the right paths. Or, at least, they knew what paths to follow. What did my homeboys know?

The last letter from Gabi had been at the beginning of December. Overnight Wallingford had been blanketed with almost a foot of clean white snow. Chappie, the ex-army sergeant who worked at the Academy and who had appointed himself keeper of the "boys," gave me the letter along with an overstuffed envelope from the University of Wisconsin. Wisconsin was my second choice of schools after Brown, and I opened that letter first. It said how glad they were that I had applied and told me to fill out the enclosed forms for financial aid. Nothing special, no definite aid, or admission.

What I wanted was for all of my letters to Gabi to be special, to be the kinds of letters someone years in the future would read and wonder about. Even before opening her letter I had imagined my reply, how the snow had fallen in the night and how beautiful the trees around the pond, their bare limbs dressed in the white fluffiness of clean snow, had been in the morning.

Gabi's letter had been long and rambling. She talked about her mother getting on her case and people talking behind her back. There was an oddness in what she was saying, almost an anger. She said that she wished I had made it home for Thanksgiving.

I was sorry I didn't make it home for Thanksgiving. I was sorry that I didn't know why I didn't make it home for Thanksgiving. Was my need to work so compelling? Were the pumpkins in the windows of Wallingford's quaint stores so inviting?

I tried to think about what I would say to Gabi. I called her number and was told the phone was still disconnected. Going down to Harlem would only take a few hours and I could have borrowed the money, but I didn't.

I called Mom and asked her if Gabi had been by, and when she said no I asked if she would go over to her house. She said she would. Later she called me and said that Gabi's mother was ill, and that was probably why I hadn't heard from her.

Gabi had called the next day from a pay phone. She laughed off the letter, saying that I sounded like a soap opera character. She said she had been offered a scholarship to Columbia, and would I consider going there? Yes, of course I would if I could get in, I had said. But Columbia had been a surprise. I hadn't known she had applied.

"Who do you think I should invite to the party?" Chanelle's voice broke through my thoughts. "I don't want it to be just kids from the Academy."

"What kind of party do you want to have?"

"Something that doesn't end in kids puking and crying," she said. "You think a poetry slam would be too corny?"

"Not if you know enough poets," I answered. "You remember the poetry slam they had in the Hall and nobody brought any poems?"

"And Brand dissed the whole thing with his stupid rap? I remember that part," Chanelle said. "I'm just getting depressed going home. Holidays are not my thing. Especially Christmas."

"Why especially Christmas?"

"Because it's here now," she said. "If it was April it would be especially Easter."

The train stopped and two young nuns got on. They were dressed in regular clothes except for their headgear. One of them, very pretty but overweight, smiled at us. I thought of a Guy de Maupassant story in which a nun was hijacked by a robber.

"I could be a nun," Chanelle said. "I don't think it'd be so bad."

"First you live with me for a year on a desert island," I said. "Then you join the nunnery."

"Mr. Witherspoon!" Chanelle put on her *Gone With the Wind* accent. "How you do go on!"

The train started again and the conductor was telling us how many minutes we were from Bridgeport. Chanelle got up to go to the cafe car and asked me if I wanted anything. I said no and she looked at me for a long moment before she left.

The nun who had smiled at me before smiled again and I smiled back.

"Are you on Christmas break?" she asked. "I see your books."

"Yes."

"Us, too," she said.

I hadn't thought of nuns being on Christmas break and it amused me. When Chanelle came back I told her that the nuns were also on Christmas break, and she started talking to them and found out they were both beginning teachers.

Co-op City. The huge, ugly buildings loomed against the gray sky, emphatically announcing CITY.

"You have my number, right?" Chanelle looked up from her book.

"Yes."

"Can I have yours? Is it all right? Maybe we can all have lunch or something? Is that all right?"

"Yeah. Sure."

"No, really, you don't seem too cool with it," Chanelle said.

"I'm cool with it," I said. "You know, I'm just a little nervous."

"Then I won't call." Chanelle shrugged, her hands turned outward.

"No, I don't mean about you calling," I said. "I'm just a little nervous about going home. Is that weird, or what?"

"Why are you nervous?"

I shrugged. As we went into the tunnel leading to Pennsylvania Station I could feel my stomach tense. And suddenly I knew there was a reason I hadn't been home since August. It wasn't exactly clear to me, but I knew it had to do with the mix. Chanelle, Brand, even Julie had all taken the train or driven from New York up to Wallingford, but the distances had been different. They had taken their lives, their successes, with them, and I had left mine behind.

The train stopped at 34th Street, under Madison Square Garden, the home of the New York Knicks. The station was crowded. The escalator up to the main floor. A black man with a paper cup and a toothless grin.

"Can you spare two quarters for a brother?"

"You okay?" Chanelle asked. There was a crowd, moving smoothly through the station, going a hundred different directions, busily weaving the shadowed mosaic of New York. "You're always so laid back and everything. You sure you're okay?"

"I'm okay," I said. "I'll call you."

Chanelle smiled, put her hand on my arm as she kissed me on the cheek, and turned toward the taxi stand.

For a moment I was confused. I told myself that everything was indeed all right.

HARLEM, 356 WEST 122ND STREET

It was New York, my New York, but it felt different. I had only been away a few months but I had already lost the feeling for the crowds, the faster pace. Intending to go straight home, I had taken the A train at 34th. Then I remembered what Chanelle had said about having to explain what I had been doing in school. My parents would expect the same, and I wanted to see Gabi first. I got off the train at 125th and walked down to her block.

The brownstones on 122nd had been converted to two apartments and sometimes more on each floor. Morningside Park was across the wide avenue and gave an airy feel to the block. A wide variety of brown-skinned girls were jumping double Dutch on the sidewalk. Some young boys were sitting on a stoop, a boom box just above them spewing out a rap song. They stared at passersby, daring them to make a comment on either the volume or the string of profanities. I looked to see if Gabi's younger brother, Rafael, was among them; he wasn't.

Gabi's bell was still broken, with the wires coming from the wooden door frame. As I had a hundred times, I took the wires in my hands and touched them together to ring the bell. A moment later I heard the buzzer and pushed open the door. The hallway was musty, and the smells from a mixture of different foods cooking competed in the vestibule.

There were flights up to the top floor and her apartment. The book I had bought Gabi was still in my overnight bag, and I wished I had giftwrapped it even though it was only a used copy of Gabriela Mistral's poems, translated by Langston Hughes. Gabi had been named, by her grandfather, for the Chilean poet.

The door opened. Rafael.

"Yo, what's going on?" Street tough. We touched fists and he moved away from the door.

"So, what's up?"

"The world is still spinning," Rafael said. "And I ain't fell off yet so I must be doing something right."

Rafael was thirteen and smart, but didn't want anyone to know it. He pointed to a chair and told me to "cop a squat" while he went to get Gabi.

The kitchen was small. The shelves were lined with yellow and green placemats that had been cut to fit them. The stove was old enough to look like an antique, and I remembered when Gabi and I had touched up the green enamel and painted the black iron legs. When the gas oven was on full blast it looked like a portable inferno, which came in handy on those winter days when the landlord didn't send up any heat.

"She'll be out in a minute," Rafael said as he came back into the kitchen. He was pulling on his jacket. "I got to go check out my peeps."

"See you around."

Rafael left and I sat alone in the kitchen for a few minutes. Then I heard a door open and heard a man's voice.

"¿Hola? ¿Gabriela?"

"Hello," I said, standing as the old man entered the room. "I'm Anthony Witherspoon, Gabriela's friend."

The man stopped in the doorway, as if he were unsure of his bearings. Then he called Gabi's name several times. He held onto the doorframe as he spoke, and I realized he was either blind or couldn't see very well.

A moment later I heard footsteps and Gabi, in a housecoat, her hair combed out and haloed around her head, came into the kitchen. She put her arm around the old man and said something to him in Spanish. He nodded and held out his hand.

I shook his hand. He had a good grip. "You don't speak Spanish?"

"No, I don't," I said. "Gabi's promised to teach me, but she's fallen behind in her lessons."

"Spanish is a beautiful language," the old man said. I figured he was the grandfather who had come to live with them. "Sometimes, near the waterfront, I used to have my tea in the afternoon and listen to the little girls talk as they played. When Spanish is spoken like that it doesn't have to be fancy talk to sound like music."

"That sounds good to me," I said.

"Maybe I'll listen to the radio," he said, putting his hand on the wall, feeling his way out of the kitchen.

As the old man headed toward the bedroom Gabi followed, her hand on his shoulder, smiling back at me. I felt suddenly awkward, too large for my skin, too clumsy to be in her presence. She disappeared down the hallway and a moment later I heard the sound of the radio being tuned to a Spanish-language station.

She came back quickly and put both arms around my waist and squeezed me. "When did you get home?" she asked.

"I haven't been home yet," I said. A hint of perfume, the feathery touch of her hair against my face, the warmth of her body against mine, sent a rush of blood to my head.

As we kissed she ran her fingernails lightly across my chest. "It's so good to see you," she said. "You want tea? Juice?"

"Juice is fine. How are you?"

"Mom is in the hospital," she said, looking into the refrigerator. "Just an overnight thing. She's got a touch of the flu. Some woman she knows told her not to get shots, so she comes down with everything. Plus we've got a little stress with Abuelo living with us."

"You look good," I said. She was wearing an old housecoat, dark brown with a floral design. As she moved from the refrigerator a glimpse of almost golden thigh contrasted with an off-white silk slip. But once again it was the glance, those dark eyes pinning my butterfly heart with a sudden thrust, that recreated the memory of who she was. *You look good.*

"How long will you be home?" She put the juice and a glass on the table.

"Ten days. I'm off all next week," I said. "I had wanted to plan something, but . . . How's your time?"

"With my mother in the hospital and Abuelo living with us I'm running a bit," she said. "But if you're still Spoon, and I'm still Gabi, I have time for you."

"Good. Good." I was searching for words. "How's the writing going? Are you still working around themes?"

"You want to take a walk?" she asked. "I'll get dressed."

"Sure."

She smiled again and went toward her bedroom. From the other room I could hear Abuelo's radio. Strings. A plaintive reed finding a melody and then the same melody repeated in the strings. An image of the old man listening to the music and feeling its colors with his mind. Another image, from Morningside Avenue, the distant silhouette of Riverside Church, the red light at its very top to warn low-flying planes. Why the image? Why not think about Gabi?

Thin. She was thinner. Or was she? Could I have remembered her fuller than she was? She had said that her mother had the flu. Was she also ill?

"Spoon?" Gabi standing in the doorway, the angles of

her body interrupting the rectangle of the door. "I was thinking, maybe I should stay home in case the hospital calls. We can make it a long day tomorrow. Maybe I'll even get up the nerve to read you some of my poems. Have you been writing?"

"No. I've been hitting the books so hard . . ."

"Is the Academy really all that hard?"

"Not really," I said. "But the students there all have a real kick-butt attitude that says they're the best. And I keep telling myself that I don't have anything to prove. You know what I mean?"

"Yes, I think so. You'll tell me all about it in the morning? Come over early and I'll make you breakfast, okay?"

Yes. We agreed upon a time and she kissed me at the door. The kiss was tender, but not eager. I was nervous and thought that she might be, too. How long had I been away?

"Gabi?"

"Yes?"

"Are you still . . . you know?"

She touched my lips with her fingers and nodded yes. Her mouth tightened as she looked up at me and nodded again. "We're still," she said.

In the street I felt good, but slightly wary. It was as if I were looking around a place I hadn't seen before. I passed the girls double Dutching and pretended I was going to jump in and one of them cut me down with a look. The walk from 122nd Street to my folks' place on 145th and Bradhurst was a long one, but I started it.

I thought of Gabi again. She had made me feel good saying that we were still close, but I had felt the need to ask her. Back at the Academy I had thought so many times about touching her again, about slicing through the colors of discovery and settling into some sphere we would both recognize as where we should be now. But I had been hesitant, and it had been Gabi who had put off our being together until tomorrow.

The streets were crowded. Walking along St. Nicholas Avenue I was surprised to see so many people just standing around on the sidewalks, just doing whatever business they had to do, shopping, talking, sitting on folding chairs in front of the small stores. At the Academy we were always conscious of the luxury of sitting in the square or around the pond. It was a good thing to do, to be outside. I sensed a rhythm that my feet felt awkward stumbling through. It was funny. I had been away for only a few months from the place I had spent almost all of my life, and suddenly it was ahead of me, like a shadow on the cracked concrete sidewalk, mimicking my every move.

THE BLOCK — 145TH STREET

The street was incredibly busy and I felt hemmed in as I weaved my way through a sea of people. What I had packed in my memory of Harlem, had taken with me to Wallingford, had been the colors: vibrant Gauguin hues almost bursting from the squared city canvas, barely subdued by the earth tones of people gliding gracefully through the streets. Now there were arrays of the disheveled, eyes dulled from wine or boredom, soft angles against the dark bricks, watching from the stoops as I passed by. Young men, puffed up by bulky jackets, stared from their posts like lions in the high grass watching a passing herd of antelope. I walked faster. Could I remember the cadence of the strut? Could I have forgotten it so soon?

On the corner there was a pile of black plastic garbage bags. Children played around it. The gray metal garbage cans along a railing had eyes painted on them. One of the eyes was winking. Art.

As I approached my stoop I saw Junebug, Ray, and Brian. Brian saw me first and pointed. Not realizing I was tense, I felt myself begin to relax.

"Yo, man, we heard you was in jail!" Junebug put both palms out and I slapped them. "You on parole or you escaped?"

"I'm home for the holidays," I said, sitting next to Ray. "What you guys up to?"

"Ain't nothing going on," Brian said. He looked down the street as if he were looking for somebody. I knew he wasn't. "The biggest thing that happened around here was that Clara got pregnant."

"Clara? You mean light-skinned Clara, live on the Ave?"

"Yep," Ray said. "That's the one. And she's not saying who the baby's daddy is, so you better stay away from her."

"I thought she was supposed to be Miss Perfect," I said.

"I sure didn't expect to see her on the sports pages," Junebug said.

"You see my man Scott around?" I asked.

"Yeah, he's going to art school at night. Downtown somewhere," Brian said. "You play any ball up in that school you going to?"

"A little," I said. "I'm working part time."

"My father said if you get into a prep school you can get a scholarship easy," Ray said. "I was thinking about going to one of those schools, but I don't think I could deal with all the rules and stuff."

"They got a lot of rules?" Brian asked.

"Not really," I said, standing up. "Let me go on upstairs and check out the folks. I'll catch up with you guys later."

"You can catch up with me and Junebug," Ray said, a broad grin across his face. "Don't hang out with Brian because he's one of them bad elements the parole officers keep talking about."

"Man, get out of here." Brian narrowed his already narrow eyes even farther and Ray played it off with a grin.

I had known all of them, Ray, Junebug, and Brian, for years. The day I had left they had been sitting on the stoop. I started into the hall and had almost reached the elevator when I heard somebody coming up behind me. I turned and saw Brian. He had gotten taller, at least six two, maybe six three.

"Yo, man, I just want to tell you something," he said. "You know Rafe, right?"

"Yeah, Gabi's brother."

"I heard he was gang banging right after Halloween," Brian said. "It probably don't mean nothing, but I just thought I'd pull your coat."

"Gang banging? Rafe? Yeah, thanks."

Brian and I exchanged high fives and I got into the elevator. Was it smaller than it had been? Were the light brown metal walls more depressing?

Fourth floor. My thoughts jumbled into each other. I needed to see my parents, to re-connect with them and, at the same time, make sense of what Brian had said. What was Rafe doing trying to get into a gang? Somehow the world seemed to be spinning in a different direction.

The door opened. A brown-skinned man, glasses halfway down his nose. He turned and called into the apartment.

"Eloyce! It's a guy selling encyclopedias. You want any?"

"No, we've got one on the computer," my mother answered.

My father pulled me into the apartment and hugged me and suddenly I felt like crying I was so glad. We went into the living room. The evening news was on and Mom turned from it when we entered the room.

"Oh, baby!" She jumped up and ran to me. More hugs, more kisses. It was so good to be home and I let the warmth of it rush over me.

"So, say something smart!" my dad said. "All the time you've been gone you should know everything."

"How are you doing up there?" Mom asked.

"I'm doing all right," I said, flopping down onto my old seat on the right side of the couch. "We're going through the college square dance now. I told you I applied to Brown and a few other colleges, right?"

"You should think some more about accounting," my father said, nodding in agreement with himself. "You got the qualifications to be a certified public accountant. You get your certification and you got a job for life."

"If you don't love accounting you shouldn't get into it," Mom countered, riding her mom's horse to the rescue. "Anthony has to make up his own mind and find something he truly loves."

"I'm not telling him what to do, Eloyce," Dad said defensively. "But he should know his options. When I was his age I didn't know a thing about a job. If I had I might have been a lawyer or something."

"Is that what you wanted to be?" I asked. "A lawyer?"

"No, what he wanted to be was an explorer," Mom

said. "You know, Matt Henson lived right up the street in the Dunbar Apartments and that's what he wanted to do. Run off to the North Pole or something like that. Isn't that right?"

"You just can't get into the exploring business," my father said, settling into his chair. "Anyway, there's a difference between something like that and a real job. When he finished exploring, Matt Henson worked for the government, same as I do."

The conversation was a net, loosely thrown out to gather the nostalgic moments we tossed into the middle of the room. They kidded me with a hundred questions. Mom had asked them all on the phone, but now she sat in front of me, her hands in her lap, and looked at me as I answered. I wanted to ask her if I'd changed. She hadn't. She was still pretty, still younger than the age on her driver's license. In her voice there was still the faint lilt of Saint Kitts. I still thought my father had been lucky to find her before she realized how beautiful she was.

"The thing I had to learn," I said, "was that the kids who do well study all the time, not just when they take tests. It's like a habit for them. Once I got that into my head I could deal with the academics. I also found out that some of the kids who didn't study were being passed anyway because nobody wanted them to flunk out. That's the dark side of the Academy. They need to make everybody look smart."

"You have to study," my father said. "That was the last thing I said to you before you left for school."

"That's right," I answered.

It's what I was supposed to do, to tell him that I understood the wisdom he offered, and I did.

There were four small porcelain elephants on the upright piano. The first one was slightly larger than the others, and they graduated in size until the smallest one, barely an inch high. On the mantle there were porcelain dogs and cats. They were so familiar, I had counted them a hundred times and knew that, around the room, there were twenty-seven porcelain animals. But now I saw them.

Dad had had a few beers and dozed off in his chair. Mom got him up and, after another hug for me, he was shuttled contentedly off to the bedroom. She came back and asked me if I was tired.

"You trying to put me to bed?"

"I'd like to see you snuggled safe and sound in your own bed," she said, revisiting Momtalk. "Yes."

"I stopped by Gabi's house on the way home," I said.

"Her mother's very sick," Mom said, folding her hands in her lap. "I don't think her family is doing well."

"Oh?" I was disappointed that I hadn't sensed that Gabi's mother was so ill. "I didn't know that."

"I know Gabi's very special to you," Mom said. "When somebody is so special you don't always listen closely enough to what they're saying."

Mom tiptoed over and rubbed her nose against the underside of my chin.

"A man's stubble," I said, using my most manly voice.

"Poof!" she answered.

In the darkness of my room I replayed my homecoming. Five months was not that long, but it was long enough to shift perspective, I thought, to discover new shadings and to question old ones.

I thought about the 'hood. In the morning it would fall into place again, jumping with life, with brightness, alive.

My parents were the same, and not the same. My mother, so sweet, was still the safe haven against any storm. But now I saw her as the dark and gentle guardian angel that she was. My father's rituals, his search for the proper things to say, him reminding me that I needed to think about making a living, had moved beyond the annoyance I used to feel into a kind of comfort zone.

The stone steady stoop was the same. The guys had laughed about Clara being pregnant. It was really sad, and they all knew it. In a way they were all disappointed, but sadness doesn't wear well in the 'hood, and so they had thrown it out as if it didn't matter. As if nothing was so serious that it couldn't be laughed off. But Brian hadn't thrown away what he knew about Rafe.

And here was Anthony Witherspoon, the big Spoon, the great observer.

"Mr. Witherspoon, do you find yourself amusing?" a math teacher at the Academy had asked when I had missed an easy problem.

Sometimes I did. Yes.

TAR BEACH

Y ou want me to come up with you?" Rafe had asked.

"No," Gabi had said.

Gabi and I had taken a folding table to the roof. There were already two milk crates up there and Rafe realized we were going to have breakfast. It was so much like Gabi, finding private moments on top of the world. Someone had rigged up an electrical connection and she plugged in the hot plate.

"How do you want your eggs, kind sir?"

"Sunny-side up," I said.

Gabi's roof overlooked 122nd Street in front, and a patchwork of yards in the back. The yards, some with trees, others with clotheslines, were marked off by fences. A black cat crept along one of the fences and stopped when a dog, it looked like a pit bull, strained forward, barking. The cat stayed frozen for a few seconds, then realizing that the dog was not able to reach him, walked slowly the rest of the way into the next yard.

"My mother's really sicker than I thought." Gabi sat at the table, her coat open, her wide dress tucked between her legs. "I called the hospital this morning and the doctor said her infection flared up again."

"How sick is she?"

"It comes and goes. They found a few cancer cells in her stomach lining and she's been taking chemo just as a precaution. Sometimes it doesn't look so bad, sometimes it does. It's just when she gets home she gets depressed," Gabi said. "It's depression on top of the illness. So she's cramping up and crying for God to help her and then she's saying that she'll be glad when it's over. I keep telling her that if she takes care of herself physically she'll feel better inside. Last week she called my father and asked him to come back. Can you imagine that?"

"He's married again, right?"

"And she knows that," Gabi said.

She was eating bread and strawberry preserves and there was a crumb on her cheek. I took it off and touched her lips with my fingers.

"Is he okay?" I asked. "Your father?"

"Her life is getting to be like a huge puzzle." Gabi went on about her mother, ignoring my question. "She goes to church three times a week, she lights candles, she goes to a woman who reads her tea leaves, everything. I started a poem about her, I wanted to call it 'Black Clouds,' but then I switched it to 'Nubian Clouds' and it became a poem about black warriors. Isn't that stupid?"

"You think she's going to make it?" I asked. "Is the chemotherapy working?"

"The doctors say that she'll be okay if she's strong." Gabi closed her eyes and tilted her head back. "I don't really know, but sometimes I think she has too many paths in her life."

"Maybe it's good her father came to live with you," I said.

"Do you know how easy it is not to be strong?" she asked, suddenly opening her eyes. "Sometimes she says she wants to give her life to God. But when those words come from her mouth I only hear 'giving your life.' I know she's thinking about her life in the DR, and that has a meaning to her that I don't even know about. She's faithful to my father even though he's moved on with his life. She even lights candles for him. She thinks she's led a good life, like a *campesina*, a peasant woman, and all she wants is for God to tell her what to do.

"She's not that complicated a person when you get right down to it, and all of this, when you add the sickness to it, is like some giant labyrinth that she's stumbled into. She takes a step and then pulls her foot back. Whatever path she takes makes her worried about the ones she didn't."

"That's got to be a downer."

"Maybe. But she has to do something. There's no use in feeling sorry for yourself. You live, you have choices, and you have to make them."

The eggs, sunny-side up with onions and salsa, were good. Gabi tried to make tea but the hot plate wouldn't get hot enough to bring the water to a boil. I asked Gabi if she had made up her mind about Columbia and she shook her head no.

"It was more talk than anything real," she said. "The guidance counselor is telling me — what did he say? — that if I apply I'm sure to get it, and I'm thinking that it's like the lottery, a dollar and a dream, only what are your chances? You know what I mean?"

I knew what the words meant. I didn't know why she turned away as she spoke, or why her voice cracked.

"I'm checking the mail, waiting to see what offers are out there," I said. "But I think going to the Academy might un-blacken me to the point where I don't get an offer."

"What are the girls like up there?" She was smiling now, but her eyes had reddened.

"How would I know? All I do is study."

"That's not all you did when you were in Harlem," Gabi said. "And you haven't said anything about missing me so I guess you've found somebody new."

In the street below a fire engine, its horns blasting, passed. I looked around to see if anyone could see us if we kissed on the roof, and figured no one would.

"You know, I was thinking what I would say to you when I saw you," I said. "I had lined up all my 'I love yous' and was even trying to figure out a way to use 'darling' in a sentence. Nobody ever really says 'darling' in real life."

"¡Mi querido!"

"It doesn't count in Spanish."

"So why haven't you said it in English?" She looked at

me intensely, as if she were trying to find a truth in my face.

"I feel shy about it," I said. "We haven't talked much in the last couple of months. It's almost as if we have to get the beat going again. The night before coming back to the city I thought about what we would say, what we would do. I thought about kissing you. Holding you."

"Now I'm the one feeling shy."

"Maybe we should have this huge kissing and hugging session and get a lot of momentum going and see where it leads," I said.

"Let's take it slow, Mr. Anthony Witherspoon," Gabi said. "You can have one kiss today, two tomorrow, and we'll see where that leads. We'll use a quota system. Then we won't be rushing into anything we're going to regret."

"So do you have the urge to throw some 'I love yous' my way?"

"Before you left I thought that you were the most special guy in the whole world." Gabi turned to me, her hands between her legs, her head slightly to one side. "I still feel that way. But when you left and things got really hard here — my mother, my grandfather living with us — life took a little turn. I'm even surer how I feel about you, maybe a little less sure about how I feel about myself."

"When do I get the kiss?"

44

She smiled, and stood up. "Now, because I have to go downtown to do some business for my mother."

"I'll go with you."

"No."

"Why?"

"It's personal."

"I don't care."

"I do."

She shut off my objections with her hand across my lips. Then, moving her face close to mine, she pulled her hand slowly away. An embarrassing rush of lust swept over me as I felt her tongue slip into my mouth.

We parted and I felt myself trying to catch my breath. "Will I see you later?"

"It depends on my mother," she said. She was stacking the dishes in the center of the card table. "Sometimes she's not too rational. I don't always want to do what she asks me, but she's my mother."

We took the table and dishes down to her apartment. I wanted to kiss her again, and told her. She said no, that she wanted something to look forward to.

"I'll call you tonight, if Mom is okay," she said. "About seven?"

"How's Rafe doing?"

"He's real good," she answered. "He runs the streets a lot, but he's not really getting into anything too heavy. He helps out in the house, too. I'm really proud of him. He just doesn't have that macho thing going on."

I didn't want to go home. I wanted to hang with Gabi and do things for her mother. I wanted to climb her and swim her and find the words she did to say how I felt. I wanted another language to speak to her, to say all the things I was too shy to say in English. I wondered if I would make love to her before I went back to school.

I hadn't wanted to press Gabi about Rafe hanging with a gang. She seemed definite about him being cool and I wondered about it. When I got back home the apartment was empty. My parents were at work and I got out my texts to study. That lasted a minute and I put them away and looked up Brian's number in my address book. He answered the phone and I told him that Gabi had said that Rafe wasn't in a gang.

"I don't know if he's in it or not." Brian's voice sounded nasal on the phone. "But I know he was walking with some bangers."

Lying across the bed, staring up at the ceiling, I felt numb. I told myself that I would speak to Gabi about what

Brian had said. Brian wouldn't like me putting his name in the street, but I decided I would.

The phone rang. Chanelle.

"Come over for pizza tomorrow. Just a few people, mostly kids from the Academy. Bring your girl. Anytime after six, okay?"

Gabi called from a pay phone and I told her about going over to Chanelle's. She said it sounded like fun, that she would love to go.

"I want to check out the Anglo competition," she said.

"It was really good seeing you today," I said. "I especially dug having breakfast on the roof. It was like our little romantic balcony overlooking the Danube, or whatever river they have in the latest James Bond flick."

"Yeah, you've still got it going on," she said. She sounded tired. "I like cooking for you."

"You sound tired. How did it go today? You were doing something for your mother?"

She said it had gone all right, something to do with the Department of Welfare, but that it had been tiring. "And now I have to fix my grandfather's dinner," she said.

I asked if I should call her back later, and she said no, that she would call me in the morning.

"Where are you now?" I asked. I could hear trucks passing by in the background.

"On the way home," she said. "I'll see you tomorrow. Come to my house and we can go to the pizza thing together."

She was off the phone and I felt the distance between us.

Was it Einstein who said that time can be thought of as a fourth dimension? I had been in Wallingford for about five months and now, back in Harlem, the physical dimensions were all the same, the angles still set at the right pitch, the distances still true, but there was change. What bothered me most was that I thought Gabi might be seeing somebody else.

17 WEST 54TH STREET

New York at night has the illusion of magic, but it is shallow, like the oyster's suggestion of mystery. There is no magic, only the hard shell and the promise of a pearl that is never realized. But even the illusion has resonance in the timid heart and I fought against it as I turned down Fifth Avenue onto Chanelle's block.

Where is the character? I asked myself. How do you grow up in this asphalt cocoon? I imagined Chanelle being taken from one event to another, never once wondering what she would see when she left the house, never questioning if the event would be on time or if she would be well received. I was being condescending. Dee-fense! Dee-fense!

The doorman stood in front of me, his large body blocking the entrance, trying to look intimidating.

"What do you want?" he asked. There was no respect in his voice. The servant assuming the airs of his master.

"Chanelle Burnitz," I said.

"So what do you *want*?" he repeated. He had become derisive. A derision that bordered on the defensive.

I was already mad because Gabi wasn't coming, so the anger bubbled up easily. "Hey, man, she expects me," I said. "So why don't you just do what you need to do and let her know I'm here."

Expected. He looked at me, wondering how to regain the upper hand. We stared at each other for a long moment, both needing a win. He knew that I could not possibly live in the building he was hired to guard. He turned away and picked up the phone. I looked away as he dialed Chanelle's number. Could he possibly have known how he had defeated me?

The elevator. The lackey had already pressed the button for the seventeenth floor. He was telling me that he didn't trust me not to press another button, to hop off the elevator at a floor at which I was not expected and molest the rich white people. Did he know how he had defeated me?

Chanelle's apartment was light, airy. The living room walls were a bland gold, outlined by an equally bland white trim. The furniture was plain, with clean straight lines. The polished walnut table along one wall reflected the small chandelier. The room was nothing until the eye caught the three enormous round windows with their wrought iron and wood design. They were what the room was all about. After the statement of the windows, everything else was just gesture.

I did my counting thing. Me and Chanelle, eleven whites, and an Indian-looking girl in the living room. On a side table there were soft drinks, beer, and what looked like white wine. Chanelle kissed me on the cheek and said she was glad that I'd come. I recognized several faces from Wallingford. There was James Brand, pushing himself into the center of every conversation. Amy Martinson, tall, perfect teeth, perfect moves, perfect casualness. And Chanelle. She was wearing a brown sari. It wrapped around her body, silky and sensuous, and I imagined its coolness against her skin. I tried to think of something else before I fell over.

"So, you down for some ball tomorrow?" Brand asked me.

"Sure, I guess. Where and who?"

"Some brothers from the Drive," he said. "I think three of them played in some church league this year."

"They don't play out of Riverside Church, do they?" I asked.

"What's the difference?" Brand's smile is a practiced crooked.

The difference, I said to myself, is the difference between a great basketball program like the Gauchos and some pickup team. Brand doesn't know basketball in Harlem. He doesn't have to know it, either.

We made arrangements.

There was music from a smoking system. I danced self-consciously with girls dancing self-consciously with me. Chanelle avoided me. She didn't ask me why Gabi hadn't come.

"I'm really stressed out," Gabi had said. "I think I'm coming down with something. Maybe mono, I don't know. Drop by afterward if you want. Can you forgive me this time?"

"Sure," I'd answered.

There had been a time when her kisses had been wolf-hungry, her body eager to push against mine. She would have wanted to see me, to talk to me, to spin out our dreams. Now I was jealous of whoever or whatever had her time and the feeling made me stiff, awkward.

Can you forgive me this time?

The glasses tinkled and the guys hovered until they came to the collective conclusion that they had not discovered anything magical about Chanelle's party, that the girls were not going to be steered into empty bedrooms, and no one was going to have an adventure to talk about for months, or even weeks, to come.

I spent the hours shifting from foot to foot. It wasn't just the white doorman downstairs that made me feel out of place, it was the world that had white doormen and sixteen- and seventeen-year-olds who wore expensive jewelry and dresses that cost as much as some people uptown made in a week. I could dance as well as anyone at the party, even better. But I still felt as if I didn't belong.

"Your girl didn't want to come?" Chanelle finally asked. I was leaning against the wall. Amy and another girl were in the bathroom, and both were crying. I imagined one of them had just lost a lover or an earring. Chanelle put her hand on my forearm and was telling me good-bye.

"We could be drifting," I said. "I don't know."

"So what are you going to do?"

"Well, if I could find a volcano, I could throw myself into it and then she'd be sorry," I said. "Naturally, I'd leave a note. Haiku."

"Do you think she was uptight with the party being down here?"

I shrugged and wondered why I had always thought that the differences were only viewed from bottom to top. Chanelle leaned against me and rubbed my chest with the flat of her hand.

"You're a good guy, Spoon," she said. "You have to keep that in mind."

The elevator again. I was mad at myself for not staying longer, for not making a play for Chanelle.

Why? Why not? What else did I have going on?

You have Gabi, and you love her.

I took the downtown E train at Fifth Avenue and 53rd Street to 42nd Street. Then the uptown A to 125th, and to Gabi's house.

The streets were quiet, dark. There were Christmas lights in the store windows, a huge wreath in the apartment complex on 124th Street. A radio played "Jingle Bells" in Spanish and that lifted me. I rang Gabi's bell and there was no answer. After a second ring someone pulled back the curtain on the vestibule door. It was Rafe.

"Yo, man, it's late."

"I know," I said. "I have to see Gabi."

He didn't answer as he let me in. On the way up he said she was sleeping. I thought I'd made a mistake, that maybe I should leave and come back in the morning. But Rafe was moving faster than I could muster my casual air and so I followed him up.

In the apartment Rafe sleepily pointed me toward Gabi's room. Everything I thought of that was romantic was also corny. I thought of calling her name, kissing her lightly before she was fully awake, then leaving so it would only be a partial memory that would bother her forever. I didn't.

On her dresser was a small plaster statue of the Virgin Mary. There was a candle in front of it and, next to the candle, the reflected light iridescent on its narrow shaft, was a hypodermic needle.

I froze. My heart pounded in my chest. I turned toward where Gabi lay in the middle of the bed, the sheets twisted around and through her brown legs. I called her name.

"Gabi?"

She murmured and reached out her hand. I took it and sat by her on the bed.

"How you doing?" I asked.

"Spoon." Eyes still closed, she put my hand against

her cheek, then, turning, kissed my fingers. "What time is it?"

"Late," I said. "I shouldn't have come by so late."

She pulled the sheet up in front of her. "You shouldn't be seeing me half-naked," she said.

Her shoulder was bare, and I kissed it. We said each other's names at the same time and both smiled.

"How was the pizza party?"

"There's a needle on your dresser," I whispered to her. "Why is there a needle on your dresser?"

One brown leg over the side of the bed. Her foot touched the floor and she lifted herself to see the needle. She sat back down heavily, her head drooped forward. Seconds passed. Perhaps minutes. From the street below her window the constant hiss of cars energized the night.

She lifted her head and pushed her hair away from her face. I could only see the outline of her cheek and the candlelight reflected in her eyes. "Spoon, I'm only skin surfing. Really! Oh God!"

She buried her face in her hands and began to sob. Skin surfing. The words were heavy and dragged me down hard. The vocabulary of drugs was familiar to me. I imagined her "skin surfing," sliding the needle beneath the soft brownness of her skin. Where did she put it? In her thigh? Her arm? It was all violation. A needle sliding between skin and muscle, between trust and despair.

Nearly still in the darkness, her sighs marked the passage of time. I looked at the dresser, the sad Virgin. The flickering candlelight. Our moments were strung together, futile, despairing, like the continued silence between heartbeats.

"Gabi, what can I do? How can I help?"

"*'En una pura noche se hizo mi luto . . .'*"

"Don't go Spanish on me!" I said. "Don't!"

"'In one pure night my mourning shaped in the labyrinth of my body,'" she said. "Spoon, I have to go to Spanish, or to poetry. I can't stay in this awful place!"

"Gabi, what can I do?"

"Go home," she said. "Think about me. If you can talk to me in the morning, it'll be enough."

Her eyes were half shut, her words slurred. She turned away from me and pulled the sheet over her head.

As I walked into the Harlem night the signs of Christmas were all around me. There was an excitement in the air that was available in even the meanest street. But somewhere, Herod was killing babies.

HARLEM HOSPITAL

I called Gabi in the morning, but the phone was still not working. I spent the day with my mother. We were polite to one another when I knew she wanted warmth. Once, she asked me what I was thinking about, and I couldn't bring myself to tell her.

As we shopped for food my mind raced through one scenario after another. It was my whole life on fast-forward. There was a scene in which I lectured Gabi before I strode triumphantly away. There was a scene in which I took Gabi back to Wallingford with me, and we were reading quietly at the edge of the pond. There was a scene in which I was sitting at her feet, my head resting on her knee as I told her how much I loved her.

But loving her was different now. It was no longer something that could be done from long distance. It had to be the here and now, the immediate. I suddenly understood the words of the marriage ceremony. Do you take this woman? But it is more than that. Do you take this life, these hard streets, or do you run back to Wallingford and tell yourself that the miles between there and Harlem will always protect you?

I was desperate to talk with Gabi again, but I had to spend some time with my parents. I tried to be casual as I kidded with my father, but he knew I was watching the clock and asked me if I was going out. I told him I was thinking about it. Whenever the phone rang I thought it might be her. The smell of frying onions had filled the house, and on the television tiger kittens were being pushed around a sty by a pig when my father called my name.

"Gabi's on the phone," he said, watching for my reaction.

I smiled weakly.

The first thing she said was that Nestor had been stabbed. She asked if I could meet her at the hospital. I said I could, in fifteen minutes. Mom wanted me to eat something before I went. She had already dished it up.

"Will you put it in the refrigerator for me?" I asked.

Of course. I kissed her and started to leave. Dad called me aside and asked if I had any money. I didn't and he gave me twenty dollars. Then he asked me if Gabi was pregnant.

"Not by me," I said, smiling so that he knew it was a joke.

He was upset, and it wasn't fair of me to leave without telling him more. But what would I have said? That Gabi had touched the Black Plague?

Nestor. I remembered a skinny, sallow kid, a friend of a friend, who played clarinet in the school band and later with a Latino group in Elmhurst. Gabi had treated him like a little brother and had tried to get him to write raps in Spanish for the school newspaper.

The hospital emergency room was filled with Saturday-night people. Vine-thin children struggling to breathe through their asthma-congested lungs. An old woman in her night-gown with a swollen face. I heard her say that her daughter had punched her. Her mouth was bleeding. On a small table in one corner stood a pathetic little Christmas tree, its lights blinking on and off, the little brown angel on top leaning to one side.

A nurse looked around the room, trying to pick out the worst cases. She saw a pudgy kid with his foot wrapped in a towel. She touched his foot and he winced in pain. She carefully moved the towel, looked at the foot, announced aloud that the foot was broken, and told him he'd have to wait. There were worse cases.

The kid was pleased.

Gabi came in with Nestor. It was the Nestor I remembered, bent over at the waist. There was an incredibly ugly bloodstain on the front of his chino pants. Gabi was talking to a male nurse as I walked over to them.

"What happened to him?" The nurse was big, thick. He lifted Nestor's head and looked into his eyes.

"He was stabbed," Gabi said. "He can't walk any farther. You have to get a gurney for him."

The male nurse walked away, stopped at a desk, and picked up the coffee container he had left there. No, he didn't have to do anything, he was saying. Life was that cheap.

Gabi looked around for someone else to talk to. She saw a prim woman sitting behind the desk and, leaving Nestor leaning against a pole, went to talk to her. The woman handed her a clipboard with a form to fill out and turned away. I looked at the male nurse and thought he was smirking. I walked over to him.

"Excuse me, I wonder if you can give my friend a hand," I said. "He's really hurt badly."

Satisfied, he said he would see what he could do.

He pulled a gurney from against the wall and wheeled it over to Nestor. I helped Nestor up on it.

"Yo, Spoon." Nestor made a fist and I hit it lightly. "Gabi said you were back, man. Glad to see you, bro."

"Glad to see you, man."

The nurse wheeled him down the hall. Gabi followed them. I didn't know what to do, and so I looked around for a place to sit.

"If he walked in on his own two feet he ain't going to die." This bit of wisdom from a man my height, but heavier than me, maybe two hundred pounds. "When they come in like that it means they haven't lost so much blood they're going to pass out. Then they can patch you up.

"The way he bent over — you see the way he was bent over?"

"Yeah?"

"They got him in the stomach. You get some blood in the stomach, some bleeding and whatnot, but they'll find that."

"Oh, good."

"I bet you're wondering what happened to me, right?"

"Yeah." No.

He pulled his hand from his side and I saw that it was

bandaged heavily. Slowly, like a striptease artist, he started unwinding the gauze. When he got to the end I saw that he'd cut off the tip of his finger, and the last of the gauze was stuck to the bloody stump.

"They'll put some antibiotic on it, put in four or six stitches — they always put in an even amount so they know they don't miss none when they take them out — and I'll be out of here," he said, rewrapping the finger.

Wonderful.

Gabi came out and said that Nestor was taken to X-ray, and that they were going to keep him overnight.

"I'll come back later to see if he's okay. I want to tell his mother."

"How come she doesn't know already?"

"Because she lives in the Bronx and nobody has told her," Gabi said, her voice edged with a sudden annoyance. "When he was hurt he came by my house looking for Rafe. I saw the blood and knew I had to get him here. Help doesn't grow on trees around here, not even Christmas trees. I figured you would help if I needed moral support, and I know we needed to talk."

"You want to go for coffee across the street?"

She said yes and we walked across 135th to the diner. It was fairly crowded, with packages and shopping bags between the seats. Gabi ordered black coffee and I ordered a hamburger.

"So, what do you want me to say?" Gabi looked at me and then quickly away. "You want me to say that I'm mad at myself for using drugs? Say that I know it's all wrong? What do you want me to say?"

"I don't know what I want," I answered. "On one hand I'm thinking speeches, and on the other hand I'm feeling hurt. You're talking as if I'm coming down on you and the real deal is I'm just put out to dry. The woman I love is using. Wow! It's almost too heavy to deal with. What would you say if I told you I was on drugs?"

"I'd say, 'Get off.'"

"Hey, man!" a customer at the counter yelled toward the small clerk at the register. "This sausage ain't even done! I ain't paying for this crap!"

"Free," the man responded, a toothpick dangling from his lips. "You can just walk into Harlem Hospital for free. You don't need no pass or no wounds or nothing. Just tell them you want to be in there for a while."

"I'm talking about these damned sausages, man!"

"I'm talking about this damned shotgun, boy."

He lifted the shotgun from behind the counter, held it up for a few seconds, and put it down again. The customer went through his pockets, found the money for his meal, and left complaining that he would never be back again.

"I spent all day thinking about last night," I said. "It's like something sneaked into my life when I wasn't around."

"The only thing I can say right now is that I'm not a street person." Gabi's lips quivered and she looked away a second, and then back to me. There were tears again. "I always thought I was stronger than the streets."

I didn't know how to answer.

The hamburger came. Tasteless, on a dry white bun, surrounded by soggy iceberg lettuce and a pale tomato. I told Gabi that it was horrible, and she smiled.

I finished half of the hamburger. Gabi finished her coffee and said that she was going back to the hospital. I paid the bill and we went across the street. I sat outside on the bench while she walked down the corridor looking for someone who could tell her about Nestor.

Three white cops came in with a man in handcuffs. There was a knot on the side of his head and blood all down the front of the white shirt he wore. He was cursing and spitting at the cops and anyone he caught looking in his direction. One of the cops, the beefiest, announced that it was a "nut case."

A pretty girl with sweet, pouting lips told the deranged

man that if he spit on her she would cut his heart out because she "didn't play."

The hospital security guard pointed to the clock and mentioned that it was only a quarter past nine. The cops and the guard laughed.

Where was the world I had left behind? What had happened to it? Had something changed, something that wasn't in the papers, that wasn't on television? Or was it me? Had I changed?

Gabi came back. She said that a nurse told her that Nestor was going to be all right and that she had got his mother's number. We went into the other waiting room and Gabi called her.

"Where's your mom?" I asked Gabi as we walked out into the cold December air.

"Downtown," she said. "I spoke to her today."

I took her thin hand in mine. We walked slowly down Lenox Avenue. On 130th Street there were street vendors selling knit hats and T-shirts. Other pushcart people, cooking on makeshift grills, filled the sidewalks with the scents of sausages, onions, and sweet potatoes. When we reached 125th Street we turned and started crosstown to the West Side.

"When I was young my mother said that she used to

love this street because of all the nice things in the store windows," Gabi said. "She said she would give herself an imaginary budget of $100 and pick out things she would buy if she really had the money."

"I've done that," I said. "But that's a long time ago, a different reality."

"And you want to know what's real now, right? Well, what's real is that there are places for everything," she said. "School was in one place, and college applications sat over there, and my mother was over there, and my father and my grandfather were in their places. And you were there, too. Old, shiny, and handsome Spoon, with your nice muscles and your good ears that liked my poems.

"And there was this road through it all, and I could see it." She sighed heavily. "Do you know what I mean?"

"A road?"

"Like you know all of those things are in your life, and you know you need to make sense of them somehow. Then one day you get up in the morning and begin your walk, you say now you need to look at the road, to see how you should move on. And then the road is gone.

"One day . . . no, not one day. One week perhaps, maybe one month, I don't know, it just all stopped being clear. And when it wasn't clear anymore I stopped knowing what was real and what wasn't. The road suddenly became a maze of twisting, winding paths going nowhere. My mother talked to me about leaving school and taking care of Rafael. Abuelo came to live with us. From 'doing all right' we had slipped down to 'just holding on.' I didn't know what to do. What I had been good at doing was thinking, and now I didn't know how to think anymore. All I knew was that I didn't want my life to be my life. I wanted to have somebody else's life. Can you understand that?"

"I want to," I said. "But I can't." We had reached her stoop and sat on it. "I don't understand how you can know something one day and not know it the next day."

"It doesn't make a lot of sense, sometimes, but that's the way it seems when I sit down and try to sort it out myself. I even thought about you and everything you were doing," Gabi went on. "When we were saying good-bye you were so clear. You had plans and places to go and things to do. I think there's a time when we want to think that we all have plans and places to go, and sometimes we really don't."

"Like boys who say they're going to play in the NBA?"

"Or like girls who think they're going to college," she said.

"You don't start using drugs . . ."

"When you know so much?"

"Yeah, that's right," I said. "When you see it all around you and know what it's really like."

"If you see the Beast, you run away," she said. "I didn't run fast enough."

No. No. It wasn't that simple. It wasn't about strange roads and poetry. It was about drugs.

"And Rafe?"

"He's not using drugs. Not now, anyway. But he's running the streets and I'm afraid for him. I keep telling him all the things I should have been telling myself," she said.

No. I wasn't buying it. "Gabi. Gabi. When I say your name, it's more than a name. It's what I think about love. It's what I feel about family. Maybe you've been my idea of a road or a path. And now I'm so confused. It's like . . . it's like you hurt someplace but you don't even know where you hurt."

"Oh, Spoon, I don't want to hurt you. . . ." She was crying. Deep animal noises came out of her and she was clutching at my arms and my chest, as if she wanted me desperately but was afraid to hold on. "Let me . . . let me put the words on paper. I'll burn them into the paper for you. I need to get all the words right. Give me that chance, Spoon. I'll see you tomorrow, or the next day. You'll make me say the words and it'll make me get it back in order. Please. Please."

I took Gabi to her door. "Do you want me to come up?"

"No, I need you to be away from me, and think about me," she said. "Right now you're asking me why I'm messing up my life and I don't have anything to say that's neat and clean and logical. I see you looking at me and I want to tear my heart out when I see the disappointment in your face. God knows I want to be special for you, Spoon. God can see my heart and He knows I want to be special for you."

"You are special, Gabi. You are special."

Good night. Lips touching lightly, Gabi's head against my chest, moving away from me ever so slowly, as if she were afraid to let go.

I took the train uptown. By the time I reached 145th it was raining. A woman asked if I had two quarters to spare. I was offended. I walked away and instantly felt guilty, too guilty to turn around and give her the two quarters, which is what I wanted to do.

Mom was doing a crossword puzzle. She asked me how Gabi was doing.

"Not well," I said. "Can you know where a person is, and still think they're lost?"

"I know you care for her," she said, "but . . ." Kindly, she let the words trail off. But they were there in the night air and we both knew we would find them again.

THE STOOP — 145TH STREET

The light on Christmas morning was a harsh gray. From beyond my bedroom window, there were dueling radios. I recognized Handel. When I got up to go to the bathroom, my parents were already in the kitchen, and I was greeted by the comforting smell of freshly brewed coffee. The cold water on my face felt good. I told myself I would have a wonderful day.

"Are you up?" Mom called.

"Will be in a minute!" I called back.

Sitting on the edge of the bed, I told myself not to go to Gabi's. I knew how it would go: Rafe answering the door, telling me he'd get Gabi, then coming back and saying she'd call me later from the pay phone on the corner.

She wouldn't call.

I thought of the sweater I'd bought her from the school store. It had a big W on the front for Wallingford, but I had planned to tell her that it stood for Witherspoon. We were supposed to laugh.

I looked at myself in the mirror above my bureau, and saw that my eyes were teary. Did crying come so easy? When had it started sneaking up on me so naturally?

I had coffee with my parents. Mom made nice-nice over the book I'd bought her, and Dad, somehow, was touched by the football I gave him. They gave me a great fountain pen. We chatted quietly through the morning, like three friends, and it felt good. Later, no longer able to bear the silent telephone, I went back to bed.

"Yeah, Christmas was okay," I said. Scott and I were sitting on the stoop, edging our way into a conversation, when Lavelle came over and asked us to unload some groceries from a truck. Lavelle, tall, black, his head shiny bald. He had been looking out for kids on the block for as long as I could remember. Like all old men on the block, he expected us to know something.

"I got to get the truck back downtown," he said. "It won't take you no time and you got ten dollars apiece."

I liked doing stuff with Scott so I said okay and we went to the back of the rental truck. Lavelle had a helper from his little restaurant come out with a handcart to help us.

"So, man, we need some serious hangout time," Scott said. He was on the truck handing out boxes of frozen fish. They were wet and stinky.

"Your mom tell you that I called?"

"Yeah, she did." Scott tried to pick up two boxes at once, then put one down. There were a lot more boxes than we'd thought there would be. "We went to services yesterday and she asked me if I had called you."

"Yo, where do you think Lavelle got all these frozen fish?"

"I don't know," Scott said. "I don't think his refrigerator is big enough for all of them, either."

The helper was standing on the sidewalk next to the handcart and I asked him if he was crippled. He caught an attitude and said something under his breath, but he didn't help with the unloading, just the wheeling of the boxes into the restaurant.

"You see Gabriela?" Scott called down.

"Yeah, have you seen her around much?" My stomach tightened.

"No, I don't get downtown and you know I left school."

Left school? I didn't answer. No, I didn't know he had left school. Scott was my main man. We had been tight for years. When I left we had promised to write to each other, but we hadn't. Somehow I was always too busy, or too tired, or didn't have anything to say. The weeks had slipped by, and then the months, and then we were on the block unloading frozen fish.

"When did you leave school, man?"

"Right after midterms," he said. "A bunch of us left then."

"Why?"

All at once the street was filled with noise. A blast from a siren. Brakes screeching. Startled, I looked around. Two dark cars had stopped, one with its front tires on the sidewalk. Men were jumping out of the cars, guns in the air.

"On the ground! On the ground!"

I fell to the ground and put my hands out by my sides. I could feel my heart racing.

"Don't move! Don't move!"

"Yo, Spoon, it's not us." I heard Scott's voice next to me and sensed his body. I realized I had shut my eyes. I opened them, looked up, and saw a crowd on the sidewalk.

I got up and saw that the men with the guns had badges

on chains around their necks. Some of the guns were still drawn. In between the sea of legs, there were two people on the ground.

"That's Leon," Scott said.

Leon. Good jump shot. Couldn't handle fractions.

"Man, get my fish unloaded before it goes bad," Lavelle hissed.

I was wondering if the fish was stolen. Why was it in a rental truck? Scott got back up in the truck and we continued to unload it as the commotion on the sidewalk played out. I saw they had Leon against the wall. One cop had his knee in Leon's back and was pushing him against the wall while the others searched him. There was a struggle on the ground with the other person.

The truck was half unloaded. The rest of the food was canned groceries. I was relieved. Why was I relieved to see cans instead of frozen fish?

The next thing I knew Leon was handcuffed with his hands behind his back. A cop, young, white, tough-looking, held the cuffs high, forcing Leon to bend over. They rushed him into the back of one of the cars. The guy on the ground was lifted to his feet. It was Ray. There was dog crap on the front of his shirt.

Ray. Couldn't play no b-ball but could sing up a storm. Had all the finest ladies.

They spun him around, bent him over, and finished searching him. Ray fell and the cops, finding nothing on him, took off the handcuffs and left him lying on the sidewalk. They got into their cars and in a moment squealed away toward Frederick Douglass Boulevard.

"Welcome home, brother," Scott said.

"Is Leon dealing?" I asked.

"Guess what? I don't keep tabs on all the dealers," Scott said. He seemed offended. He wouldn't have been offended before I left.

We finished unloading the boxes in silence and Lavelle asked us how much he had promised us. Neither one of us answered him and he "remembered" that it was ten apiece.

Back on the stoop, Scott was kidding about me getting on the ground.

"You're out of the 'hood two days and you forget the routine," he joked.

I was grinning but uncomfortable. Down the street, in front of the record store, Ray was talking to a small crowd. He had taken off his shirt and thrown it into the gutter. Some men from the barbershop had come out and stood at the edge of the group.

I turned back to Scott. "Hey, man, you never did tell me why you left school."

"I decided to go to Cooper Union at nights," he said. "Get right into the arts thing. I needed some money to get started next September."

"How are you going to Cooper Union if you don't finish Douglass?"

"Just taking some art courses so I can get a j-o-b," he said. There was a studied casualness to his gestures as he spoke. "Maybe I'll go to regular college later. But what I want to do is art. Most artists don't finish college. You know, my thing isn't that conventional. I mean, my vision has changed. I'm seeing behind objects and through them. I'm still into the drafting thing, I know I can draw, but what I want to see is what makes something beautiful, or what makes it ugly. I can't learn that in school; I have to get it out here in the streets."

I didn't understand him and left it there. The silence that crept between us was heavy, cumbersome, and we both changed positions to deal with it. Scott drew up his legs; I leaned back and put my hands behind my neck. More silence as we searched for words that we might want to say.

"So what's up with Wallingford?" he finally asked.

"Just about what we thought. Rich white kids, some

Asians, a few of us. They run it like a college more than a high school. It's okay."

"You miss Douglass?"

"Yeah, a little." I wondered if he would have left if I had stayed at Douglass. I didn't want to ask.

"Things are the same on the block," he said. "I bet if we went back in time fifty years, and came to this block, it would be the same. Just different people. Maybe fewer cars. Other than that it's just everybody drifting into the same ol' same ol'. Running down their raps about why they're watching the world go by."

We watched as some of the guys who were talking on the sidewalk started to drift into the barbershop. Scott tapped my elbow and pointed to where Ray had thrown his shirt. A dog was peeing on it and we both laughed.

"Suppose that fish was stolen," Scott said. "And we were arrested. Can you imagine how that would look on the front page of *The New York Times*? 'Frozen Trout Thieves Busted in Harlem!' You could never live that down."

"So how are you going to get a job in art?"

"What are you, the FBI now?"

I didn't answer. A beat. Scott put his hand on my knee and rocked it gently. "I don't know, man." His voice sounded like a huge sigh. "My life is getting raggedy. Nothing much seemed to happen. It just slid from correct to raggedy."

"Everything is looking so different to me," I said. "Hear Clara is pregnant?"

"Yeah." He shook his head. "She was like a symbol of all the right things to do."

"So, let me try this on you —" Ball in the left hand, stop, pivot, fake right, ball in the right hand. "Why don't you come up to Wallingford one weekend and take a look around. I can find you a place to squat."

"Sure, that sounds good." Scott stretched his legs. "I can get to meet all the preppies."

I would have liked to have Scott come to the Academy, to see the pond, the grounds, maybe to sit and rap with me in Hill House. I would have loved even more for things to have been as easy as they used to be with us, so I could tell him about Gabi. *Gabi is using.* I wanted to say the words to somebody, to hear them coming from my lips so I could try to make sense of it.

"It's not all that," I said. "I mean, Wallingford, it's not all that."

"You like it?"

"Yeah. I like it. I haven't checked out all the corners yet. I'm still one eyeing into the fish store, but I think I like it."

Two kids, maybe three or four years old, playing with a pink rubber ball, knocked it toward us. Scott grabbed it and just crossed his arms. One of the kids, big eyed, looked at me and then at Scott and took a tentative step toward us "big guys." Scott stared the kid down until he put both hands behind his back.

"You want this ball?" Scott asked. He tried to look mean, but he was smiling.

The kid nodded and Scott held it out. The kid approached slowly, grabbed the ball, and then gave Scott a defiant look.

"A baby gangster," I said.

Scott pointed down the street. I looked and saw Leon going into the barbershop.

"Let's check out what's happening," Scott said.

Inside Leon was already telling his story.

"So they said a guy who looks like me ripped off some valuable baseball cards from a white dude downtown." The left side of Leon's face was swollen and his words weren't clear. "So they're saying they heard I sold baseball cards at the flea market and what did I know about this dude's cards. I didn't know nothing about the cards."

"You were never officially arrested?" A heavy dude in horn-rimmed glasses.

"No," Leon said. "They just said I better let them know if I see the cards."

"So, we'll file a report," Horn-rimmed said.

"What good is that going to do?" Leon asked.

"It's going to say that the New York Police Department cannot just slam people around and terrorize people without a response," Horn-rimmed replied. "And that might not do any good. And it begins a proceeding that will lead to a police department hearing and that might not do any good. But it will also show a community unity, a willingness to stake our claim for this neighborhood, and that will do some good."

The young brothers talked about what they really wanted to do, but they were deferential to the men in the barbershop.

Scott and I went back to the stoop. All along the street there were small groups of young men standing and talking. And watching. They were a little stronger now that the elders were involved.

"You hear anybody say who Clara is going with?" I asked.

"The tide," Scott said. "Things drift with the tide and she drifted with it."

The tide. I was hearing talk of tides that drift and carry

people away, of roads that turn into mazes, of paths that disappeared.

"So much has been going on in the 'hood since I was gone it makes me feel funny," I said.

"You see something going on?" Scott asked, looking away from me. There was a sadness in his voice that couldn't be answered.

RIVERSIDE DRIVE AND 96TH STREET

Riverside Park was bright and cheerful. Big-eyed, round-faced kids ran in wild circles, showing off their new Christmas toys. I tried to put everything in its place, to make everything seem right. Gabi was wearing the sweater I had given her under her parka. She was beautiful again. With the cascades of children's laughter as a backdrop, I imagined what our child might look like. Perhaps a girl lighter than me, darker than Gabi, and beautiful. Earlier there had been a few snow flurries, which I'd hoped would decorate the park for us, but they had given way to a light, chilling rain.

"You seem different today," I said.

"How?" Gabi asked.

"You've brought our lunch in a bag, you're smiling, you seem so happy."

"'*Cuando yo te estoy cantando, en la Tierra acaba el mal. . . .*'" Gabi leaned her head against my shoulder. "'When I am singing to you, all the evil in the world stops.'"

I wanted to believe her. I held her hand and squeezed it, wanting the moment to last forever, wanting evil to end. There were a lot of children in the park. They were all brown. Even the white ones seemed somehow on the verge of brown.

"I think I'd like to have three children."

Gabi put her hand over her mouth. "I am so surprised at you, Spoon! Only women are supposed to think things like that."

"I don't even know why I said it."

"Children are innocence," Gabi said, sounding suddenly very serious. "Sometimes I see myself with a child and being very happy. Then sometimes I see myself looking at a child and wondering what right I have to such an innocent person. I believe that if you have a child, you must either put that child in a frame, put a label on it immediately, or wait to discover who she is. If you wait, then you have to be afraid. The child will be a stranger, looking at you with no evil in their heart. Looking at you as if they wanted you to share their innocence."

Where are you going, Gabi? What do you want to tell me?

Skateboarders. Five in a row, their first doing his tricks, the others following, trying to copy the leader. He was good. Gabi stopped and watched them. Her face was serious, almost stern. Then she turned away with a wave of the hand. Skateboarding was not the stuff of life.

The drizzle had let up. We stopped and sat on a bench. Gabi took a tinfoil dish and a thermos jug out of a plastic shopping bag. There were fried chicken wings and potato salad and yellow Filipino bread. We ate and she told me what our child would be like.

"If he is like you he will be too serious. Even when he's in diapers he's going to be too serious," she said. "And he's going to wear glasses."

"I don't wear glasses."

"He's going to wear glasses just to prove he's more serious than you."

"What are we going to do?" I asked.

"Two things." Gabi held up two fingers. "First, we have

his glasses tinted, which will at least make him look cooler. Then we get him a baby girlfriend, maybe one of those little cuties in the soap commercials. She'll loosen him up."

"I meant about us," I said.

"Whatever you want."

"I can't do whatever I want if I don't know what's going on with you, Gabi. We can't just say that everything is the same. It's not."

Tears. *Lagrimas.* She had given me the word years ago. I had said something wrong to her, had hurt her, and she had written it down on a piece of paper and handed it to me. "*Lagrimas,*" she had said, pointing to the tears that streamed down her face. "Hold on to them."

Now her tears screamed at me. *What do you want?* they shouted. *Why are you looking at me like that? Where are your answers?* I put my arm around her and she leaned against me.

"How's your mother?" I asked, searching for neutral ground.

"Worse," Gabi answered. "The doctor thinks she doesn't have the will to live. She's hallucinating. Yesterday I went to see her and she said that my father had just been there. I know he has never gone to see her.

"They say that she can come home soon. I know it's because they can't do anything more for her. It's sad, but whatever happens will happen and I'm ready for it. Maybe you'll come with me to the hospital. You have the stomach for it?"

"Sure." I didn't want to go.

"I got the phone put back in. It's mostly for my mother. I don't want her to die without speaking . . ." She paused, then pulled herself together. "I don't want her to die without speaking."

"To say good-bye?"

"Or whatever troubles her mind," Gabi said.

I didn't know Lucila, Gabi's mother. She was a shadow woman, always standing just out of the light, never quite in focus when I looked for her. I was sorry that she was dying. I was sorry that she would die without me ever really knowing her. I tried to push her death out of my mind as I walked Gabi home.

When I kissed her at the door Gabi said she had been sure that I was going to hit on her when I came home.

"Do you think about me that way?" she asked, standing against her door in the dim hallway. "Do you want to do nasty things to me?"

"Yes," I said, sliding my hand down from her shoulder.

She took my hand, the one seeking its own adventure, and kissed it.

WEST END AVENUE, ST. MARK'S SCHOOL GYMNASIUM

The narrow running track ran in a tight circle under stained glass windows that badly needed washing. Below the track the gymnasium floor, some of the boards along the wall lifting from the hard bed beneath, was unpolished and uneven where indifferent repairs had been made over the years. There were dead spots where the ball wouldn't bounce properly and the curvature of the track prevented shots from the corners. I thought about the athletic center at Wallingford with its synthetic surface and natural lighting.

Brand had tried twice to set up the game before getting it on. He was a whiner and I also thought he was a snob but somehow I had found myself in the same circles he was in at the Academy. He had picked up three other white guys, one who looked to be six five or so, and me. The "team" we were going to be playing against was all black. One of them was the son of the janitor at Brand's apartment and that's how the game got started. We were playing at St. Mark's because the guy was also the janitor there and had the use of the gym at night. I didn't mind playing ball, not even with Brand, but for some reason it annoyed me to see Chanelle and Amy show up with him.

Brand had himself playing point guard with me at one of the forward positions. On defense he wanted to run a two-one-two zone, which was all right with me, because it forced a pattern to the game that could be useful.

Brand introduced me to the janitor's son, in his mid-twenties, with a round moon of a face that flowed effortlessly into his double chins. He said his name was Wilson without differentiating whether it was a first or last name.

"Where you live?"

"A hundred forty-fifth," I said.

He said he used to have an aunt who lived near 145th and I said, "Oh, good."

Brand gave us a silly pep talk, unofficially designating himself as captain, and the game was on.

Wilson's team consisted of two kids who looked like they could have been fourteen or younger, and two men who were at least thirty. One of them wore long shorts down to his knees. They brought the ball down first and they looked like a mixed bag. The dude with the ball dribbled it through his legs for no reason, made useless passes as if he were trying to set something up, tried a drive between two defenders, then threw up a twisting jump shot that missed the rim altogether.

The guys who Brand brought had played together. One of them had mentioned Trinity, the Episcopal prep school, and I figured that all of them might have played there. They were good, not great, but they didn't throw the ball away.

Wilson couldn't play, but he hustled, a jerky, awkward kind of hustle that was all knees and elbows and sweat popping off. I found myself on him several times, pushing him away from the basket with my chest, and him not having enough floor moves to get around me.

Chanelle and Amy were keeping time. It was supposed to be two twenty-two-minute periods with no time-outs.

Amy marked off the period by running onto the court, waving her arms, and pointing at her watch. Even with us having the biggest man on the court and fewer turnovers we were only up by three points, 31–28, at the end of the first period.

We sat down and Brand started in his whine about how far ahead we would have been if we were calling fouls.

"I think I would have had at least nine foul shots," he said.

I was wishing Scott were there. He would have been the best player on the court.

The second half started with us in a one-two-two. They had only taken a couple of outside shots the first half and so I thought it would probably work. As it turned out Wilson and another of their players pooped out after five minutes and were bent over, with their hands on their knees, gasping for air. I thought that the whole game would cool out. I was wrong. Brand and the other three guys on my team were suddenly more intense, calling plays instead of freelancing, setting harder picks, pushing the score way past the point that they were going to be caught. I wanted to laugh when one of them started calling numbered defenses, as if we were playing some professional team in the playoffs. They weren't just winning a game, they were beating a team they would talk about during the school year, elevating the level of competition in their conversation as if they had really taken on and conquered some real players. I imagined phrases: "These street hustlers from the city," or "Some mean black dudes that tried to beat us to death." Basketball as a landscape for white triumph.

Game over. Final score 58–38. High fives all around. The guarded landscape of advantage and winning. Chanelle and Amy congratulated us. Wilson's team came over to where we were putting on our street shirts and shook our hands.

"You guys were kicking some butt at the end," Wilson said.

I looked to see if he was serious. He was and I moved away from him, uncomfortable with his accommodating the situation.

Brand was going home with one of the Trinity players. He said he'd call me if we played again. We shook hands, with me deciding that after thinking they were making too much of the game, I was doing the same thing. Wilson was checking the windows as we began to drift out to Amsterdam Avenue.

"They're probably going to drink beer," Chanelle said. "Come on by my place and get some ice cream. You feel like walking?"

I had arranged to go to Gabi's house at six and then to the hospital to see her mother. It was three, and I wanted to shower and told Chanelle so. She suggested that I shower at her house.

"My mother's not going to mind," she said.

Somewhere in the back of my mind a dormant layer of lust was stirred. I tried to disassociate it from Chanelle, telling myself that I had time to kill and, perhaps truthfully, that I didn't want to tell my mother that I was going to the hospital with Gabi. Mom already suspected that all wasn't right between Gabi and me. She didn't know what was wrong, but her ears were perked and waiting for any opening.

We took the number 1 train down to 59th Street and walked the five blocks to Chanelle's house. I was thinkng about a hundred things as we entered the building. I wasn't thinking about the doorman. His eyes pierced me, and I looked away.

"I'm really looking forward to going back to school," she said in the elevator. "I just want to get this new semester going and do some serious thinking before I start college."

"You decide on a major yet?"

"My dad is pushing finance, and I think that's just be-cause my mom is so lame with money. He's working the same strings. Get back at her through me. My brother wants me to get into home decorating — you know he's studying architecture at UCLA?"

"Yes." Into her apartment.

"He's got some idea that we could go into business together. But that home decoration is so, like, the little woman's thing. I don't want any part of it. You want me to get you a clean T-shirt from my brother's room?"

"Sure, how big is he?"

"He's big," she said.

In the bathroom I took off my shirt and T-shirt. Something told me to leave. Chanelle was talking on a cell phone as she handed the shirt to me.

"You want to go out for dinner?" she said into the phone. "About nine or so? Okay, see you then."

I held up the T-shirt and it looked to be my size.

I felt Chanelle's arms around my waist and saw her head as she looked around me into the bathroom mirror. She was smiling, making a funny face, giving me a chance to back away. I grasped her two hands in one of mine and held them together, lifted one arm, and turned around so that I was facing her. The smile was less silly as she looked into my eyes.

"Can I reach your lips if we're both standing?" I asked.

She lifted her arms and pulled my head down to hers. Then we were kissing, and then she was pushing me away.

"We'd better cool down," she said. "Why don't you take a shower and I'll have the ice cream ready when you're finished."

"You sure you don't want to take a shower with me?"

"No, I'm not sure," she said. "But I won't go all the way, so I'd better not start taking anything off."

She backed out of the bathroom and closed the door.

I was dizzy with wanting her. A dozen scenarios flickered through my mind. Chanelle coming back into the bathroom, into the shower. Me coming out with just a towel wrapped around my waist. The two of us going into her room.

The warm water didn't help and I turned the cold water up until my shoulders were covered with goose pimples. More scenarios danced through my mind, this time with the scenes of lust interlaced with scenes of her father coming through the door in a rage. Why did I imagine him with such a large head?

I showered for as long as I could stand it, saw that Chanelle was not going to make an instant move, dressed, and came out to find her watching television.

"The ice cream was brick hard," she said. "It's edible now."

"Should I be sorry I kissed you?" I asked.

"I'm not," she said. "But I'm sure you knew that."

Where was my head? As I ate the ice cream I couldn't think of anything but wanting Chanelle. It didn't make any difference what we were doing, as long as she was female and I was male and we were alone.

"Why are you smiling?" she asked.

"I'm surprised at how you make me feel," I said.

"We're going to have to be very careful when we get back to school," she said, smiling. "I don't want to get pregnant in my senior year."

Careful? Pregnant? What was she suggesting? That we would be a couple at Wallingford? That we would be lovers?

We sat on the edge of the couch, with Chanelle sitting in the corner and turned to me, and me sitting on the middle cushions. Our knees touched lightly, now and again, as we spoke quietly. I traced small circles in the palm of her hand with my middle finger. I wanted to say something with the weight of the moment, but my thoughts flickered nervously, like the dying neon sign that spelled out Pentecostal on a storefront church I could see from my kitchen window when I was a kid. Where Chanelle's hard body pushed against the fabric of her jeans, Gabi's thin body retreated beneath the unseasonably light clothing she wore. I thought of Gabi as I stumbled uneasily between my thoughts of her and my body's memory of pressing against Chanelle.

"Sometimes the senior year can really be stressful," she said. "You end up getting into situations you don't want to be in."

"You smell nice," I said. "A hint of flowers."

"You smell like soap," she said. And then, "Do you think you might want to join the choir? I love your voice."

"Could be," I said. "We'll see."

For a moment we were silent, and close to each other. I saw her eyes, brown, baby-doll wide, a strong lower lip making her look older than the roundness of her face suggested.

Time for me to leave, and she walked me to the door. We worked at being casual as we walked to the elevator. As the doors opened she kissed me again and murmured that we would have to be careful when we got back to the Academy.

On the way out I stopped for a moment to return the doorman's look. It was unexpected and he raised his eyes to the ceiling.

I was in a different world, and it was easy to be in. The paths were somehow clearer downtown. At 59th Street, still lust high, I took the uptown train.

LA PLUMITA, DOMINICAN REPUBLIC

Rafe let me in and then told me he had to leave. The old man was sitting at the kitchen table, a half a cup of tea in front of him. The teabag, carefully laid on the paper it had come in, was next to the cup.

"Gabi in?"

"She'll be back soon," Rafe said, glancing at the old man, "any minute. I have to run to the store."

I watched as Rafe nervously scooped change from the top of the refrigerator. He was a blur as he rushed past me and, over his footsteps already in the hall, I heard him calling that he would be back shortly.

"I'm Anthony Witherspoon, sir," I said. I reached out

my hand for his, realized he didn't see it, and brought it back to my side. "We've met before."

No response.

"I'm Gabi's . . . friend," I said.

He nodded.

"Do you mind if I sit?"

He gestured, a palm turned that said "If you please," and I sat across from him. Immediately I searched for conversation. He was blind and couldn't comfort himself with visual judgments. He had to listen, and I didn't have any words.

The red second hand of the clock on the wall moved silently. Five seconds. Ten. Fifteen. An eternity.

"It's not that cold today," I said. "Yesterday was a lot colder."

He nodded slowly. His face was not brown, but suggested brown. He was lighter than Gabi, and I imagined him walking arm in arm with a tall black woman. He was handsome and she sensuous. Immediately my mind switched to Chanelle.

"Who are your parents?" he asked.

My parents. "My father's name is Sidney and he works for the Internal Revenue Service in Brooklyn. My mother, Eloyce, works for a finance company."

"And they are who they work for!" He hit his fist lightly on the table. "That means they are Americans!"

We both laughed.

"When I was young I wanted so to come to New York. I was teaching English and geography in La Plumita — that's how things are done there — and I had seen drawings by a Cuban artist, Miguel Covarrubias. I said to myself, could these people be so free, so alive with all that I had heard about them? I wanted to know. But in my city, La Plumita, there was no way for me to find out.

"I thought — it was a young man's thought — that if I ever got to San Pedro I would find out. San Pedro was only eight miles away, but it took my family twenty years after they first thought about it to move from La Plumita to San Pedro. Then they hated it."

"Why?"

"Because it was different from La Plumita," he said. "For a simple people *la diferencia* is enough. But I still wondered about America. What I knew about your country was New York, Hollywood — and I thought it was two words — and where the black people lived."

"Harlem," I said.

"Now I am come here and I can't see it," he said. "I

don't know if there are mountains here, or lakes. I don't know if swallows go from tree to tree all day."

"There aren't any mountains or lakes in Harlem," I said. "Take my word for it."

"But those are your words," he said. "Those are the visions you have seen. It means nothing to me. My only visions are of La Plumita and of San Pedro."

"They're good visions, I hope."

"They are wonderful. I am a romantic. And so I see my grandmother, she was so small, working in our garden. We called her Chiquitina and she loved it. Each morning she would go to the well and draw fresh water and then she would come home and work in the garden. The garden was special to us. My father, a rather hard man, would work all day in a factory that made rum to send to the United States. When he came home he loved to sit in the garden and hold his guitar across his lap."

"He enjoyed playing the guitar?" The old man was fishing, but for what?

"He couldn't play, but he enjoyed holding it in case God would send down a miracle."

"You never saw him play?"

"What did I see? Now that I am blind I ask myself that

question a hundred times a day. What did I see? Did I really see fields ten acres wide swaying with lilies? Were all the women in La Plumita really so beautiful? Or am I seeing now with my heart what I never saw with my eyes? When the boy leaves in a rush all that I see is a shadow across my eyes. From then on it is what the heart sees."

"Teenagers are always rushing someplace," I said. He was telling me that his heart saw something wrong. Did he think I'd tell him what it was?

"When we're young we think we have to hurry," he said. "When we're old and to the place to which we were rushing, we know we didn't have to bother."

"Sometimes I wonder what I'm seeing," I said. "The place I go to school, in Connecticut, is so different from Harlem. I come back here and I'm seeing things that I've never seen before."

"There is a danger whenever you go back to a place that you remember from a distance," he said. "The danger is that you only look with your eyes. You see a friend you haven't seen in twenty years and what happens? You see an old man and not the swimming together on early mornings. You see a woman with a limp and forget how you shared a piece of fruit with that same woman when you were young.

"The eyes are not always faithful to the heart. Are you seeing with your heart?"

"I'm not sure what I'm seeing with."

"Not being sure is good, too," he said. "Do you want me to make tea?"

"No, do you want me to make tea?"

"No, do you want me to make tea?"

We laughed again. I liked him and, I thought, he liked me. I watched him as he got up, found the teapot, and filled it with water.

"In the center of La Plumita there is a town square," he said. "On Sunday nights everyone came there. Young girls dressed in their finest, young men in clean shirts and slicked-back hair, families. The old women would sit and watch the young girls, to make sure they acted decently. If you lived in that little town you could tell your age by what you did in the square on Sunday evenings. If you played with your friends, you were a boy. If you put oil in your hair and washed your hands ten times to get the dirt from under your fingernails, you were a man. Then, if you just sat and rested, wondering how Sunday, your day off, had gone by so quickly, you were a family man."

"It sounds like a good life," I said.

"But was it true?" He tilted his head back and I saw that his eyes were grayed over. "Was any of it true, or is my heart as blind as my eyes?"

"I think it's true."

We waited and the small talk between us became smaller and smaller. The tea grew cold. An hour went by and then another. Twice he asked me the time, and I told him. I wondered where Gabi was. Was she rushing through the darkness, her smooth walk a jazz adagio over the asphalt streets? Did the moonless December night frighten her? Our minds, mine and the old man's, were rushing about the small kitchen. Finally, I said to him that I should be going home.

"Your parents will be worried about you," he said, nodding.

"My mother worries about me even when I'm in the house," I said.

"Ah, that's who she is," he said, "not a job."

I took the subway uptown. The car I was in was nearly empty and I started to read a newspaper I found on one of the seats but thoughts of Gabi distracted me. She seemed so different than she had been, as if she had been somehow wound tighter than a person ever should be, as if any moment she would either spring loose into a thousand parts or stop altogether. Somehow I had lost my understanding of her.

I found my parents watching television. My dad asked me how things were going, and I said they were going well.

"I guess you're ready to get back to school?" he said, not looking at me.

"Not that ready," I said, glancing at Mom.

I was tired and thought about going right to bed, but I knew what my father was saying, that I hadn't spent much time with them. I stayed up and we talked about the television shows we were watching. Mom laughed too hard at all my comments and Dad was being distant, cool. I only had a few days left before I had to go back to school. I made myself some promises to hang out with my folks.

Dad went to bed first, and I sat next to Mom on the couch and put my arm around her.

"Watch it," she said. "I'm a married woman."

I was dreaming when my father woke me. The lights were on in my bedroom and for a moment I didn't know where I was. My father's shaking was strenuous, urgent.

"What's up?"

"Grab the phone," he said. "It's that girl."

The phone was on the dresser, and I swung my feet over

the side of the bed to reach it. In the mirror I saw my father watching me closely.

"Hello?"

"Spoon. Spoon. I'm sorry to call you so late, honey." Gabi's speech was slow, distant. "What time is it?"

"I don't know what time it is," I said.

"Four-fifteen," my father said.

"It's four-fifteen," I repeated. "Where are you?"

"I'm at a girlfriend's house," she said. "Mami died last night."

The image of a thin woman, her dark hair pinned away from a face that seemed too young to belong to my girlfriend's mother, flickered through my mind.

"Gabi, why don't you go home?" I said. "Are you all right? Can you go home?"

"I'm on my way home now," she said. "Will you come by later?"

"Yes, of course. You were with her?"

"I was sitting by the bed. I think I dozed off and . . . oh, man. Spoon, I'm broken. I'm broken!"

"Gabi, you have to . . ." No, there was nothing that she *had* to do. "Do you want me to come over — I'll come over now."

"No. Wait until I call you. Give me some time. Let me tell Abuelo," she said. "I'll see you later, baby."

The phone went dead and I hung up.

"She drunk?" my father asked.

"Her mother died last night," I said.

"And she was drinking?"

"It sounded like it," I said, almost sure that she was high, but not from booze.

"You need to wait until daylight before you go over there," my father said. He loosened the belt on his robe and refastened it. "Nothing you can do right now."

"I think you're right," I said.

My father took my hand. "You need me, I'm there for you, Anthony," he said. "You want me to shut out the light?"

I nodded and he flicked the switch. In the darkness I thought about Gabi. She had called me "baby." It was too small a word for her. I had seen people high before, fading in and out, hanging on to the surface chatter to communicate.

Gabi, I am so sorry your mother died, and I am so afraid for you. I am so afraid for you.

The sun was coming through my window when I woke again. My parents were already at the table. My father asked if I wanted him to stay home. He said he had some sick days coming. I said no, but that I appreciated him offering. Mom had to leave for work first and Dad asked me again if I wanted him to stay. Again I said no.

I showered and rummaged through my closet until I found a decent pair of pants to wear. The street was just coming to life when I got downstairs. The super was wrestling some garbage to the curb; across the street a delivery truck was already unloading cases of soda at the grocery store. The rest of the world was going about its business.

Gabi would need comforting, I knew. So would the old man. I remembered that Gabi had an aunt who sold advertising for *La Prensa,* a Spanish-language newspaper. But what did she know about Gabi?

THE LABYRINTH

A cold December morning. People leaned into the wind as they maneuvered the hill toward the 145th Street station. In the station there were still touches of holiday spirit. Somebody had put up a mural of children's drawings, which brought smiles. The new year was only days away and there were still touches of Christmas color among the otherwise dark clothing of the huddled passengers. A few of the women were carrying shopping bags, and I imagined they contained goodies for office parties.

The downtown train was a mixture of rumble and

squeal as it jerked its way into the station. People positioned themselves to get on, shifting their weight, pushing toward the doors while being careful not to violate the tiny cocoon of personal space each demanded. I allowed myself to be herded onto the train and grabbed the overhead rail. As the doors closed I felt a slight chill, and then an uneasiness in the pit of my stomach that made me think I would throw up. For a second I thought it was the lack of air in the jammed car, but then I realized that it was not just nausea that I felt, it was fear.

Gabi and I had always been there for each other, had always managed to understand each other's feelings, and find the right words to reassure and help. But we hadn't dealt with drugs before, or death. We had always projected our lives onto a larger, more expansive screen, one which we could paint with the comfortable background of what would happen next and the immediacy of the poetry we shared. Now we were coping with the here and now. Where once we were living largely in the realm of our collective imaginations, now we were forced to live in the present, and the present had no promise of forgiveness.

I got off at 125th and walked toward Gabi's apartment. From somewhere I conjured up a scene in which I was holding Gabi, and she was crying and explaining how her mother's death had torn something from her. We would hold each other, be impossibly close to each other, and things would be all right again.

When I crossed Manhattan Avenue I saw Rafe walking down the block away from me and I called his name. He turned, saw me, and waited.

"I got milk for coffee," he announced, holding up the container in a plastic bag. "You seen Gabi?"

"She's not home?"

"She hasn't been home since the day before yesterday," he said. "I don't know where she is."

"Hey, Rafe. I'm sorry about your mom, man. You okay?"

"Yeah, I guess."

"Look, you hang in there. I'll look for Gabi," I said. "Any idea where she might be? She called me early this morning and said she was at a girlfriend's house."

"I don't hang with her," he said, shrugging.

"Yo, Rafe, you know Gabi's using, right?" I was attempting to put on my Harlem street voice but it came out hesitantly, weak.

Rafe looked down the street and I was almost tempted to look in the same direction, too, to see what he might be searching for.

"Yeah, man, I know, but I don't know where she gets her stuff or nothing," Rafe said.

We stood for a brief and awkward eternity, shifting our weights on the corner, as the condensation from our breaths mingled and dissipated in the morning air. I sensed that Rafe was not all that concerned with Gabi, or even with his mother's death. He had his own demons to contend with.

"Tell your grandfather I'll call when I find her," I said. "You going to be around the house today?"

He gave me an unconvincing "Yeah" and headed up the street.

Where to start looking? Gabi had called at a little after four, saying she was at a friend's house, and I didn't think anything had happened to her. I tried to imagine her high, and pushed my thoughts away from it. It was too soon to call the police or even the hospital. Nothing came to mind except to walk around places that I knew she liked. I went over to Mt. Morris Park and remembered the days we'd spent there. Once she had asked me to come with her to the park and to bring some poetry. We'd sat on one of the benches and read to each other. I had read Derek Walcott and she had read some short pieces by a Cuban poet, Carolina Hospital. We were enjoying the poems and each other, and then she had announced that she had one more poem for me, one that she had written, and then we would have to leave.

"Don't ask me to translate the poem into English," Gabi had said, taking my face in her hands. "I'd be too embarrassed."

The words she'd recited, ever so slowly, just above a whisper, in a language that I couldn't reach, had so filled me that day, I'd become suddenly heroic, had been able to fly, to soar over the familiar gray of the city into the heavens. It was when I had loved her the most.

I sat on the same bench and watched as pigeons pecked at a dirty bag near the water fountain.

I didn't think she would be at St. Cecilia's, but I went over there anyway. I told myself that I was doing the right thing, no matter how fruitless it seemed. What I wanted was for her to just show up, alive and well, and ready to restart the business of living, no matter how painful. I hoped that she would lean on me, and that I would be strong enough to carry the weight of her grieving.

One Hundred and Twenty-fifth Street. How many times had we walked down this street solving the problems of the world? It was already crowded. I went east until I reached Park Avenue. There were sidewalk evangelists already preaching on the corners, some day workers with their toolboxes waiting to be picked up, a man with a grocery store shopping cart filled with scrap metal rummaging through some discarded boxes.

On one corner there was a woman, incredibly thin, her dark skin dull and pockmarked, nodding out on the corner. She leaned to one side, her eyes closed, and dipped to an impossible angle before jerking herself upright. People walked by her as if she wasn't there. A patrol car cruised past and the policeman turned his head away from her. I watched as I glanced at a clock in a bodega window and saw that it was ten-thirty.

I walked and walked. I called Gabi's house at one, and then again at four. She hadn't shown up.

Gabi's mom had died late Wednesday, she had called me Thursday morning, and no one had seen her since, or heard from her. I called the house and spoke to her grandfather twice and I could hear the hurt in his voice. He told me the funeral was to be Tuesday afternoon at St. Joseph's and asked me if I knew where it was. Yes, of course, I had passed it on 125th and St. Nicholas a thousand times. Yes, I would be there for the funeral.

By the weekend I was sure that something had happened to Gabi.

Sunday afternoon I called the police and a sergeant took her name and a description in a coldly matter-of-fact way. When I asked him what else I should do he said to just ask around the neighborhood, that her friends should know something.

Chanelle called in the evening and asked me when I was going back. I told her I was going to try Tuesday night but that I had a problem. I told her Gabi's mother had died and we hadn't been able to find Gabi.

"Are you mad at me for what happened the other day?" she asked.

"No, of course not," I said.

"I just wondered why you hadn't called."

"It's this thing with Gabi and her mother," I said.

"Oh," Chanelle said. "I understand. I guess you'll be busy for New Year's?"

Rafe called Monday and asked if I had heard from Gabi, and I told him I hadn't. He said that their grandfather wanted to be sure I would come to the funeral on Tuesday. I said I would be there. I didn't say that my stomach tightened up when I thought about going, or that there was no way I wanted to go if Gabi hadn't shown up. I asked Rafe again if he knew of any places that Gabi could be, and he said no. I called him a jerk for not knowing, and he surprised me by saying he knew he was, but that none of his friends had seen her.

I had been to all the places I had once shared with Gabi, and hadn't found her at any of them. I knew, if she wasn't ill or injured somewhere, that facing her mother's funeral would be hard for her, but facing herself if she didn't go might be even more difficult. Gabi was in trouble, and if I was going to help her, it had to be soon.

I've always believed in barbershops. The one I found in Gabi's neighborhood had framed newspaper photos of boxers on one wall and basketball players on the other. It was two o'clock when I went in, trying to frame the right combination of words. There was one man in a barber's jacket sitting in one of the chairs, reading a paper, and two older men playing checkers.

"Hey, you got here just before the line got long." The barber looked up from his paper and started folding it. "You even get your choice of seats."

"I've got a problem," I said. "I'm looking for my sister. She hasn't been home for three days and we're really worried about her."

"You been to the po-lice?" one of the checker players asked.

"I have, but they don't know anything. Look, she uses drugs, so I think she might be in some place where drug people hang out."

"Then you need to let her stay there," the other checker player said. "Because nothing you're going to tell her is going to get her away from those drugs. And that's what God loves, the truth!"

"Do you know if there are places around here . . . ?"

"Man, you need to get on out of here!" the first checker player said. "We don't use that mess and don't want anybody in here that do!"

I felt incredibly stupid as I turned and started for the door.

"Hey, how much money you got in your wallet?" the barber asked.

"You need to get him on out of here, Frank." The first checker player looked up. "Those people attract trouble like shit attracts flies."

"How much money you got in your wallet?"

I looked in my wallet and came up with twenty-six dollars, all money my father had given me.

"Just a minute," the barber said. "He ain't no junkie. If he was he'd be out here buying dope. Didn't Sister Scott say something about there being a dope place on 121st Street?"

"Yeah, she did," the first checker player said. "She said they go in and out of one of them buildings. But if he ain't buying no dope they liable to kill his skinny butt and eat him. That's the caliber of people you got using that stuff."

The barber went to the phone, looked up a number among all the numbers scribbled on the wall next to it, and dialed it. I heard him say hello to a Sister Scott, ask her if the hot towels had done anything for the pain in her knee, and then ask her what was the number of that dope house she was talking about. He talked to her a little longer before hanging up. He tore off a piece of his newspaper, wrote something down on it, and handed it to me.

"Like Smitty over here said, you messing with dope people you taking your life in your hands," the barber said. "That's the number she give me and it's a basement apartment. If you get yourself messed up don't come crying to me."

"Thanks a lot," I said, taking the paper.

"Don't thank him yet," the first checker player said. "You ain't got your sister, and you ain't come out alive."

The address on 121st Street was less than a block away and I hurried to it. It was an abandoned building. The windows were covered by boards, and there was junk strewn in the well of the basement apartment. A woman sat on the stoop next to it. She was reasonably pretty but blade thin and I figured her for a user. I tried to act casual as I sat down next to her.

"What you want, honey?" Her voice was low, raspy.

"I'm looking for a girl named Gabi. You don't know her, do you? Pretty, dark eyes, light skin?"

"They don't pay me to be seeing people," she said. "You got two dollars you can let me have?"

I didn't answer.

"You looking for a good time?"

Not from you, I thought. "I'm looking for this girl," I said. "And I think she might be inside."

"Give me two dollars and I'll go find out for you." She nudged my knee with her own. "I'm Monica, everybody in there knows me."

I gave her the two dollars.

"I need four."

"You can get it," I said. "But I need to know if she's in there."

"I need it now," Monica said, her voice hardening.

I stretched my legs in front of me and crossed them at the ankles without answering her. She started talking to me again, telling me how she really needed the money, and I looked the other way.

"Why you looking for her?"

"Why? Because she's — Look, do I have to give you my résumé or will you settle for the two dollars?"

"Don't be nasty, baby. Life ain't that long we gotta be taking crap from anybody who come along."

I felt so tired. I could hardly hold up my head. "Look, Monica, I was away at school, and when I got home my girl was using. She says she's just skin surfing —"

"Skin surfing, smoking, whatever, it's all the same."

"Yeah, well, I still love her and —"

"And you don't know what the hell to do."

"And I don't know what the hell to do."

"Did her mama die or something like that?"

"Yeah." I caught my breath. "You know her?"

"Come on with me," she said, taking my hand.

My heart was pumping furiously and my mouth went dry. I didn't want to go with her into the house, and almost pulled away. She rang the bell, two short rings and two long ones. The door opened and beyond it was a wrought-iron gate and behind the gate a face, half concealed in the shadows, its features indistinct. He looked us over quickly, hardly more than a glance, then pulled the gate aside.

The only lights were dim and red in holders along the

walls. I could see bodies lounging around on chairs, some asleep. There was some activity in a corner. A young boy, I figured he was a sticker, was examining the arm of an older man. I looked away quickly. The sound of slow blues came from somewhere. The room was filled with people and yet, somehow, seemed almost to be one huge being. I imagined I could hear its breath, as if some massive creature was crouched in the darkness. The sickening smell of pot filled the air like the smell of fresh blood in a slaughterhouse.

"What's your girl's name?" Monica whispered.

"Gabi," I whispered back. "She's Dominican."

Monica stepped away from my side as she looked around the room. I opened my mouth to suck in what air I could and prayed I wouldn't pass out.

"What you want?" A big dude came up to us. He was in overalls, the kind with the big pocket on the chest.

"Two rocks," Monica said. "Give the man the ten dollars, honey."

Crap. I was too scared to even look at the guy as I took out my wallet, found the twenty, and handed it over. He reached into one of his side pockets, pulled out a bag, and shook the rocks into Monica's hand.

"Where that girl was talking about her mama died?" Monica asked.

The big dude pointed to a dark corner. Monica took my wrist and led me to the corner. In the chair, sleeping with her legs folded under her, was Gabi.

THE BEAST

Gabi opened her eyes and murmured my name. I pulled her upright and she leaned against me, lightly holding my arm. The big dude who had sold Monica the rocks came over and stood menacingly nearby. With one hand around Gabi's waist, I started to leave. He tried to move Gabi's hair away from her face to see what she looked like, and Monica pushed his hand away hard. I kept moving as I felt the small woman's other hand urging me toward the door.

Gabi was unsteady as we hit the street. A light breeze blew bits of colored paper along the sidewalk and the low rumble of distant thunder echoed between the once elegant brownstones. Halfway down the block Monica pointed toward a stoop and said to sit Gabi down for a minute.

"Let's check her pulse," she said.

Gabi was taking deep breaths and tried to put her head down, but Monica pushed her upright and took her wrist. She felt for her pulse, waited a moment, and then said she was all right.

"I don't know what she was using, but if it was blow sometimes they get a fast heartbeat and you have to be careful," Monica said. "Her heartbeat's normal. Give her a minute and she'll be okay."

I looked around and no one seemed to notice us. I thought it would be good to get Gabi off the street, but I didn't want to take her home looking high. I took off my jacket and put it around Gabi's shoulders and she leaned against me. Monica sat next to Gabi and nervously scratched the backs of her hands. It was growing colder and Monica pulled the drawstring on the hooded sweatshirt she wore.

"Yo, Monica, nice looking out," I said. It sounded lame.

Monica looked away and I could see her profile against the changing blur of nighttime traffic. She couldn't have been more than sixteen or seventeen. She noticed me watching her and smiled. Nice smile.

"You ain't never been in no mess like this before, have you?" she asked. "Head joints, people selling dope right out in the open?"

"I've seen some of it," I said. "Never been this close before."

"Ain't nothing pretty about it, that's for sure. And if you stay in it long you won't be pretty, either."

Her lips firmed. For a moment her eyes seemed to tear, and then they were suddenly dry, as if she had, for the moment, willed away the pain.

"How did you . . . ?" I searched for words.

"Get caught up in this mess?"

"Yeah."

"I don't know. It was like, one moment I was walking down the street thinking I was real, thinking I was part of life, and the next moment I wasn't part of it. I was walking and breathing but life had just slipped on away from me. I looked around to see what was happening and I knew it sure wasn't me," Monica said. "And when I fell into the shadows I sure didn't have nobody come looking for me. I don't know if it would have helped if they had."

"Yeah, but drugs are like killing yourself," I said.

"No, it ain't, baby. If you kill yourself you ain't around to say you did it." Monica looked directly at me. "You can use this stuff and make believe you still alive."

"Make believe?"

"Hey, honey, how you doing?" Monica looked past me to Gabi.

"I'm okay," Gabi answered.

"Take her on home and let her get some sleep." Monica stood. "You got cab fare?"

"It's only a block and a half," I said. "We can walk it."

"Stay sweet, baby." Monica touched me on the shoulder, turned, and started down the street.

"Monica. Thanks!" I called after her.

As we started to her house Gabi seemed subdued but alert. At the corner I stopped again and told her that I thought her aunt might be at her house.

She nodded, and kissed me on the cheek. "I'm so wrong," she said, and the tears in her dark eyes spilled over onto her face.

"You walk as strong as you can, and we'll get you home and deal with whatever we have to," I said. "Can you do that?"

She sucked in more air and took my arm.

At the house I rang the bell, and there was no answer. Gabi went through her pockets, found her keys, and gave them to me.

We got upstairs and went in. There was a note on the kitchen table. I picked it up. It was in Spanish and I gave it to Gabi.

"They're going to sit at my aunt's house for the night," she said, after reading it. "They're telling me where the funeral will be."

Gabi sat at the end of the table, put her hands in her lap, and began to cry. I watched as her whole body shook. Looking around, I found some instant coffee and put on the kettle.

"I can't even go to the funeral tomorrow," Gabi said. "I don't have one decent dress. Not one decent . . ."

Tears again. Sobs that filled the small kitchen space, that slowed the hands of the clock on the wall, that framed the pans and dishes on the drain board.

The radio alarm suddenly came on, startling both of us. I looked at the clock, saw that it was nine, and turned off the radio. I made coffee and put a cup in front of Gabi.

"You want to talk to me, Gabi? We've always had good things to say to each other."

Silence. And then me again, pulling a chair next to her,

sitting close and touching her hair. "Gabi, please talk to me. Please try."

"I don't have any excuses," she said, her voice trailing off. "I'm just so wrong. I know everything, but still I went the wrong way."

"I'm not asking you to be right," I said. "I'm just trying to understand this thing. Remember when I broke my toe that time, and you and my mother took me to the emergency room?"

"Your mother doesn't like me," she said.

"She likes you, Gabi. Enough to think that I would want to run off with you and not go to college. She just didn't understand you asking me to tell you about the pain, about how much I was hurting. I understood it, and it helped. It helped to search for the words, to bring it into some kind of perspective."

The phone rang. Gabi closed her eyes and picked it up. She spoke in Spanish, and I sensed she was explaining to somebody else where she had been.

"I'll stay here tonight," she said, in English. "I'll see you tomorrow."

She was crying again even before the receiver hit the cradle. "I don't even know somebody to borrow a dress from," she said.

"I'll get you a dress," I said.

"I don't want you to —"

I put my finger on her lips. I knew she had to go to her mother's funeral. I went through my pockets until I found Chanelle's number. I called her and told her I had to borrow a dress for a funeral. She asked me if it was for "my friend," and I said yes.

"What size?" I repeated Chanelle's question to Gabi.

Gabi signaled no, that she didn't want to borrow a dress.

I put my hand over the phone. "For me? Gabi, will you do it for me?"

She told me she wore a size six and I relayed it to Chanelle, as well as the address and how to ring the downstairs bell. Chanelle said she would try to find something.

I tasted the coffee. It was bitter and weak.

"Do you want to lie down or something?"

"Are you going home?"

"No."

The low hum of the refrigerator shut off and I realized I was hungry. I looked in and saw that someone had brought donuts. I took them out and put them on the table in front of Gabi.

"When you were getting ready to leave I was so happy for you," she began. "I went around thinking of wonderful things to write to you. I was going to invent poetry that you would read and be so glad about me, and about my letters.

"After you left things started falling apart. I kept starting letters and throwing them away. The words wouldn't come, and after a while I knew they wouldn't. You were thinking about me like some kind of amazing poet and that's what I wanted to be. But I wasn't an amazing poet or amazing anything. I'm not. Sometimes I would copy poems from books and string them together in letters. But I couldn't mail them to you. It would be a lie. Like the way you think about me is a lie."

"You're not a lie, Gabi." I took her hands in mine. "You're real and you're here and I do love you."

"That's funny, because I don't love me anymore."

She began to cry again. Softly at first, and then — no louder — but so much harder. So much harder. I felt so helpless. Gabi was hurting and I was sitting right next to her, and I still couldn't reach her pain.

"When Mami found out I was using she got worse. She would stand at the foot of my bed, screaming at me. 'You are a Dominican woman!' she yelled at me. You should have seen her face. Twisted and angry. 'Dominican women don't do this filth!'"

"I'm sorry."

"Then one day everything got to be too much for me. It was too hard to comb my hair. Too far to travel to get to school. Any book I picked up was too heavy. The words were drifting away from me. I could read them, but they had lost their meaning. How can you read words and not know the meaning? How can you walk down a street you've been down a hundred times and not know where it's going, just stumble along until you are lost? Sometimes I thought about being a different person, of going away from you, or you going away from me. I even dreamed of you killing yourself because I had left you."

"I remember the story you told me about Gabriela Mistral," I said. "How her lover had killed himself when she was young. But that doesn't — am I just too out of it to understand this thing?"

"Understand how I could use drugs?"

"Not living in this neighborhood," I said. "Not with all you know."

"The first time I let myself not think," she said. "I was at a party and some people were smoking and some were shooting up. 'Oh, come on, Gabi, this one time won't hurt you. It's not like you're putting it in a vein or something.' I should have left the party. If you had been there I would have left the party."

131

"I wish I had been there."

"It's no way your fault, Spoon. I couldn't find my way out of my life, and so I just tried to get out of the moment. Every time after that I swore I was going to quit and that I just wanted to get through this one day, this one hour even. I knew you would be disgusted with me. I'm disgusted with me. You know it makes me sick every time? I puke my guts out and then I hate myself even more than before I use the drugs."

"Are you addicted?"

"I don't know the chemistry," she said. "What I know is that I can't let go of the explanation for my life."

"Which is what?"

"Which is the drugs. Can you believe that I feel better thinking that I can't help myself than saying that I just stopped loving myself?"

"The drugs aren't an answer," I said, hating the simplicity of the statement.

"I know," she said. A sparrow's voice. A twig snapping beneath the foot of God. "I didn't ever believe they were."

She asked me for a glass of water from the refrigerator and I got it for her and watched her drink it down quickly. She rubbed the cold, empty glass against her forehead.

"Do you need some sleep?" I asked.

She murmured no, but laid her head down on the kitchen table. I thought about trying to get her to the bed, but I wasn't sure if that was the right thing to do. I remembered movies of people keeping drugged people awake.

I thought of Monica. Of her sitting on the stoop with us, and checking Gabi's pulse. I wondered if she liked herself. People who were kind, I thought, and Monica had been kind to us, liked themselves, or at least wanted to like themselves.

"So what are we going to do?" I asked. "That's what it comes down to, Gabi. What are we going to do?"

"That sounds so hard," she answered. She had her eyes closed and her head resting on her hand.

"How are you feeling?"

"I'm okay," she said. "I'm just so tired. But I need talk. Can you talk to me awhile?"

Gabi's breathing was slow and I thought she was falling asleep. I really didn't know what to say, what to think, or even what I understood.

"Now that I'm home I feel like everything has kind of shifted," I said. "There was a time when the older guys were just hanging around, just drifting through life. It was always the older guys getting into trouble, or the older girls getting into trouble. Now it's my friends — guys like Brian and Leon and Scott — they seem as if they're wandering around in some monster maze. And they're all so cautious, as if any moment they'll either be out in the clear again or something will catch them in the darkness."

"You'll get it all straight," Gabi said, running her hand through her hair. "I believe in you."

I went to the refrigerator and looked for something besides the donuts. There was a pot and I looked in it and saw peas and carrots. I took it out, decided it would be too much trouble to heat them up, and put them back. I was wondering if I had enough money to go out and buy Chinese food when the doorbell rang.

I pushed the buzzer near the door and waited. I thought it would be Rafe or someone else from Gabi's family. It was Chanelle. She stood in Gabi's door, her eyes wide and looking around the apartment.

Gabi stiffened when she saw Chanelle step into the apartment with the shopping bag. I made a brief introduction and Chanelle said she hoped the dress fit.

"I should try it on," Gabi said. She stood as tall as she could; she was much taller than Chanelle as she held the dress up in front of her. "I hope it doesn't fit."

"Gabi!"

"I'm sorry," she said, glancing again at Chanelle. "Let me go wash."

Gabi laid the dress across the back of the chair and went to the bathroom that was just down the hall from the kitchen. I knew she would be crying again.

Chanelle sat at the table and told me that the dress belonged to a girl in her building. She tried not to look around the apartment but couldn't help herself. I wondered what she saw.

We heard water running, and then nothing.

"Do you want me to take it in to her?" Chanelle asked.

"I'll take it," I said.

I took the dress to the bathroom and knocked on the door. There was no answer and an image of Gabi, bending over the sink and bleeding, flickered through my mind. I opened the door.

Gabi, in her bra and underpants, was sitting on the edge of the tub, her head down. Chanelle moved by me and sat next to her. Gabi looked up and managed a small smile.

"I'm just so tired," she said.

I closed the door and went back into the kitchen. I was exhausted, too.

As I waited for them, I thought about all the changes

that had taken place in the few months that I had been away. Clara had gotten pregnant, Scott had dropped out of school, and Gabi, my Gabi, had been using drugs. It was as if so many dreams had suddenly been abandoned, so many lives had been set adrift. I wondered if Monica had once had similar dreams, had once read poetry in the park with someone who had promised her the stars. What were we going to do? I had asked the question of Gabi. What were we going to do? Now that we were glimpsing our whole selves, our selves with blemishes and faults, with saints that sometimes failed us and beasts that sometimes brought us comforts, what were we going to do with these new selves? Could we truly reinvent our dreams? Could we, coupling and tripling with our fellow travelers, find a gentler, easier path to walk upon?

Gabi and Chanelle came out of the bathroom.

"She's beautiful," Chanelle said.

And she was.

ST. JOSEPH'S
ROMAN CATHOLIC CHURCH

I n the first row there were five women, a boy, and a blind
man. The women were dressed in black, their faces
veiled. The man was pale. The yellow streaks in his silver
hair reminded me of old newspapers. The boy, Rafe, looked
smaller somehow. The suit he wore hung loosely over his thin
shoulders. He looked around uncomfortably, as I did, avoiding
the dark wooden casket in the front of the church.

Beyond us, beyond the steps and the communion rail
and the rows of candles, was the organ. A young black man
sat before it, gently touching the keys, almost as if he were
trying to awaken them. He was playing from memory, the

stiff chords of St. Joseph's intermingled with the soulful monotony of gospel. In this place, at this time, there was a strange mixture of black and Catholic, each claiming the other, each failing.

Gabi was at my side. She was ravishing in black. I was ashamed of my thoughts as she suffered through the funeral liturgy.

Somewhere, in the ordered geography of the church, my parents sat. My father didn't know what to do about me, what to say. He wanted to be understanding, and he was, but his understanding was of another time and, perhaps, of other people. Gabi and I sat apart from the others and I was surprised to find it was me who felt a sense of desperation as I clutched her hand.

The censer swung in a small circle, filling the still air with mist and mystery. It was done with purpose, this putting away, this turning away from life gone stale. There was holy water, a soul refreshed for a final journey.

Gabi leaned against me and her tears burned my eyes.

There were words, the poetry of King James, and they slid through me without touching nerve or sense.

Heavenly Father, bless Lucila and receive her into
    Thy kingdom.

Lord have mercy.

Mary, Mother of God, bless Lucila and pray for her.

Lord have mercy.

Gabi knew these words of ancient innocence by heart. How many languages did she know? I didn't know them and my mind, despite my efforts, drifted to the phone call from Chanelle. She was going back to the Academy tonight. What was I going to do?

I did what I understood, but what did I understand? I knew what my father understood, that the Academy was a chance I must take, for which he was willing to make sacrifices. The Academy represented what he wanted for me, a heaven for his Baptist heart. Gabi, leaning forward against the dark pew, was the threat. I imagined him sitting in the living room, his large fingers nervously strumming the arm of the plastic-covered couch, asking me to explain Gabi. How would I arrange the words in my mouth to say that she had simply stopped believing?

I believe in God the Father Almighty, Creator of Heaven and earth, And in Jesus Christ, His only Son, our Lord.

I stood when Gabi stood, and sat when she sat. I learned parts of the Mass. The rituals washed over me and I tried to let them take me away. They moved swiftly along and soon we were filing out of the church into the blinding light of the winter sun. The old man was being led by Gabi's aunt. He walked stoically, a stone man who had learned to grieve within. I imagined tears, like gray pebbles, falling behind his blind eyes.

My parents came to touch Gabi's arm before they returned home. They were sincere and Gabi managed a wan smile. I told them that I was going to the cemetery, and my father said he would see me later.

At the cemetery we waited in cars until the priest was ready, and then we gathered under a small gray canopy. The coffin was already there. It felt as if we were rushing through this last part, as if we needed to get it over with. We said prayers over the grave and over the coffin. We held hands in a moment of silence and then we walked away.

It was late when we returned to Harlem and to Gabi's aunt's house. There was food, wine, and soft drinks. People remembered Lucila, how she had shocked her family by climbing a tree in her Communion dress, how she could sing any song she'd ever heard, how she had always had the prettiest smile of anyone in the family.

Gabi's father. I hadn't noticed him before but then I saw him, sitting on a folding chair, uncomfortable, silent. He joined the conversations by nodding. When people left he looked longingly toward the door. When Gabi went to the kitchen to get me lemonade he went in and spoke to her. Through the door I saw him put his arm around her shoulders. Then he left.

Business. It was decided that Rafe and Gabi would live with one aunt in the Bronx and the old man with another in Harlem. He said he would go back to the Dominican Republic but they didn't take him seriously. How would an old blind man manage? they were thinking. I thought he was already there.

Gabi said she had to go and pulled me out of my seat with her eyes.

"I'll come this weekend to help you pack," an aunt said. She looked at me suspiciously, returned my smile weakly, and turned to Gabi, touching her hair as she spoke. "If you need anything . . ."

The aunt's apartment was on Audubon and Gabi and I took the bus downtown. We didn't talk on the bus or on the walk to her house. Gabi went into the bedroom, took off the dress she had borrowed, and put on a blouse and pleated skirt.

"I'll have it cleaned," she said.

"Give it to me," I said. "I'll get my mom to have it cleaned and send it to Chanelle's house."

"Can you thank her for me? Should I call her?" Gabi asked. "I don't even know her."

"I'll thank her," I said. "How do you feel?"

"A little bit afraid," she said. "I've always been a daughter, 'Lucila's girl with her nose in the air,' my aunt used to say. And now I'm in a new place. But I think that somewhere deep inside I am strong. I am the Dominican woman my mother thought I was. I can do this life, this vagabond road."

"It's going to be hard."

"I know, Spoon, but it's easier when the hard part is in your face. When you don't have choices," she said. "When Mami wanted me to leave school and work and help out with my grandfather I just saw it as the end of my world. I didn't know where to turn. Now, I'll just do the best I can, and maybe it will be enough. Maybe, without her to lean on, it'll be easier somehow."

"I don't know if easy lives here anymore," I said. "I think you reach a point where it doesn't get easier, you just get stronger. I came down from Wallingford looking to find the world I'd left, but it's all changed. You spoke about believing in yourself, and I realize that I've been hearing that question over and over since I've been back."

"I thought you were going to say since you've been back home."

"I am home, Gabi. But home is not what it used to be for me. It used to be simply a neighborhood I played ball in and a building I lived in and where my parents lived. All of a sudden it's a place in which I question everything, mostly who I am. I'm asking myself what does it mean to play ball? What does it mean to sit on the stoop? Can we reach a point where there's just no place else to go?"

"Do you have a different dream when you're at school?"

"I had a different dream," I said. "Wallingford is all about what's going to happen tomorrow, or a thousand to-morrows in the future. It's like when we were kids dreaming about what we wanted to be when we grew up."

"And then one day a really hard "now" awakes us from our nap," Gabi said, putting her hand on mine.

"'And then one day a really hard 'now' awakes us from our nap,'" I repeated.

"What is your 'now'?" Gabi asked. "You got any verbs and adjectives to feed a starving poet?"

"I don't know," I said. "I'm not even sure what there is to know."

It was growing dark. Gabi's half-shadowed face in the dim light reminded me of a woodcut of an angel I had once seen. For a long time we sat in the silence we had drawn around ourselves. Outside the street noises were subdued, only the hissing of tires along the avenue suggesting that life was still pushing relentlessly forward.

"Gabi, I love you," I said.

As the words left my lips the space they vacated was filled with an image by Goya — an aquatint in which soldiers drag women beneath the dark hollow of a bridge. One of the women was Gabi. What did she have to do to get the drugs?

"I love you, too," she said.

"I think, in the end, that matters most," I said.

As the words left my lips the space they vacated was filled with an image by Goya. It is called El Gigante, but it is not of a giant; rather, of a minotaur: half man, half beast. In the corner of the image there is a woman, only half conscious as she lays on a couch. Gabi.

"Gabi, are you going to be okay?"

"Yes, and you have to leave," she said. "You don't have a choice. You have to make these next steps. Finish high school, start college, chase your dreams. It's what I want for you. It's what I want so much for you.

"And I swear to you," she was crying, "I swear with this Dominican woman's brain and with this Catholic heart, that from this moment on I will at least try to be okay."

I went to her and she stood very still and we clung to each other in love and fear.

"If I were a magician I would wave my wand and make everything clear for us," I said.

"If I were a magician I would turn you into a mango and eat you," she laughed. "Then I'd know that I would have you safe inside of me and making me stronger."

It was a nice image. I thought her poetry might be coming back to her. But now it was my throat that felt swollen, my tongue that felt heavy and useless in my mouth. I had to say the words we were avoiding.

"Gabi, how about the drugs?"

She sighed heavily. "I'm not as afraid as I was," she said. "I've been there, if only to visit, and I've seen the beast. There's nothing there that I want. I can't fool myself again."

When I left I was exhausted. My mind drifted through the day, helping Gabi to get ready for her mother's funeral. The church. The singing. But most of all that moment at the cemetery when we had turned away from the coffin, leaving it under the tent for the workers to deal with, when Gabi and I had walked away, neither of us looking back. I felt that I was walking away again, and this time it was Gabi who stayed alone in the darkness. I wanted to think she would be all right, but I didn't know. I didn't know.

I believe in the Holy Ghost, the Holy Catholic Church, the communion of saints . . .

    I believe . . .

RETURN TO WALLINGFORD

The change in Miss Mathews' voice was perceptible. Where it had been warm at our first meetings, now, on the phone in Harlem, it was edged with suspicion. I explained, slowly, carefully, how I understood the seriousness of taking off an extra week. She repeated her feelings of disappointment in me, and said that my lack of an explanation was distressing.

"I can't excuse your absence," she had said. "And I'm sure there won't be much of an opportunity for you to make up the work you'll miss."

She ended the conversation with a good-bye that

sounded forever final, as if she really did not expect me back at all. Maybe she would have had more understanding if I had told her that I would spend the week sitting with Gabi in hospital corridors and rehabilitation centers, searching for one that would take her without health insurance.

The interviews were exhausting and frustrating. We ran into waiting lists, sometimes six months or longer. Sometimes there were special conditions, such as being an expectant mother or assigned by the courts. Sometimes, they were just painful.

"Have you been tested for AIDS?" an older woman, thin, her lips smeared with a bluish shade, spoke loudly as she looked up from her papers.

"I don't have AIDS," Gabi said quietly.

"I didn't ask you if you had it, honey," the woman said. "I asked if you've been tested for it."

"No."

"IV?" the woman asked, certain of her questions.

"I just injected under the skin," Gabi said.

"You used a needle," the woman said, tearing some forms from a pad. "We have outpatient counseling available. Have a seat and fill these out. And this card. Do the card first and give it right back to me. Then a counselor will call you."

The half-filled waiting room was a grimy yellow. There

were couches and a few individual chairs, all green vinyl and chrome, along the windowless walls. Gabi filled out the card with her name and address. There were two boxes, one that said AIDS COUNSELING and the other DRUG COUNSELING. She checked off the drug box and took the card back to the receptionist.

"It's going to take a while." The receptionist raised her voice, making it even uglier than it had been. "You don't have to wait with her if you don't want counseling."

"If you go I'll kill you!" Gabi whispered.

I wanted to go. I wanted to be away from the sordidness of the place, away from the others waiting in the green chairs. A woman, somewhere between twenty-five and ninety, stood and walked across the floor to the magazine rack. Her steps were awkward, stiff-legged, as if there was something wrong with her hips.

"What magazines they got over there?" her companion, a man with heavy shoulders, a beer belly, and spindly legs, asked.

"The usual ones."

"Yeah, okay, bring a couple over."

I kept my head down and followed Gabi's progress as she filled out the questionnaire. How many times married? How many children? Had she been arrested for drug use?

Gabi finished the form and then, with her felt-tip pen, wrote on the palm of her hand *I am crying.*

I kissed her palm, and held her hand, and tried desperately to hold back my own tears. It was a half hour before she was called into one of the offices.

"Hey, man, is she going to intake?" the big man with the spindly legs asked me.

I nodded yes.

"Don't sweat the wait," he went on. "They're slow here and not too many people know about this place. But you come here once a month and they give you your pills for six weeks, which is two weeks better than most of the clinics. You can get three months up near 14th Street but if you got to restart, say, you don't take your pills or your count goes up, they don't switch you to a new regimen right away. That's their problem, they ain't flexible. You know what I mean?"

"Yeah."

"No, you don't know now," he said. "But after a while you'll know."

I knew he was talking about AIDS, not drug counseling. I knew he was welcoming me to the antechamber of the labyrinth. This is what you have to know when you live here, he was saying. This is the language of the beast.

When, fifteen minutes later, Gabi appeared from one of the frosted doors, she was smiling.

"Is it better-looking on the other side of those doors?" I asked.

"No," she said. "But I think I'll come here. I think I'll get along with the counselor. At least she didn't lie to me when I was in there."

I said good-bye to the others as we left. One of the white men called me "brother" and waved a fist at me. Right. Outside Gabi said that she felt as if I were putting her into day care. We laughed. On 8th Street and 6th Avenue we bought frankfurters and orange drinks and wandered into the bookstore across the street.

"Do you think they have a 'Happier Times' section?" Gabi asked.

My parents were upset that I hadn't returned to school. I was upset, too. I had never felt so alone in my life, so unsure of myself. From somewhere an image formed itself in my mind. It was me standing on the stoop in front of my house, with my homeboys — with Junebug and Scott and Brian. We huddled together to comfort one another in the shadows of the tenements.

"No, she's not pregnant," I'd answered my father when he asked.

On the way uptown I asked her if she would really go to the counseling sessions. It was three afternoons a week at first, and later once a week. They did weekly testing, and there was no methadone, so it looked good to me. She said she would. I thought one of the parts of the program, in which people expressed their feelings in journals, would be good for her.

I told my father that I was finally going back to school and he wanted to hire a limo for me. I told him I could manage with the train.

Pennsylvania Station had never been so big as Gabi and I stood waiting for the train to Wallingford. Every time I tried to talk I choked up.

"I want you to be sad to leave me," she said. "One time, when I was young, I saw a snake in a pet shop window. On top of the snake there was a little white mouse. Any moment the mouse knew the snake might eat it. It was shaking and trying to be still at the same time. That's how I feel. I want to believe in myself. I want to believe in myself."

"I am sad," I answered. "Sad and unsure of myself."

"Unsure . . ." She traced a finger from the center of my forehead, down my nose, and onto the center of my lips. " '*Beso que tu boca entregue a mis oídos alcanza.*' 'The kiss your mouth gives another will echo within my ear.' "

"I don't plan to be doing a whole lot of kissing in Wallingford, Connecticut," I said.

"It's almost time for you to go," she said.

"I'll call you," I said. I picked up my bag with one hand and put my other arm around her.

Gabi threw her arms around my waist and clung desperately. "Call me all the time. Write to me."

"I will. I promise," I answered.

We held on to each other on the station platform until we saw the conductor looking down the platform, ready to close the doors.

Gabi looked so small standing by herself, so small and so still, the ever-busy New Yorkers passing in front and behind her until it was only them in a colorless blur as the train plunged into the darkness.

"You going back to school?" The blond man sitting next to me indicated my books with a nod.

"Yes," I said. "I'm a little late getting back, too."

"You kids have it made today," he said. He smelled of aftershave lotion. "If my generation had had the Internet I think we would have done two things: prevented the Vietnam War and solved the civil rights problem a lot sooner."

I was trying to study and wanted to keep my mind on the textbooks, but he had sucked me in.

"How?"

"Okay, first the war." A stubby, well-manicured finger went up. "We could have prevented Nam by actually dropping computers, maybe laptops, right into North Vietnam and giving those people actual lessons on how to farm. That was the major problem there. The Vietnamese were struggling to survive. That's your basic cause for all war. You get a man's belly full, and he won't walk down the street for a war.

"Then the civil rights thing. You realize that most people in America didn't have any idea of what segregation was all about?" The same finger went up. "You saw a few signs, Colored and White, that kind of thing, but most Americans didn't know about what you people were going through until Malcolm X came along. That's when we found out that a lot of blacks hated white people. Your basic liberal, north or south, didn't know that."

He went on, and I closed my book and let my mind wander. I wondered if he knew any black people now, or anything about black life. What would he make of my father? Of Miss Mathews worrying about the black kids without ever mentioning race? What would he have thought of the men in the barbershop or the sister who had spotted the drug house?

I thought of Monica, all skin and bones and heart, pushing her way between the muscle man and Gabi. Could he ever know these people? Could I really know them?

"What's going to revolutionize the Internet," he was saying, "is when they reach a saturation point and realize that they need to charge for people to have Web sites. Then you'll get rid of a lot of frivolous stuff and dead sites . . ."

The truth was that I didn't want him to know about black people, or how we lived in Harlem. These were my people, my parents, my barbershop, my girl, my old lady who sat in the window and looked for crack houses. If he couldn't tell that he was boring me, how could he discover the humanity that seemed so different from the world he knew?

Chanelle had promised to meet me at the Wallingford Station and "tell me the dirt" before I got back to the Academy. I was glad to talk with her on the phone and mildly surprised to hear that I wasn't expected back.

"You know how rumors get started," she had said. "How's she doing?"

"I think she'll make it," I said. "And, Chanelle, thanks for being there."

"Hey!" she said. I had expected more to the sentence, but it hadn't come.

". . . we'll all have devices we wear on our belts to instantly access the Internet wherever we are in the world." The finger was in the air again. "Good grief, are we at New Haven already?"

Downtown New Haven looks better from the train than the streets. My Internet expert began to gather his things and told me to "watch the way the wind blows." I promised that I would.

The conductor announced that the cafe car was closed and there would be a fifteen-minute layover in New Haven. I went out to the platform, found a telephone, and called New York. The phone rang five times as I held my breath.

"Central Intake." The voice sounded vaguely West Indian.

"Gabriela Godoy, please."

"Just a minute."

The on-hold music was B. B. King and I wondered how they had decided he was appropriate at a drug rehab center. I listened to several choruses, then panicked when the operator asked for sixty-five cents more. I fished through my pockets and found two quarters and a dime.

"Please deposit five cents for the next four minutes."

I was desperately looking for another nickel when the

voice came back on. "I'm sorry, she's in a session right now, can you call back in an hour?"

I said I would and hung up. The phone was ringing again, probably the operator looking for her nickel as I got back on the train.

Chanelle was wearing black low-cut jeans and a sloppy green sweatshirt. She smiled as I came over to her and she tried to take my bag.

"I think I can manage it," I said.

The day was unseasonably warm and I didn't have much to carry, so we walked to the campus. The main street in town was trying too hard to be picturesque; the gray, squat buildings down the side street showed the beginning of another season of rainy New England weather.

"You glad to be back?" Chanelle asked.

"Yeah, I am," I said.

"And glad to see your friends?" she asked.

"Delighted to see my friends."

I told Chanelle about Gabi going to the rehab center and voluntarily taking drug counseling. She said she knew a psychiatrist who did drug counseling for show business people, and I thought that was funny.

"Why's that funny?" Chanelle smiled. "That's what he does."

"Maybe it's the way you said it," I answered. "Just one of those things, no big deal."

That bothered her, and she grew quiet. The instant distance made me realize how close we were.

The campus. The tree limbs were still brushed with snow, making them stand out against the black winter sky. The lights that circled the still pond glowed warmly. The pond was still frozen over and a handful of skaters, in twos and threes, glided effortlessly along its surface. But somehow it all seemed less magical now, less inviting. We sat on a bench near the small end of the pond and, in spite of myself, I asked Chanelle what she thought of Harlem.

"I can deal with it," she said. "What did you think of 54th Street?"

"I can deal with it," I said.

"Good." She held out her hand for me to take and, suddenly, I was hesitant.

Chanelle stopped and looked at me, puzzled. I took her hand and held it for a moment against my cheek. And then I kissed her hand, and then I kissed her upturned face as softly, as very softly, as I could.

I was back at Wallingford, away from the landscapes I was only beginning to see with my heart. The journey from the pond to Harlem that I had thought was ended had only begun. At that moment I didn't know what to say to Chanelle, or what to write to Gabi, except that I knew, or was beginning to know, that all journeys are harder than they appear, and that there are often hard roads to climb and beasts to slay along the way.

"Life ain't always simple, is it?" Chanelle said.

"No," I answered. "It ain't."

THE VAN WICKLE GATES, PROVIDENCE, RHODE ISLAND, NINE MONTHS LATER

S *mile."*

"You bring me to a strange city, put me up against a fence, and then tell me to smile." Gabi has her hand on her hip. *"How do I know what you're up to?"*

"Try a smile," I say, still looking into the camera. *"It won't hurt."*

She smiles. A beautiful smile. A radiant smile. A smile that pleases the angels. A smile that pleases me.

I graduated from the Academy over the summer and was accepted at Brown. Gabi had a much harder struggle, graduating but with no scholarships in sight. Then came the realization that Rafe, too, was using drugs. I watched her fight to free herself and her brother from the physical agony and emotional despair of their addiction. It was a draining experience for her. We spent little time together during the summer. She said that she needed to find the strength within herself, that she couldn't lean on me. I remembered what her mother had said, that she was a Dominican woman, and that Dominican women are strong. I didn't know if she would be strong enough, for herself or for Rafe.

At first I didn't know what to do. Twice I walked the streets with her looking for her brother. Once we found him in an empty lot, a needle still in his arm, and sat with him until an ambulance came to take him to the emergency room. It had been a hard summer, a summer of too much pain and too much stumbling through the impossibly mean streets of the city. These were the streets that either sharpened us with their richness and depth or trapped us within endless corridors of desperation.

Gabi had found a job as a stockroom clerk in a bookstore on 12th Street, close enough to the rehab clinic to make all of the meetings. She had stayed with it. I worked on 126th Street at an insurance company and we saw each other some evenings and weekends, but we hadn't been close. She had isolated herself from the world, and from me. I'd understood what she needed to do, how she needed to be strong, to re-examine her life, to recognize the demons that threatened her and Rafe. But I had been put adrift as well. We sat together in the park, or in the library, or in the coffee shops along Columbus Avenue and exchanged small talk, but we had lost the closeness we once had, or perhaps were too cautious to re-explore it. For the first time in my life the streets frightened me. I knew that if Gabi — Gabi with her dark eyes that could stop time, who strung words into casual hymns — if she could lose her way, then so could I.

The summer sped by and soon I was headed to Providence for Brown University's minority students orientation. Gabi had asked me not to make any promises to her, and I had made as many as I could think of. On the morning that I left for Providence my dad picked Gabi up and drove her to work. He parked the car on 10th Street and went to get a newspaper so that Gabi and I could say good-bye.

"He is so old school and corny," she'd said.

"We're supposed to be kissing or something," I answered.

We kissed. We held hands as we walked toward her job. We said good-bye.

I called her from Providence and told her about Brown. In my heart I knew she would have loved it, too. I could sense the disappointment she never mentioned, felt it when she showed up at the railroad station with a slim volume of poetry and a small overnight bag. She had gained some weight and I told her it looked good on her.

"Oh, now you think I'm fat," she said.

"No, I didn't say you were fat," I answered. *Why was I afraid to kid with her?*

We had a tasteless vegetarian lunch in town and I watched Gabi check out all the students around her. I imagined her picturing herself among them.

"They all look so smart and ready," she said.

"Ready for what?"

"For whatever comes their way," she said, staring admiringly at a tall Indian girl in a sari.

She was right. They were ready for whatever came, or at least thought they were. They weren't waiting on street corners, or on stoops, to see what rounded the corners of their lives.

After lunch we walked around the part of town where most of the students hung out. A few spoke to me and I pointed out a couple of others who were in my dorm.

"What are you reading?" she asked.

"Mostly some esoteric stuff that I don't understand," I said. "It looks like everybody here has to bring their own 'I'm smart' flavor to the scene and it has to be different from everybody else's. It's funny."

"It sounds like fun."

"I guess so."

"There are so many different-looking people here," she said. "East Indians, Chinese, a few Middle Easterners. What do you think that guy over there is?"

We are two dancers on a stage, moving without touching, making only the surest steps, not daring leaps.

"I know him, he's from Tibet. You want to meet him?"

"No."

"No problem," I said. I knew these are not Gabi's people. I sensed her discomfort as I touched the straight line of her cheek. "How's Rafe doing?"

"Good," she replied. There was a slight rise in her tone, which made me believe that Rafe was doing well.

"I think that one day we'll put all of last year behind us," I said. "It'll be like some wrong turn that we took."

"I don't think so," Gabi said. "Everything you do becomes part of you. Drugs become part of you even after you leave them behind. They're always there. We don't leave anything behind."

There is an image in my mind, black and white, a dark etching of beasts sleeping in a forest clearing. There is a girl with them. She is awake. What has happened that she will not leave them behind?

We found our way to the Van Wickle Gates and I took pictures of Gabi in front of them. An African student came by and I asked him to photograph us. He took several shots, urging me to put my arm around Gabi, then telling me to put it around her waist when I had chosen her shoulders. Afterward we walked up and down the hills toward the school of design, with me trying to pick out the Brown students from the art students.

"Where is Chanelle going?" Gabi asked.

"UCLA," I said. "She switched schools at the last minute."

"That's a long way," Gabi said. "She'll have to call you."

"She won't *have* to call me," I said.

"She will."

"You jealous of some girl 3,000 miles away?"

"She's not that far away from where you are," Gabi said.

The dancers stop. They measure the distance between them and realize they are supposed to be dancing together. The music slows as they look at each other from across the stage.

"I was thinking how it would be when you came up," I said. "I was imagining you on the train. The first part of the trip was the same as the trip to Wallingford. I was thinking about you looking out of the window and seeing the same things I've seen."

"I was nervous coming up," she said.

"Yeah, so was I. I want things to be good with us."

"It can be good with us without us being, you know . . . having some kind of huge commitment or anything." Gabi tensed her lips, and I wanted to un-tense them with a kiss but was too far away from them. "You'd be a cool best friend."

The music has stopped. I think about Chanelle. About a two-hour phone call from Los Angeles and the two of us recounting the Christmas break in small details as if we had been talking about a movie of someone else's life, as if the Christmas break had been an unfinished documentary. It had been an easy conversation, free of the grainy images of Gabi's apartment or of Harlem Hospital or of the huddled figures on the stoop. It was easy, and seductive. Like sunshine on the pond at Wallingford, like the hot water running off my body in Chanelle's bathroom, like filling in the outlines of pain with the crayon colors of memory, instead of blood.

"I think I don't want to be your best friend," I said. "If what that means is that you won't be part of me any longer." We were passing a coffee shop with outdoor seating, and I pulled her down onto one of the chairs.

"I can't drink any more coffee," she said. "I already have to pee."

I sat down while she went into the coffee house and found the rest room. I could feel my heart beating faster, feel myself becoming nervous. A waitress, buoyant, plump, asked me what I wanted and I stood and said I was just waiting for a friend. She shrugged and went back inside.

I thought about telling Gabi that I really liked Chanelle, but I hadn't allowed myself to love her. I instantly recognized that I hadn't yet thought it all through, and decided not to say anything to Gabi until I had, if ever. What I wanted to remember on this bright day in Providence was how much Gabi meant to me.

She came back from the bathroom and I saw that her eyes were red from crying.

"You okay?" I asked.

"You have to ask me that a lot, don't you?"

"I need to know."

"Are *you* okay?"

"I'm not sure of where we're going," I said. "But I'm

thinking that it's okay not to be sure. I want to be unsure with you, Gabi. I want for you to take a chance being unsure with me."

Gabi swung her head down and away from me. The words had been from my heart, but they hadn't been enough. She needed more.

"Gabi . . ." I reached for her. She turned to me, her smile so sweet, so angelic. My hand was suspended in midair for a long moment, and then she reached for it and took it in her own. She needed a god, and I was only human.

"When I was on the train I played out all these little scenarios between us in my head," Gabi said. We were walking arm in arm, going nowhere in particular. "You were going to beg me for my love and then fall down on your knees, toss a rose over your left shoulder, which would instantly transform itself into an impossibly bright moon, and declare that you are willing to die for the touch of my lips."

"That sounds good," I said, wanting to be the hero of her dreams.

"But you saying that you want to be unsure with me sounds even better, because I know it's from the heart," she said, putting her face against my arm. "I know it's from your heart."

What is from the heart, and what is from the mind? I

didn't know anymore. For a long while we didn't speak. It was almost a relief not to have to find the right words, not to have to measure and weigh how much we both felt. It was turning cool. Leaves danced along the curbs on the evening breeze and the colored pennants outside of the small shops began to flap.

"You know, I have some bad news for you," she said. "It's about Monica."

"What happened?"

"You know I was working with her over the summer and she was really trying to get straight again. I saw her last week and she's way back, man. She saw me and almost ran across the street so I wouldn't see her, but I did."

It was bad news, but worse than the news was that I had expected it, had expected Monica to fail, to go back to the streets, and to whatever she was taking to make her journey easier. I felt sorry for Monica. Grieved for her.

We walked around the campus for another hour, until the early autumn shadows stretched across the cobbled pathways and the summer sun disappeared with an appropriate flourish. Gabi began telling me what she was reading, a new poet published by the Indiana University Press. The excitement rose in her voice as she described the poet's language.

"It's as if she's discovering the simplest words for the first time," she said. "The simplest words, and the simplest emotions, but she brings them alive. Oh, she's simply wonderful."

It was the rich landscape of Gabi's mind that made me want to drop to my knees and throw a rose over my left shoulder, hoping that it would be a moon with enough light to lead us to where we wanted to go.

As she talked, the words rushing from her full lips, we were drawing close again, talking about our dreams. There was the fleeting thought that I might one day lose her again, that now might not ever be forever, that I might never find all the beasts that lay in wait. But I pushed those thoughts aside and told myself to believe in a heart that sees beauty and a soul that prays for love.

We talked until we were exhausted, and then we held one another, and then the day ended with the fat promise of a new one to come.

ABOUT THE AUTHOR

Walter Dean Myers is the author of many highly acclaimed books for young adults, including *Motown and Didi: A Love Story*, *The Young Landlords*, *Slam!*, and *Somewhere in the Darkness*, all winners of the Coretta Scott King Award; *Scorpions*, a Newbery Honor Book; and *Monster*, a National Book Award Finalist, a Coretta Scott King Honor Book, and winner of the Michael J. Printz Award.

Walter Dean Myers grew up in Harlem, but his travels have taken him to the Far East, South America, and the Arctic. He presently lives in Jersey City, New Jersey. He is a member of the Harlem Writers Guild.

Explore every side of life with acclaimed autho
Walter Dean Myers...

  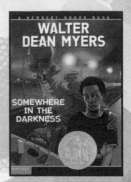